THE EVERYTHING

PARENT'S GUIDE TO

CHILDREN WITH DYSLEXIA
2ND EDITION

Twenty years ago, I did not know how to help my son. He was bright, but every school day was a struggle as he could not master the basic elements of reading. I feared a diagnosis of dyslexia, thinking it would mean that something was terribly wrong with his brain. Instead, I learned that dyslexia is merely one facet of something wonderfully right with my son's brain—it is the flip side of his extraordinary creativity, his wonderful sense of humor, his quick grasp of mathematical concepts, and his knack for solving problems.

I found a way to help my son, and by age eleven he was an avid and enthusiastic reader. He excelled in high school, earned a college degree, and now is attending graduate school and raising a son of his own.

I also found a way to help others, as the webmaster for the "Dyslexia, the Gift" website at *www.dyslexia.com*. Every year, I receive thousands of e-mails from parents like you seeking help for their kids. Some have success stories to share, but others are overwhelmed by the confusing and often contradictory information and choices that they face.

I cannot give you a crystal ball to predict your child's future, but I hope that I can guide you through the maze. I hope you will find this book to be a valuable reference and starting point, and that it will lead you toward the answers you need. Your journey will be different from mine, but if you have faith in your child, I think you will find that you are just as richly rewarded at the end.

Abigail Mar

D1052067

WELCOME TO THE
EVERYTHING®
PARENT'S GUIDES

Everything® Parent's Guides are a part of the bestselling Everything® series and cover common parenting issues like childhood illnesses and tantrums, as well as medical conditions like asthma and juvenile diabetes. These family-friendly books are designed to be a one-stop guide for parents. If you want authoritative information on specific topics not fully covered in other books, Everything® Parent's Guides are your perfect solution.

 Alerts

Urgent warnings

 Facts

Important snippets of information

 Essentials

Quick handy tips

 Questions

Answers to common questions

When you're done reading, you can finally say you know **EVERYTHING®**!

PUBLISHER Karen Cooper

MANAGING EDITOR, EVERYTHING® SERIES Lisa Laing

COPY CHIEF Casey Ebert

ASSOCIATE PRODUCTION EDITOR Mary Beth Dolan

ACQUISITIONS EDITOR Pam Wissman

DEVELOPMENT EDITOR Brett Palana-Shanahan

EVERYTHING® SERIES COVER DESIGNER Erin Alexander

Visit the entire Everything® series at *www.everything.com*

THE

EVERYTHING®

PARENT'S GUIDE TO

CHILDREN
WITH
DYSLEXIA

2ND EDITION

Learn the key signs of dyslexia and find
the best treatment options for your child

Abigail Marshall

Adamsmedia
Avon, Massachusetts

This book is dedicated in loving memory
to Elizabeth "Misty" Davis

An Everything® Series Book.
Everything® and www.everything.com® are registered trademarks
of F+W Media, Inc.

Published by Adams Media, a division of F+W Media, Inc.
57 Littlefield Street, Avon, MA 02322. U.S.A.
www.adamsmedia.com

ISBN 10: 1-4405-6496-5
ISBN 13: 978-1-4405-6496-3
eISBN 10: 1-4405-6497-3
eISBN 13: 978-1-4405-6497-0

Printed in the United States of America.

10 9 8 7 6 5 4 3 2 1

This book is available at quantity discounts for bulk purchases.
For information, please call 1-800-289-0963.

Acknowledgments

This book would not have been possible without the contributions of dozens of parents and educators who continually share their ongoing experiences via the DyslexiaSupport Egroup; special thanks to the group creator Annette Marshall, and to moderator Mary Yohn. I continue to be guided and inspired by the hundreds of members of the Davis Dyslexia family, too numerous to list; I am especially grateful for the support of Ron and Alice Davis, and my good friend Dorothy Owen. Special thanks to my son Ethan and daughter Elise, who taught me everything I know about being a parent.

dys•lex•ia (dis lek´ sē ə)

n. **1.** a learning difficulty primarily associated with problems with written language such as reading, writing, spelling, and in some cases, working with numbers, stemming from naturally occurring variations in brain structure and function.

Contents

Introduction

Dyslexia is not the same as reading failure. Teachers often see only that aspect, because reading instruction is their concern. They are trained to measure a child's progress against a "norm" or "grade level" or "expected reading age." When the child does not meet the standard, they intensify early reading instruction, assuming that reading is an essential skill that must be acquired early.

Children invariably grow up, but few researchers have charted the developmental path of dyslexia over time. One who has is Professor Rosalie Fink, who tested and interviewed more than sixty prominent adults with dyslexia who had become leaders in fields requiring extensive reading, including medicine, law, business, and sciences. This group of adults included a Nobel laureate and a member of the National Academy of Sciences. Each tested above twelfth-grade level on word recognition, oral reading accuracy, and word meaning; more than 40 percent tested well on spelling and did not need extra time to complete reading tasks. As a group, they performed significantly worse than their controls when reading nonsense words, a test commonly used to measure decoding ability and to diagnose dyslexia.

On average, these high-achieving adults learned to read at age eleven. They learned through reading about subjects that fired their imaginations and excited their passions. Their reading was supported by their intense interest, which had spurred them to develop the background knowledge and vocabulary needed to use context to help interpret the words on the page. For each, there had come a time when the thirst for knowledge simply drew them past whatever barriers to reading had existed before. That time seems to correspond with the onset of the period Piaget called the "stage of formal operations" (usually age eleven to fifteen), and the rapid growth in brain gray matter and synapses known to occur just prior to puberty.

Children with dyslexia are capable learners who manifest some abilities well ahead of their peers, but their brains simply are not constructed to ease into early reading. They need an enriched learning environment to fuel their inherent curiosity and thirst for knowledge. If they cannot find intellectual stimulation at school, parents should work to provide it at home.

Reading support to build foundational skills is essential and should begin early, but it should not overshadow or impede other learning opportunities, nor should it be withdrawn as the child enters her teens. The eight-year-old diagnosed with dyslexia can reasonably be expected to begin reading comfortably in her teens; she should not be deprived of educational opportunity because of early difficulties in acquiring basic reading skills. As a parent, you must shield your child from the demoralizing aspects of school failure by providing constant support and encouragement, recognizing that your child's optimal learning periods for certain skills will not always coincide with the "norm."

The key is in understanding your child's needs and abilities, not in trying to change the child. He can be helped, but his brain cannot and should not be "rewired" nor can his dyslexia be "cured." Through observation and open communication with your child, you can facilitate this understanding, recognizing that a misfit between child and school is a failure of the school, and not of your child. Celebrate your child's talents, feed his passions, and work to cultivate his emotional as well as intellectual growth—in the end, you will have raised an empowered and enthusiastic learner.

CHAPTER 1

Understanding Dyslexia

Children with dyslexia have many strengths and talents, and grow up to be successful adults with rewarding careers. However, they are likely to struggle with learning to read, write, and spell, especially in the early years. They may need specialized help and support to enable them to achieve their goals. You cannot cure your child of dyslexia, but you can guide him and help him to find his own way to succeed in school and in life.

What Is Dyslexia?

Dyslexia is a learning disability that primarily affects a person's ability to learn to read and develop a strong understanding of language. It's more than just a problem with reading; your child may also have difficulties with oral communication, organizational skills, following instructions, and telling time. Sometimes the symptoms can be extremely variable within the same individual. For example, your child may have problems learning basic math facts and doing arithmetic; on the other hand, he may have a special aptitude for geometry and advanced mathematics. Because dyslexia stems from differences in the way the brain processes information, it can also be connected to physical clumsiness or poor motor coordination; on the other hand, your child may turn out to be especially athletic and talented at sports.

Fact

Dyslexia is far more prevalent than was once believed. In fact, dyslexia may affect one out of five children in the classroom setting. Although at least 20 percent of the population has reading difficulties, only about 4 percent of school-age children receive special education services.

While dyslexia may present certain difficulties to children, it also seems to be associated with many strengths and talents. Your child could be highly imaginative and may excel in art, music, or drama. He might be a good problem solver, and may be especially good with solving jigsaw puzzles, working with Legos, or playing games of strategy. It's possible that you may have noticed he's handy around the house and has a knack for fixing broken toys and other objects.

What Dyslexia Means for Your Child

Dyslexia is not something that can be outgrown. Over time, your child will gain skills that she struggled with at first, but her dyslexia will probably present new challenges as she grows older and school becomes more demanding. She may master reading and writing in elementary school, but have difficulty learning a foreign language in high school. She may not encounter early problems with arithmetic, but struggle with algebra. As you learn more about dyslexia, you will be able to anticipate these problems before they arise and help guide your child to use study methods that are effective and useful for her.

Reading is the most significant problem area associated with dyslexia. Your child will eventually learn to read, but it will probably take her longer than most other children. It is common for a child with dyslexia to be unable to read independently until age eight, or ten, or twelve, or even until the teenage years. Despite the delayed start in reading, your child can learn to read advanced material and can gain reading comprehension skills as good as, or better than, her peers. Having dyslexia, though, means that she'll be more likely to read slowly and with greater effort.

Dyslexia can also affect other areas of life. Your child is likely to have difficulty remembering and following directions, and have poor time management skills. She may be tremendously disorganized, or become compulsively neat as a way of compensating for her confusion. These issues can be very frustrating for you and your child, but they are also problems that can be resolved over time by using planning and learning techniques to compensate for weaknesses. For example, as your child grows you will be able to help her become more organized by relying on calendars, planners, and lists; of course, she will need to learn to read first to take advantage of these tools.

Processing Information

Dyslexia is caused by differences in how the brain processes information. These differences don't make dyslexia a mental defect or disease; they simply mean that your child has an unusual way of thinking, learning, communicating, and solving problems.

 Essential

Dyslexia is not caused by poor schools, bad teaching practices, neglectful parenting, or a difficult home life. Those factors can explain why many other children have learning problems, and they can make things worse for a child with dyslexia, but they cannot cause a child to develop dyslexia.

Before dyslexia was discovered and labeled, these differences most likely went unnoticed because it was common and acceptable for children to discontinue their education at a young age, grow up to become farmers, artisans, or merchants, or take on other jobs that did not require a formal education. With their strong ability to learn through hands-on practice and apprenticeship, young people with dyslexia probably did quite well.

In today's world, however, strong literacy skills are essential. Increasing importance is placed on school performance and standardized tests; children learn in large classrooms where the "norm" (or average) is fast becoming a minimum standard to which all students are expected to aspire. In this environment, teachers must use the methods that best reach the majority of students in their classrooms. A child with a learning barrier quickly falls behind, and so what was once merely a learning difference transforms into a learning disability.

Areas of Cognitive Weakness

Educators and researchers have isolated some factors that seem to play an important role in dyslexia. Most of these are associated with language processing difficulties or the ability to think sequentially. Mental processing speed also seems to play a part.

The most significant areas of difficulty are the following:

- Difficulties with phonemic awareness, which is the ability to break down and manipulate the small units of sound within words, such as the three separate sounds for the *c*, *a*, and *t* in the word *cat*
- Problems with word retrieval or rapid automatic naming, which is the time it takes for a verbal response to a visual stimulus or cue, such as quickly saying the names of letters printed on a chart, or names of objects when a picture is shown
- Poor digit span, which is the ability to store a short sequence of letters or numbers in short-term memory
- Difficulties with sequencing or concepts of order

- Visual perceptual confusion, such as the inability to distinguish letters, such as *b* and *d*, or perceiving letters out of order, such as confusing *was* and *saw*, or *from* and *form*

Areas of Mental Strength

Even though dyslexia can cause extreme difficulties with learning, children with dyslexia are usually bright and capable. In fact, dyslexia is not really a single problem or issue, but the name given to a common pattern of strengths and weaknesses. Individuals with dyslexia tend to be very creative thinkers, with a knack for "out-of-the-box" thinking. Many are artistically talented, and adults with dyslexia usually do well in careers such as engineering, design, or architecture. Recent research shows that children with dyslexia do better on tests of creativity and spatial memory than age-matched children without reading impairments. Another strength is the intuitive thought process; children with dyslexia often will know the answer to a problem or question, but have difficulty explaining how they arrived at it. This is consistent with a theory that they tend to rely on right-brained, sensory or image-based thinking rather than language-based mental processes.

History of Dyslexia

The term *dyslexia* means "difficulty with words," and was first used in 1887 by Rudolf Berlin, a German ophthalmologist. However, the term did not come into common use until the middle of the twentieth century. In the late nineteenth century, two doctors, W. Pringle Morgan and James Hinshelwood, began to study cases of "congenital word blindness" in children. Dr. Morgan submitted an article to a medical journal describing a highly intelligent teenage boy named Percy, who could not learn to read despite years of intensive tutoring. Dr. Hinshelwood was the first to recognize that dyslexia is an inherited trait; he believed that it was caused by impairment to the left angular gyrus, a section of brain involved in language processing.

Fact

Dr. Samuel Torrey Orton, an American physician, pioneered the idea of using multisensory teaching methods for dyslexia. He advocated tracing and writing practice along with teaching letters and sounds, so that the child's memory of the physical movements associated with forming letters would eliminate confusion about the shape and appearance of the letters.

In 1925, Dr. Orton set up a mobile clinic in Iowa to treat children with learning difficulties, including some children with normal or above average intelligence who struggled with reading. Dr. Orton coined the term "strephosymbolia" (twisted symbols) to describe the reading disability, because of the characteristic tendency to reverse or transpose letters. He believed that dyslexia was caused by a difficulty in reconciling information received from the two brain hemispheres, because of the failure to establish left-brain hemispheric dominance.

By the end of the twentieth century, most researchers and educators agreed that dyslexia stems mostly from language-processing difficulties. Some leading researchers, such as Dr. Sally Shaywitz of Yale University, looked for specific brain defects that impaired children's ability to relate the sounds of language to the printed word. Some successful adults with dyslexia, such as Thomas West and Ronald Davis, had a different perspective. They wrote books focusing on dyslexic talents, asserting that individuals with dyslexia think in three-dimensional imagery rather than words, giving rise to creative talents in fields such as art or architecture.

Defining Dyslexia

Even though dyslexia has now been studied extensively for more than a century, experts have been unable to agree on a precise definition. This is likely because the specific symptoms and severity are extremely variable. In 1968, the World Federation of Neurology defined dyslexia as, "A disorder manifested by a difficulty in learning to read despite conventional instruction, adequate intelligence and socio-cultural opportunity." Several U.S. states have enacted laws defining dyslexia, as part of the process of providing appropriate school services. Some have added a reference to difficulties with writing or spelling; others have specified that dyslexia is "a language processing disorder."

In 2002, the International Dyslexia Association adopted an alternative statement, defining dyslexia as "a specific learning disability that is neurological in origin," which is "characterized by difficulties with accurate and/or fluent word recognition and by poor spelling and decoding abilities."

 Alert

In 2012, an advisory panel recommended that the American Psychiatric Association's *Diagnostic and Statistical Manual of Mental Disorders (DSM)* define dyslexia as "Difficulties in accuracy or fluency of reading that are not consistent with the person's chronological age, educational opportunities, or intellectual abilities," to be consistent with international usage. However, that definition was abandoned. Despite objections from prominent dyslexia researchers, the word *dyslexia* is not included in the *DSM-5*.

Although dyslexia is not a mental disorder, it was described as a "Reading Disorder" in previous editions of the *DSM*. The *DSM-IV*, first published in 1994, applied that label where reading achievement "is substantially below that expected given the person's chronological age, measured intelligence, and age-appropriate education." However, that diagnosis is not included in the *DSM-5*, published in 2013. Instead, a broader term of "Specific Learning Disorder" is used to cover deficits in an array of academic skill areas, but limited to apply only where currently measured skills are "well below the average range" for the individual's age, intelligence, or education level. Unfortunately, that new definition may exclude children with moderate dyslexia or those whose skill level has improved somewhat after remediation. Dyslexia can be overcome but it does not go away. The focus on "currently measured skills" and "average range" in the new standard might make it harder for your child to receive a formal confirming diagnosis qualifying him for continued support or accommodations as his reading ability improves over time.

Different Styles of Learning

Instead of being viewed as a disability, dyslexia can be seen as reflecting a certain type of learning style. Your child's learning style is the way in which she perceives, conceptualizes, organizes, and recalls information. All children have different areas of strength; good teachers learn to consider these factors in designing their lessons. As you learn more about dyslexia and observe your child, you will also see that you can tie some of the problems she has to a specific pattern of learning. There is no one learning style that all children with dyslexia share, but there are some common patterns that are often associated with dyslexia.

Auditory, Visual, Kinesthetic, and Tactile Learning

One way to think about learning is to look at it as a process that combines elements of listening (auditory), seeing (visual), feeling (tactile), and doing (kinesthetic). A child with an auditory learning style will learn best from listening to a lecture or explanation; the visual learner needs to see pictures, graphs, or films to learn; and the kinesthetic learner needs to use her hands or have active participation to learn.

Your child's dyslexia may cause conflicts with her dominant learning style. For example, research suggests that a large majority of children with dyslexia—about 85 percent—have a predominantly visual learning style. This works well when your child is viewing a film or looking at a picture or diagram. However, it does not serve her when she is being taught to read. The visual learner tends to try to remember words by sight, rather than sounding them out, and can often remember information by recalling how it was set out on a page. However, your child's dyslexia will stand in the way of her reading ability. You may be told that your strongly visual child has a poor "visual memory" when in fact her memory for real world objects that she sees is quite remarkable. It is only her memory for letters and printed words that is impaired.

Essential

> Your child with dyslexia will learn best with a multisensory approach that simultaneously combines auditory, visual, kinesthetic, and tactile learning strategies to teach new facts and concepts. Methods that involve seeing, saying, listening, touching, and doing will help your child learn faster and enhance his ability to retain new information.

In a school setting, lessons are often geared primarily to students with an auditory learning style. The teacher relies mostly on talking to convey information: She lectures, explains, and answers questions. If your child is a visual or kinesthetic learner, she will miss a lot of information; she will simply not be able to learn without strategies that reach her strongest learning modes. On the other hand, if your child has dyslexia but is an auditory learner, her strengths may mask her dyslexia. She may do well in school, relying on her superior listening skills to keep up in class, and learning the content of books by listening to others read aloud. Her dyslexia may go undetected until the later grades, when she will be expected to learn more from independent reading.

Left-Brained Versus Right-Brained

Some people break down two main styles of learning as being left-brained or right-brained. Researchers know that many functions related to language use and reading are typically localized in the left hemisphere of the brain. The right hemisphere is associated more with intuitive thought and creativity. Of course, the two sides of the brain are designed to work together, and most people develop the ability to use both sides, depending on the task or activity they are engaged in.

Psychologist Linda Kreger Silverman has worked extensively with gifted children, and she describes these two styles of learning as being auditory-sequential and visual-spatial. The auditory-sequential learner thinks primarily in words, learns step-by-step, attends well to detail, learns phonics easily, and excels at rote memory. The visual-spatial learner thinks primarily with images, learns concepts all at once, sees the big picture, learns best by seeing relationships, and learns complex concepts easily but may struggle with basic skills.

One possible explanation for dyslexia is that some children who are right-brained learners find it much easier to think about new information and solve problems using their visual-spatial strategies. Over time, they reinforce their own tendencies toward relying on imagery and intuitive thought processes, and fail to develop strong brain pathways for thinking with the sounds of language. Thus, when it comes time for these children to learn to read, their brains simply aren't ready.

Multiple Intelligences

Dr. Howard Gardner, an American developmental psychologist, describes eight different modalities of intelligence; your child will be stronger in some of these areas than in others. The different intelligences are:

- Linguistic intelligence ("word smart")
- Logical-mathematical intelligence ("number/reasoning smart")
- Spatial intelligence ("picture smart")
- Bodily-kinesthetic intelligence ("body smart")

- Musical intelligence ("music smart")
- Interpersonal intelligence ("people smart")
- Intrapersonal intelligence ("self smart")
- Naturalist intelligence ("nature smart")

In schools, most instruction and testing are geared to the first two intelligences—linguistic and logical-mathematical. If your child has dyslexia, she is probably weak in those areas and could struggle in school and do poorly on standardized testing. On the other hand, dyslexia does not impair the other six types of intelligence in any way. Your child is probably strong in one or more of those areas, and those inherent strengths can help her succeed in many activities in childhood, and go on to have a successful and rewarding career.

Genetic Factors in Dyslexia

Dyslexia is partly inherited, as the tendency to develop dyslexia runs in families. When a parent has dyslexia, there is a 40 to 60 percent likelihood that her child will also develop dyslexia. Studies of identical twins have shown that when one twin has dyslexia, the other will have dyslexia about 55 to 80 percent of the time, depending on the type of dyslexia.

By studying genetic markers in extended families with a high incidence of dyslexia, scientists have now identified at least nine chromosomal regions as having some role or connection with dyslexia. In some cases, they have identified the specific genes involved. Some, like the DCDC2 and KIAA0319 genes on chromosome 6, code for proteins that seem to influence the way that neurons migrate during brain development. A genetic variation on chromosome 2 seems to be associated with the structure of white matter connections in the brain.

Some genes may be tied to specific symptoms of dyslexia. For example, one team of researchers studying six extended families found that genes on chromosome 6 seemed to be associated with the phonological type of dyslexia, but genes on chromosome 15 were connected only to single word reading. Other researchers noted specific genetic factors tied only to spelling difficulties.

 ## Question

Can genetic testing help determine whether my child will inherit dyslexia?
It is not yet possible to perform a reliable genetic test for dyslexia. The genetic factors that influence dyslexia in some families seem to have no effect in others. Researchers believe that dyslexia is caused by the combined interaction of multiple genes.

However, some gene variations that appear to have a strong influence among some families have no impact on others. For example, the DYX1C1 gene on chromosome 15 was found to be associated with dyslexia in families of Finnish and German descent, but a British study found no correlation with dyslexia among individuals who carried the same variant.

No single gene is involved in all cases of dyslexia. Dyslexia is at most an inherited tendency, increasing the likelihood that a child will experience common symptoms. However, environmental influences, such as diet or stress, might trigger or suppress the action of specific genes. Your child's learning experiences will also play a role as to the severity and type of symptoms.

CHAPTER 2

Characteristics of Dyslexia

The symptoms of dyslexia are extremely variable. In fact, your child's symptoms may not even be consistent from day to day. Children with dyslexia might seem careless or as though they are not trying hard enough. At home and at play, they might be very adept, but at school, children with dyslexia might struggle to master the most basic material. This chapter will help you recognize the signs of dyslexia so that you can better understand your child's needs and take appropriate action.

Early Signs of Dyslexia

Because dyslexia is primarily associated with difficulty in learning to read, it cannot be reliably diagnosed until your child reaches the age at which reading typically begins. Although most children are ready to begin to read at about age six, individual development is variable. It is normal for some children to pick up basic reading skills as early as age four, and it is also normal for many children to be delayed in learning to read until age seven or eight.

Symptoms of Dyslexia

Identifying signs of dyslexia can be a difficult task. Many of the problems that are telltale symptoms of dyslexia in older children are part of normal development in a three-year-old. In order to assess whether your very young child could have dyslexia, it's best to look at her overall learning pattern. Following are some common characteristics that may be signs of dyslexia in preschool-age children:

- Jumbling sounds of words in speech, such as saying "pasgetti" for *spaghetti* or "mawn lower" for *lawn mower*
- Confusing words signifying direction in space or time, such as *up* and *down*, *in* and *out*, *yesterday* and *tomorrow*
- Forgetting or confusing the word for known objects, such as *table* or *chair*
- Delayed speech development
- Unusual speech patterns, such as frequent hesitations or stammering
- Difficulty with behavior or learning
- Difficulty remembering and following directions
- Extremely low tolerance for frustration
- Difficulty getting dressed, buttoning clothes, and putting shoes on the correct feet
- Excessive tripping, bumping into things, and falling over
- Difficulty with catching, kicking, or throwing a ball; with hopping and/or skipping

 Fact

Studies show that if a child has a parent or older sibling with dyslexia, there is a 40 percent chance that he will also have difficulty in learning to read. If dyslexia seems to run in your family, you will want to be alert to possible symptoms before your child begins school.

Reading and Writing

If you've noticed that your child has difficulty learning to form letters or frequently reverses letters, it makes sense for you to be concerned. However, many small children do not have the small-motor coordination needed for writing, and reversals of some letters in writing is common in many children up until age seven. Reversals of entire words—"mirror" writing—are less common, but are not significant in isolation. They are a sign of dyslexia only if accompanied by other symptoms. Although most children will learn to recognize some letters of the alphabet in early childhood, many are unable to learn to recite or write the letters of the complete alphabet until they reach school age.

Here are some problems with prereading skills that may be early signs of dyslexia:

- Difficulty learning nursery rhymes and rhyming words
- Difficulty in learning (and remembering) names of letters
- Enjoys being read to but shows no interest in letters or words
- Difficulty with clapping a simple rhythm

Keep in mind that it is important to look at the overall pattern of learning, including strengths as well as weaknesses. Many children simply are not ready to read until they are somewhat older than average; that does not mean they have dyslexia.

Speech and Language

A child who shows significant language delays or difficulties with speech can and should be evaluated by a speech and language therapist. If you or your child's pediatrician suspects a possible hearing problem, you should also seek evaluation from an audiologist. Those language problems can be an early sign of dyslexia; they can also indicate hearing or auditory learning problems. If a child is merely late to begin talking, perhaps not speaking or only saying a few words until age three or later, consider how she responds to language. If your child seems to understand what you are saying to her and responds appropriately to simple instructions, her delayed speech may just be part of her normal developmental pattern.

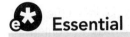 **Essential**

Expression and Articulation

You should be more concerned if your child has continued speech difficulties once she begins talking. Children with dyslexia or other language problems often have difficulty expressing themselves or with understanding what is said to them. Your child may have difficulties with articulation, which is the ability to pronounce specific words correctly. While all young children mispronounce difficult words at first, a child with dyslexia is particularly prone to making errors that confuse the order or sequence of sounds in a word or phrase.

Problematic Speech Patterns

Your child may stutter, hesitate, or stammer. This is called dysfluency, an interruption in the rhythm of speech. Some children have difficulties with voice tones, pitch, and volume. An odd or halting manner of speech can also be an early sign of dyslexia.

Your child may show signs of word retrieval problems. She may often hesitate or be unable to remember the word for common objects, or mistakenly substitute the wrong word, saying one thing when she means something else. She may frequently confuse words related to direction or time; for example, mixing up words like *over* and *under,* or *yesterday* and *tomorrow.* This word confusion may be apparent in her receptive language as well as her expressive language; that is, she may be easily confused by directions or statements that others make to her using these words.

Your child also may seem to have difficulty learning correct grammar and syntax (the arrangement of words in sentences), such as the use of pronouns. She may have a hard time learning the difference between *he* and *she*, or difficulty learning to use *I* rather than *me* when beginning a sentence. All of these problems are very normal at early stages of development, but most children show steady progress and outgrow them over time.

Persistent problems can indicate that your child has difficulty understanding and processing language. These early oral language problems can indicate that your child has difficulty thinking with and understanding the meaning of words. Even though she may outgrow the speech problems, her language issues may remain, leading to problems recognizing and understanding words in print.

Your Child's Hearing

Even if your child is speaking and understanding language well, you should be alert to other signs of any difficulties with hearing. Undetected hearing problems can affect the way that your child's sensitivity to the sounds of language develops. Many children with dyslexia suffer from allergies or frequent ear infections in early childhood. Ear infections can cause impaired hearing or intermittent hearing loss, and these may be a contributing factor to later learning problems. It is important to seek prompt medical treatment for ear infections and other respiratory illnesses.

 Fact

The National Information Center for Children and Youth with Disabilities estimates that one in ten individuals are affected by a communication disorder. In other words, at least one million children are placed in special education programs as a result of having a language or speech disorder.

Extreme sensitivity to loud noises or sounds with very high or low frequencies (such as the buzz emanated by fluorescent lights or the hum of a fan) may also indicate a problem with the way that your child hears the world around her. If you suspect a hearing problem, you can begin by consulting with your child's physician. She can examine your child and refer you to a specialist if necessary.

Your Child's Vision

Dyslexia is not caused by vision problems, but good vision is important to reading development. One in five preschool-age children has a vision disorder. Many common vision problems are preventable if detected in early childhood. According to the College of Optometrists in Vision Development, problems in any of the following areas can have a significant impact on learning:

- Eye-tracking skills (eyes staying on target, such as following a line of print)
- Eye-teaming skills (two eyes working together as a synchronized team)
- Binocular vision (simultaneously blending the images from both eyes into one image)
- Accommodation (eye focusing)
- Visual-motor integration (i.e., eye-hand coordination, sports vision, etc.)
- Visual perception (visual memory, visual form perception, visualization, directionality)

Your child can be evaluated for possible vision problems well before she reaches school age. As a parent, you should suspect a vision issue if you observe any of the following symptoms:

- One eye drifts or aims in a different direction from the other.
- Your child tilts or turns her head to see.

- Your child's head is frequently tilted to one side or one shoulder is noticeably higher.
- Your child squints, or closes or covers one eye.
- Your child seems to have a short attention span for her age.
- Your child has poor hand-eye coordination for activities like playing with a ball.
- Your child avoids coloring, working with puzzles, and other detailed activities.

It is a good idea to arrange a thorough optometric examination for your child by age three to determine whether her vision is developing normally, whether or not you suspect a specific problem. If you are concerned about your child's vision development, it is best to arrange an appointment with a board-certified developmental optometrist who specializes in evaluating and correcting these types of vision problems.

Positive Characteristics of Dyslexia

Dyslexia also comes with a set of talents and special aptitudes. These talents probably result from the same differences in brain structure and development that can make reading more difficult. For example, one researcher found that children with dyslexia could recognize letters that had been flipped or rotated more quickly than typical children; it is easy to see how this aptitude could also be the cause of common problems, such as *b/d* confusion.

However, this ability can be an asset for solving problems with real-world objects. Other researchers have found that individuals with dyslexia are also quicker to recognize drawings of impossible figures, are better at solving some puzzles involving three-dimensional objects, and are more adept at recognizing letters presented in their peripheral field of vision. Studies also show that children with dyslexia perform better on tests of creativity, particularly on tasks geared to assess original thinking.

ⓔ❗ Alert

Some traits that you may observe in your child include the following:

- Enjoys working with construction blocks or solving jigsaw puzzles
- Talented in art, drama, music, or other creative endeavors
- Learns well through hands-on experience, demonstrations, or observation
- Able to quickly provide the answer to complex mathematical problems or puzzles, but unable to explain the steps used to solve the problem
- Adept at taking apart and reassembling toys and household objects

Of course, it is possible for a child to have these talents without also having dyslexia. However, an understanding that these creative gifts are often part of the overall pattern may help you make sense of areas of difficulty as well, and will also help you advocate for your child. Your child will also feel better about himself if you can help identify the strengths that are part of his overall learning profile.

Dyslexia in School-Age Children

In most cases, you will probably not be aware that your child has dyslexia until she is in first or second grade. At that time, when reading instruction begins in earnest, your child is likely to lag behind and will begin to show signs of frustration at school. After several months, you may realize that your child simply hasn't caught on to reading in the same way as her peers. She may still have difficulty recognizing letters of the alphabet, or she may know the letters and their sounds but seem unable to put them together to form even simple words. You may notice that she seems unable to remember words that she has seen before, and struggles to sound out every word she sees.

Symptoms in Children Ages Five to Twelve

Not all reading problems stem from dyslexia. In fact, the majority of children identified by school authorities as having reading problems are struggling for other reasons, such as socioeconomic factors, language barriers, inadequate preparation for school, or global learning barriers. Because so many schoolchildren struggle with reading for reasons other than dyslexia, your child's teacher may not suspect dyslexia in your child, even if clear signs are there. Although a handful of states have laws or programs requiring early screening for dyslexia, most schools do not perform such testing. Very often children are not identified until they have fallen far behind their peers. Thus, it is your responsibility to be alert to possible signs and symptoms.

 Alert

Do not wait for the teacher to tell you she suspects a problem before seeking help. Many teachers have not been trained to recognize dyslexia, and they may not recognize the signs in a child who is bright and actively participates in many class activities that do not involve reading or writing.

Problems with Reading and Writing

The surest sign of dyslexia is simply the fact that your child seems bright and capable at home and at play, yet she struggles with reading, writing, and spelling. School-age children with dyslexia will exhibit many of the following symptoms:

- Confusing letters with similar appearances, such as *b* and *d* or *e* and *c*
- Writing that contains frequent reversals, transpositions, or inversions
- Difficulty remembering common sight words, even after repeated practice
- Stumbling, hesitating, or making mistakes or omissions when reading small, easy words like *and* or *from*
- Spelling phonetically and inconsistently (e.g., "foniks" for *phonics*)
- Complaining that letters and words on the page move or become blurred
- Complaining of dizziness, headaches, or stomachaches while reading

Even when she gains the ability to decode and recognize words and sentences, your child may read and reread material with little comprehension. As she matures and reading demands increase, new problems may arise.

Dyslexia and Math

In addition to problems with reading, your child may experience problems with math. Even if her math skills are strong, your child is likely to have poor rote memory and difficulty memorizing math facts, such as multiplication tables. She may be able to do simple arithmetic, such as addition or subtraction, but have difficulty applying or using math concepts when confronted with story problems. Even if your child seems to be good with math, she may often be unable to explain how she arrived at the correct answer or to write out the steps of the problem. All of these issues reflect an underlying problem with language; your child simply has difficulty understanding or remembering math concepts expressed in words.

Transposing numbers or making frequent errors with math symbols could be a problem for your child, such as confusing + and − signs, when copying from the board or textbook. This may reflect a perceptual problem or stem from the confusion over symbols that is part of dyslexia. Understanding time and time concepts might also be a problem.

Common Behavior Problems

Your first indication that something is wrong may be complaints from your child's teacher about her behavior or problems she is experiencing at school. Many behavior problems stem from the dyslexia itself; your child's teacher may complain that she doesn't pay attention or follow instructions, or that she is slow to complete classwork. These issues may be the direct result of your child's confusion and inability to understand much of what is going on around her.

Other behavior problems may be deliberate and could be an expression of her frustration and anger; she may intentionally try to disrupt the class to create distractions so as to avoid having to complete her work. She would rather that her classmates think of her as funny or bad than stupid. She may even want to incur punishment, if punishment means being sent to sit in the hallway or principal's office. To a child with dyslexia, such punishment can be a welcome reprieve from the torture of the classroom.

Some common behavior problems that your child's teacher may report include the following:

- Laziness, carelessness, or immaturity
- Daydreaming
- Disruptive behavior
- Being easily distracted
- Resistance to following directions
- Reluctance to work on assignments

To the teacher, all of those behaviors may seem deliberate. However, your child simply does not have the ability to conform to the expectations of a classroom when she is confused or unable to perform work at the same level and speed as the other children. You will not be able to help resolve the behavioral problem unless the learning problem is first addressed.

Social and Emotional Problems

Your child's school problems will probably also be reflected in problems at home and in interactions with her peers. Some of these issues may be directly related to her dyslexia, but many issues stem indirectly from the stress and frustration that is a constant part of your child's day.

From the age of seven, if not sooner, your child might be aware of her performance in comparison to other children her age. Struggling to understand concepts that other children find easy can be embarrassing. Showing your support and encouragement will help, but these problems will take their toll. Your child might complain of stomachaches or headaches in the morning, and while it may seem like an attempt to avoid school, the pain could be a very real manifestation of the stress and anxiety.

 Essential

You can help your child deal with anger and frustration—and help yourself—by teaching him relaxation and stress-reducing techniques and also practicing them yourself. This not only will relieve tension at home, but it will also help your child develop greater self-control and improve his ability to focus on his work.

It's easy to become short-tempered and frustrated at times, as dealing with your child may seem to require endless and fruitless repetition. It's tempting to shout, nag, and make dire threats of punishment. These responses will only make matters worse, as it will allow your child's dyslexia to become the focus of your home life. Confronting these problems will take patience, understanding, and effort. If you can lay aside your own feelings of frustration, you'll be able to provide your child with support and guidance. Try to encourage her to participate in activities she can succeed at, because her self-esteem will be crucial to her development and to peace in your household. Be prepared to set limits; your child needs understanding, but she also needs structure and support in learning to control her own behavior.

Dyslexia in Adolescents

In middle school and high school, the academic demands increase tremendously. Additionally, your child will be faced with juggling a number of classes with different teachers, each with their own expectations about homework and class behavior. Your child may need your help and support more than ever. However, your child is also feeling a natural pull toward independence. When he has academic problems, he may feel embarrassed by your attempts to confer with teachers and prefer to tough it out on his own rather than have his parents act as intermediaries.

Changes and New Challenges

As your child reaches adolescence, he may continue to have the same problems and symptoms that indicated dyslexia in his elementary school years. If he receives appropriate accommodations and services, you may notice some improvements. Often, after years of struggling and unsuccessful interventions, things seem to suddenly click at around age twelve. This can be a result of normal growth and development. Children at this age are developing a greater capacity for abstract and complex thought, and this very capacity may be the breakthrough your child needs in order to finally put all the elements needed for reading together.

Fact

Some of the changed expectations at school may benefit your child. With separate teachers for most of his classes, he may finally have the opportunity to excel in his areas of strength. It will become more common for written homework to be completed with a computer and word processor, and your child may become adept at using the computer spell checker and grammar checker. As math courses become more demanding, the use of the calculator becomes routine and expected. Your child may be able to round out his day with elective courses in art or music, and may find his niche in athletic or other extracurricular activities.

On the other hand, the social and behavioral problems that result from his frustration and low self-esteem may be magnified. As a way of dealing with their problems, teenagers may sometimes cut class or skip school, provoke conflict with teachers and administrators at school, experiment with illicit drugs and alcohol, engage in sexually promiscuous behavior, or perform criminal acts, such as shoplifting. Sometimes teens show signs of serious depression or suicidal tendencies.

These social and behavioral problems are not a direct result of dyslexia; many children will rebel and break rules in their high school years. However, a child who has low self-esteem and finds school to be stressful and unrewarding is at greater risk. As a parent, you will need to watch for signs that your child may be in trouble, and be ready to seek appropriate intervention.

The Undiagnosed Teenager with Dyslexia

Often, very bright children are able to compensate for their dyslexia in the early school years, but cannot cope with the greater intellectual demands of secondary level schooling. Some common signs that your teenager may have dyslexia are:

- He must repeatedly read and reread material in order to understand it.
- He has difficulty managing and keeping track of homework assignments and deadlines for various classes.
- He repeatedly reports that he was unaware of assignments and deadlines because the teacher "never told" him.
- He has unexpected difficulty with learning a foreign language.
- He struggles with higher math, such as algebra.
- There is a significant discrepancy between your child's school performance and scores on standardized tests.

If your child shows significant problems in any one of the above areas, it is a sign that he may have a previously undiagnosed learning disability. You should discuss these issues with him and also talk to parents of his classmates to find out whether their children are also having problems with the same subjects. Sometimes a problem with a math class or the first year of a foreign language can simply be the result of a poor teacher; poor grades in any subject can also occur with a teacher who is unusually strict in grading practices. If it is a "teacher" problem, usually other students and parents will have similar complaints. However, if the problems seem to be unusual or persistent, you should seek an evaluation for dyslexia or other learning barriers. The guidance counselor at school may be able to help arrange such testing, as well as help plan your child's course schedule to better meet his needs.

CHAPTER 3

Getting a Diagnosis

If you suspect that your child has dyslexia, you will probably want to seek a formal evaluation. The symptoms and degree of severity of dyslexia are variable; no single test will provide a definitive diagnosis. Rather, there are a variety of different approaches to measuring, defining, and understanding the learning profile and needs of each child. You may need to have your child evaluated by several different kinds of learning and medical specialists, depending on his specific symptoms and the extent of his learning problems.

Deciding to Seek Help

The first step in the process is to recognize that your child has a learning problem and that she will need extra help or intervention to overcome her difficulties. Coming to this point may be surprisingly difficult. Your child's own performance may be different from day to day, leading you to question whether there is any significant problem. Unfortunately, this inconsistency is part of the profile of dyslexia, as children with dyslexia are particularly susceptible to the effects of fatigue, stress, or frustration.

Fear of Labeling
Many parents are afraid that if their child is "labeled" with a learning disability, the label will do more harm than good. You

may fear that your child will be placed in a special education classroom with children who have cognitive or emotional problems far worse than dyslexia, or that the diagnosis will prevent your child from having access to more challenging course and enrichment opportunities. You may also be afraid that your child will be singled out and rejected by her peers. Your child may also harbor similar fears. More than anything, she wants to be liked and accepted by her peers, and to be able to learn as quickly as they do and share in the same activities. Like you, she also fears being singled out or left behind.

Fortunately, many of these fears are unfounded. Public awareness has increased dramatically, and most people now understand that children with dyslexia are bright and capable. Teachers and school administrators will usually understand that your child may be struggling in one area but capable of doing advanced work in another. A diagnosis of dyslexia is often the first step toward structuring an educational program that will lead your child toward success. In fact, for a very bright child, testing of IQ and aptitude in the course of an evaluation for dyslexia may also lead to qualification and placement in your school's program for gifted and talented youngsters. Once the learning disability is recognized, your child's innate strengths and potential might also become more apparent. In contrast, the failure to diagnose can leave your child struggling against an ever-increasing set of academic demands, with no real prospect of receiving help or understanding. Very few children can overcome dyslexia without specialized help and academic support.

Overcoming Resistance to Testing

You may find that when you discuss your child's problems with others, they may try to dissuade you from seeking a diagnosis. When you raise the issue with your child's teacher, she may try to reassure you that your child simply needs more time. She may seem to try to avoid any discussion of the subject, or actively discourage you from asking for testing, arguing that you do not want your child labeled with a disability.

You may also encounter surprising resistance from your family members. It is common for one parent to feel that the learning problems can be resolved with hard work and determination. Other family members may suggest that your child's problems stem from laziness, lack of motivation, or immaturity—and even try to blame your parenting style—arguing that your child simply needs more attention or discipline.

 Alert

You may be told that your child is too young to be tested, or that there is no test for dyslexia that can be given. If your child is old enough to attend school, this is not true. Even though a firm diagnosis may not be possible, your child can be screened to determine if he has a learning pattern indicating possible dyslexia.

Again, you need to trust your instincts. Keep in mind that if you are mistaken in suspecting dyslexia, the best way to find out is through testing and diagnosis. Even if your child does not have dyslexia, an evaluation by a qualified professional may help you uncover other issues that are at the root of your child's school problems.

When an Older Child Asks for Help

In some cases, your older child or teenager may be the one who asks for testing. Your child may find the academic demands in middle school and high school overwhelming, at least in some subject areas. She may have learned about dyslexia on her own, through the Internet or by talking to other kids. In any case, she knows that she is struggling with material that seems easy for her peers.

Your teenager may be afraid to bring up the subject of dyslexia at home. She may be embarrassed to let you know just how poorly she is doing at school, or she may be afraid that you will be angry or upset. It is important that you listen to your child and try to understand the reasons she feels she needs extra help. You might want to take a list of common dyslexia symptoms from this book or from a website, and ask your child to show you which problems on the list she feels apply to her. You may be surprised to learn that your child has been struggling for years, but has managed in the past to hide her problems through sheer determination and hard work. Your support and understanding is crucial; for a child who has previously done well academically, an appropriate diagnosis can be the boost she needs to excel in high school and gain admittance into the college of her choice.

Is Diagnosis Always Necessary?

Some families are able to help their children without formal testing and diagnosis. Keep in mind that dyslexia is not a disease or mental defect, but a learning difference that usually requires that the child receive extra educational support. You don't need a prescription to enroll your child at a learning center or hire a tutor, and the same multisensory teaching methods that are best for children with dyslexia will also tend to help other children, as they are geared to reach multiple learning styles.

If you homeschool, or if your child is attending a school with a flexible and understanding staff, you may find that her needs can be well addressed without going through the process of a formal diagnosis of a learning disability. However, diagnostic testing will help you better understand your child and may guide you to make better choices. Ideally, testing should give you a map of your child's strong and weak points, and a set of recommendations as to how best to meet her educational needs.

 **Question**

What is "stealth dyslexia"?
Physicians Fernette and Brock Eide use the term "stealth dyslexia" to describe children who appear to have age-appropriate reading skills, but struggle with writing or spelling, as well as displaying other common symptoms of dyslexia. Because these children seem to be good readers, their dyslexia often goes unrecognized.

A diagnosis of dyslexia or a related learning disability may also give you and your child important legal rights. If your child is in public school, the diagnosis can be a step toward requiring school authorities to work with you to design an Individualized Education Program (IEP) to meet your child's needs. If your child qualifies for special education services, you will be entitled to have a voice in the process and to attend regular meetings to discuss and monitor your child's progress, and to make modifications to the IEP as needed.

It's possible that a diagnosis could also prompt your child's school to offer her appropriate modifications and accommodations to enable her to experience success in school. For example, she might be allowed extra time on tests or allowed to use a calculator. These modifications help level the playing field so your child is able to keep pace with her classmates.

How Dyslexia Is Diagnosed

There is no single test for dyslexia that all experts use, or any single agreed-upon standard for testing. There is not even a definition of dyslexia that is uniformly accepted. The symptoms and characteristics of dyslexia vary significantly from one individual to the next, and the range of difficulties can vary from being quite mild to extremely severe. Some experts define dyslexia broadly to include a range of common learning difficulties, whereas others use different names and categories to describe the various academic, social, and behavioral issues that may accompany dyslexia.

Dyslexia by Any Other Name

The process of diagnosis is complicated by the fact that experts in different fields often prefer using different names to describe the symptoms they see. For many specialists, the term *dyslexia* seems overbroad when more precise terminology can be used to describe individual symptoms. Some experts might divide dyslexia into various subtypes; others might elect to call it something else entirely, such as "Developmental Reading Disorder." The specific label attached to your child's learning problems may depend on who is doing the labeling; a medical doctor, for example, is likely to use different terminology from a learning specialist at your child's school. While this can seem terribly confusing, it is important to stay focused on what the evaluators tell you about your child's learning needs.

Who Can Diagnose Dyslexia?

Dyslexia is diagnosed by a specialist who is trained and qualified in the assessment of learning disabilities. This may include:

- A clinical or educational psychologist
- A school psychologist
- A neuropsychologist
- A learning disabilities specialist
- A medical doctor with training and experience in the assessment of learning problems

Your child's evaluation might also include examination by other medical specialists. An audiologist might be involved in determining whether your child has problems with hearing or processing the sounds of language. A developmental optometrist might be needed to determine whether your child has vision difficulties that are contributing to his reading problems. Even if your child has 20/20 vision, reading might be hampered because of difficulties with near point vision, tracking, or eye teaming. A neurologist may be involved to test for problems that may stem from brain damage or problems with brain function beyond dyslexia. If your child has problems regulating his behavior or sustaining attention, a child psychologist or psychiatrist may be consulted to evaluate for attention deficit hyperactivity disorder (ADHD) or other psychiatric and emotional problems.

The purpose of all this testing is not only to determine whether your child has dyslexia, but also to consider and rule out the possibility of other problems that may contribute to his learning difficulties. Your child may have a number of different issues, some of which may be easier to treat than others.

 Alert

Your child's teacher may suggest that he be tested for ADHD because of classroom behavior problems. If your child is having problems with reading or writing, it is crucial that he also be tested for dyslexia and other learning disabilities. Medication commonly used for ADHD may help your child pay attention in class, but it will not help him learn to read or resolve a learning disability.

Early Diagnosis and Screening

Because dyslexia is primarily diagnosed through tests measuring skills related to reading and reading readiness, it is not possible to reliably diagnose a child who is too young to start school. Many common symptoms of dyslexia, such as letter reversals in writing, are also part of normal childhood development. Children grow and learn at different rates. Even though most children can learn to read at age six, many are not ready to learn to read until age seven or eight. That is why reading instruction in schools generally continues through the primary grades, from grades K–3.

That does not mean that your child cannot be helped, however. There are many reasons why a young child may be struggling in school, but extra support and reading instruction will help all children who are falling behind. A young child can be screened for early signs of dyslexia, and you can plan age-appropriate early interventions if indicated. If you are concerned about early signs of dyslexia in your preschool-age child (age three to five), you can also provide extra support at home to help build reading readiness skills.

 Fact

Two states, Wyoming and Louisiana, have laws specifically mandating that all schoolchildren in grades K–3 be screened for dyslexia. Texas also requires dyslexia screening, but the law does not specify grade level. More information about state laws and pending legislation can be found at *www.dyslegia.com*.

In some cases, screening will be done regularly by the school. A small number of states have laws requiring all schoolchildren to be screened for dyslexia. Even where dyslexia screening is not required, it is now very common for schools to regularly test children's progress in reading, typically using a test called DIBELS (Dynamic Indicators of Basic Early Literacy Skills). This is a simple series of one-minute tests that a teacher can use to monitor reading development. Although it is not a formal test for dyslexia, it will highlight specific skill areas where your child may be falling behind.

Who Pays for Diagnostic Testing

Federal law requires that all public schools provide testing, without charge to the parents, whenever there is reason to suspect a learning disability. Even if your child is in private school, you are entitled to these services from the public school district. In many cases the evaluation will be initiated at the request of a teacher or school administrator familiar with your child. However, if you suspect that your child has dyslexia, you can request testing directly. Be sure to put your request in writing and send it to the school principal.

Your health insurance may also cover the costs of some kinds of testing, particularly medical testing, such as evaluations by a neurologist or audiologist. Your child's pediatrician may be able to assist by making a referral for testing by appropriate specialists. Each health insurance policy is different, so the first step is to carefully review your policy.

You may prefer to arrange and pay for your own testing. Diagnostic testing can be very expensive, but you may feel more comfortable with the quality of an evaluation if it is done by professionals that you have selected.

Tests and Measurements

There are several different tests that may be used to evaluate your child. They are not necessarily specific to dyslexia, but when combined, they help provide a good picture of your child's development.

Intelligence Testing

An evaluator will often start with an IQ test to determine your child's overall ability level. One of the most common tests used is the Wechsler Intelligence Scale for Children (WISC-III or WISC-IV). This test is favored because it breaks down scores into two scales, Verbal and Performance, which in turn each consist of various subtests. The Verbal Scale measures language expression, comprehension, listening, and the ability to apply these skills to solving problems. The Performance Scale assesses nonverbal problem solving, perceptual organization, speed, and visual-motor proficiency. It includes tasks like puzzles, picture analysis, imitating designs with blocks, and copying. This test is given orally, by an evaluator working individually with your child, so your child does not have to know how to read to score well on the test.

By looking at the scores on various subtests, the evaluator will see a pattern of strengths and weaknesses. This sort of testing is extremely valuable for all children and can be used to indicate a wide variety of learning disabilities. Dyslexia is indicated as a possible diagnosis if the subtests show that a child has particular weaknesses in areas normally associated with dyslexia—such as verbal fluency, short-term auditory memory (digit span), or speed of processing information.

 Alert

You may be told that dyslexia is a medical term and that you will need a medical doctor to diagnose it. This is not true. Your child's pediatrician may be able to make recommendations and refer you to appropriate specialists, but she will not be able to make a determination as to whether or not your child has dyslexia.

WISC testing will also provide a "Full Scale" IQ—the number that results from combining the results of the Verbal and Performance scales. This is useful in evaluating overall cognitive ability and making recommendations for education and therapy. However, caution should be used in interpreting these results as a measure of your child's intellectual capacity. A very bright child may have a lower-than-expected IQ result due to poor performance on some of the subtests. Your child's emotional state and attitude toward testing could also result in poor performance on this test.

The evaluator may choose to supplement the WISC with IQ tests that do not rely on language ability, in order to get a better sense of your child's true abilities. If your child has scored particularly high on some of the WISC subtests, the evaluator may administer the Stanford–Binet (SB5), which can provide a more detailed measurement of the highest and lowest levels of functioning. Alternatively, the evaluator may also choose to administer the Ravens Progressive Matrices (RPM), which tests abstract reasoning by having your child complete a series of puzzles by identifying a missing item that completes a pattern.

Achievement Tests

Your child will also be given achievement tests to measure reading ability and other relevant academic skills, such as spelling or writing. The specific tests will vary depending on the preferences of the evaluator and the age of your child. Younger children will be given tests that measure prereading and early reading skills, such as simple word recognition tests. Older children may be given tests that measure sentence reading, oral fluency, and reading comprehension.

These tests are not the same as the standardized tests that are used in schools to assess classroom performance. Group standardized tests are not valid for measuring individual ability levels because they are designed for purposes of comparing the overall achievement of large groups of children. Although your child's scores on standardized tests may be a relevant piece of information to include in an evaluation, those tests are not a reliable way to diagnose learning disabilities.

Specialized Tests for Dyslexia

Your child will also be given some specialized tests geared toward measuring problems commonly associated with dyslexia. For example, a child's ability to parse out the sounds of language can be measured with tests of phonemic awareness. Your child may be asked to read a set of "nonwords"—that is, invented words with no real meaning such as *slimp* or *hife*. He may also be asked to say whether certain words rhyme, or to break apart words by their sounds, such as to say the word *bent* without the "n" sound.

 Alert

If you don't understand some of the terms or labels used in the written report, ask your child's evaluator to explain what each means in simple terms. What specific observations support the label given to your child? What type of tasks will be difficult for your child? What types of therapy or tutoring are best to address the specific problems described?

The evaluator will also likely test your child's word retrieval skills and auditory and verbal processing speed. For example, your child may be tested for rapid automatic naming, which requires the child to quickly read aloud the names of letters or numbers presented on a chart or graph. Short-term memory, or digit span, might also be tested. These tests ask children to remember and repeat a short sequence of letters or numbers or to identify a sequence of letters, numbers, or pictures after briefly viewing a picture or card with such a sequence.

Types of Dyslexia

A diagnosis of dyslexia may be classified into one of several subtypes. These subtypes are basically labels for the pattern of symptoms that emerged through testing. Understanding the nature of your child's difficulty can help guide you to choosing the right program of instruction or remediation. The labels vary somewhat depending on the type of testing used.

 Fact

Most children with dyslexia have a combination of both the phonological and visual subtypes. Research evidence shows that about 60 percent of children have symptoms of both forms of dyslexia, while about 20 percent have a pure visual form, and the remaining 20 percent show symptoms of the phonetic form only.

Some of the common subtypes are:

- **Dysphonetic dyslexia:** (also called dysphonesia; phonological dyslexia; or auditory dyslexia). Characterized by difficulties with word attack skills, including phonetic segmentation and blending. Can be identified by poor "nonword" reading skills, which are sometimes used to test phonetic skills. Spelling can be inconsistent with bizarre letter combinations.

- **Dyseidetic dyslexia:** (also called dyseidesia, surface dyslexia, or visual dyslexia). Children may have a good ability to sound out words but read very laboriously, have difficulty learning to recognize whole words visually, and have problems deciphering words that do not follow regular phonetic rules. Spelling tends to be unorthodox but highly phonetic (*skul* for *school*).

- **Naming-speed deficits:** (also called semantic dyslexia, dysnomia, or anomia). Diagnosed primarily from poor performance on tests of rapid automatic naming, which manifests as difficulty with word retrieval. Children may hesitate in speech, or frequently substitute a mistaken word for what they mean (*tornado* when they mean *volcano*). They may also frequently use generic words (e.g., *thing*, or *place*) instead of specific nouns; or they may resort to descriptive phrases (e.g., "the eating thing" rather than *spoon*).

- **Double-deficit:** Double-deficit dyslexia is a label attached to children who have both the phonological and the naming-speed subtypes. These children are thought to have a particularly severe and persistent form of dyslexia.

Many children have symptoms that overlap more than one of the various subtypes, and are not easily categorized.

Overlapping and Related Conditions

The results of testing may indicate that your child has a learning disability other than dyslexia. In some cases, the learning disability may be the same thing as dyslexia. For example, the evaluation may conclude that your child has a Developmental Reading Disorder or Phonological Processing Disorder. These phrases are merely different ways of describing dyslexia or a subtype.

It is also very common for children with dyslexia to be diagnosed as having Attention Deficit Hyperactivity Disorder (ADHD), Central Auditory Processing Disorder (CAPD), or a visual processing issue. These are different from dyslexia, but there is substantial overlap in symptoms. That is, in many cases diagnosis of these conditions will be made based on the same symptoms that support a diagnosis of dyslexia.

Alert

Find out exactly which symptoms support each diagnosis, and think about what you have observed in your child. If the diagnosis does not make sense to you, it may be mistaken. Focus on what sort of help your child actually needs, not on the label that is given to his symptoms.

For example, dyslexia is primarily a problem with processing of language, and reading problems are often accompanied by problems with using and understanding language. It is possible for a child to have an auditory processing disorder without dyslexia, but when a child has both the auditory processing issues and difficulty with reading, they probably are simply different manifestations of the same underlying language processing problem. The real issue is that the child needs help with understanding the sounds of language.

Similarly, ADHD is generally characterized by high distractibility, difficulty staying "on task," and a variety of related behavioral problems. A child who cannot read and is feeling confused or frustrated in the classroom is likely to manifest the same sort of symptoms.

However, it is also possible that a child will have additional symptoms or problems that will support a dual diagnosis. For example, difficulty with reading will not cause a child to be hyperactive, but many children with dyslexia also have the hyperactive form of ADHD. Solving one problem won't help unless the other is also addressed.

Dyslexia and the Gifted Child

As a result of testing, you may be surprised to learn that your child is intellectually gifted. It is very common for the difficulties associated with dyslexia to mask your child's true potential. Your child may have a brilliant mind, but his difficulties with verbal and written language have prevented him from expressing his thoughts in a way that others can understand. The combination of intellectual giftedness with learning disabilities is actually quite common. Gifted children have learning disabilities at least as often as other children. Research has shown that children who are highly or profoundly gifted often have predominantly visual-spatial or right-brained learning styles; this puts them at particularly high risk for dyslexia.

On the other hand, your child's strong intellectual abilities may also make it difficult to get a firm diagnosis of dyslexia. Test results may show that your child has some—but not all—of the common symptoms of dyslexia; or your child simply might not score poorly enough on any of the tests to support a diagnosis. A close look at scores on various subtests may reveal signs of specific learning barriers that are holding your child back.

Commercial Screening

There are many private-sector or commercial programs that are geared toward treating dyslexia or related problems. You may choose to go directly to the learning center or clinic providing the program for a screening test.

The screening tests offered by the clinic are usually far less expensive than full diagnostic testing; in some cases, the tests may be offered for free. The tests usually will give you some more information about your child; however, they are not the same as diagnostic testing. Rather, the screening tests are designed to determine whether the child fits whatever program or services are being offered, or in some cases to create an appropriate service plan for the child. They often use terminology that is specific to the private program. Those terms generally would not be accepted as a valid diagnosis by a school or qualified medical or educational professionals.

Some common private-program screening tests for traits related to dyslexia are:

- **Concept Imagery Disorder:** This describes a weakness in the ability to turn language into images. It is used by Lindamood-Bell practitioners to determine whether a child should receive their Visualizing and Verbalizing program.
- **Davis Perceptual Ability Assessment:** This assessment determines whether a child has the ability to mentally visualize an imagined object from multiple perspectives. It is aimed at finding a strong visual-spatial skill frequently associated with dyslexia. It is used by Davis Dyslexia Correction providers to learn more about the child's learning style, as a means of determining the best approach for teaching the Davis mental self-regulation tools.
- **Scotopic Sensitivity Syndrome:** This describes a visual-perceptual problem where the child has difficulty viewing text due to sensitivity to lighting or color conditions. It is used by Irlen Method screeners to determine whether the child will benefit by using special colored overlays or lenses while reading.

CHAPTER 4

Related Conditions

C hildren with dyslexia often have related learning difficulties. Dyslexia is usually accompanied by difficulties with expressive writing and spelling. Problems with spelling are particularly persistent with dyslexia, and sometimes are apparent even when the child seems to be a good reader. Children with dyslexia often have academic difficulties in other areas, such as math. Dyslexia can also lead to behavioral problems that overlap with other disorders, such as ADHD. Some children with dyslexia also suffer from other unrelated mental or emotional disorders that make treatment of dyslexia more complicated.

Problems with Handwriting or Expressive Writing

Dysgraphia means "difficulty with writing." Usually the term describes a difficulty with handwriting, either with printing or cursive. Sometimes there are underlying physical or neurological issues unrelated to dyslexia. Some children may have difficulty with small-motor coordination that stems from other developmental causes, or from physical difficulties that make it hard for them to properly grasp a writing implement or coordinate their movements. These children may benefit from occupational therapy.

 **Question**

Can a child who is a good reader also have dyslexia?
Yes. Occasionally, a child is able to overcome or avoid issues with reading but will still have an array of related symptoms. Usually, such a child is extremely bright with a strong visual memory, allowing her to develop good sight-reading skills despite having characteristic difficulty with phonetics. The dyslexia may become apparent because of problems with productive writing or spelling.

The term dysgraphia is also sometimes used to describe an expressive writing disorder: a difficulty putting thoughts to words when writing. Children with this sort of difficulty will find any sort of written composition to be a laborious process and may have great difficulty constructing sentences and paragraphs in a grammatical or logical format.

When associated with dyslexia, dysgraphia is a reflection of underlying difficulties with written language. Some common symptoms are:

- Fingers are cramped when grasping pencil or pen, or child uses unusual grip.
- Written work is marred by frequent cross-outs or erasures.
- Writing is inconsistent, with a mixture of upper and lower case letters, printed and cursive, variation in size of letters, or irregular formation and slant.
- Child has difficulty keeping writing on lines or within margins.
- Child writes very slowly and is easily fatigued.
- Handwriting is illegible.

Students with dysgraphia often have sequencing problems. Symptoms that appear to be a perceptual problem (reversing letters/numbers, writing words backward, writing letters out of order, and very sloppy handwriting) can also stem from difficulties with serial or sequential information processing.

 Fact

Children's writer Avi has dysgraphia. He has difficulty with writing and spelling. As a child, his teachers told him that his writing didn't make sense, and he failed most of his courses in high school. He still finds writing difficult and needs to rewrite frequently. Nonetheless, he grew up to become a prolific writer and the author of dozens of award-winning children's books.

Difficulty with Math

Dyscalculia is a learning disability with math. About 60 percent of children with dyslexia have difficulty with numbers or number relationships. However, about 11 percent of students with dyslexia excel in mathematics, while the remaining students have ordinary mathematical abilities. Thus, although strongly associated with dyslexia, dyscalculia should be considered a separate and different learning problem.

Symptoms of dyscalculia include:

- Problems with operations such as addition, subtraction, multiplication, and division
- Difficulty learning math facts such as memorizing times tables
- Confusion over mathematical symbols such as + and ×; −, ÷, and =; < (less than) and > (greater than)
- Difficulty with understanding words used to describe mathematical operations such as *difference* or *sum*
- Tendency to reverse or transpose numbers in writing such as writing 31 for 13

- Difficulty understanding concepts related to time and learning to tell time
- Difficulty grasping and remembering math rules, formulas, sequence (order of operations), or algorithms used for problem solving

Some problems associated with dyscalculia stem from the same underlying issues with language processing and sequencing that characterize dyslexia. Your child may be able to understand math concepts when working with math manipulatives, but may struggle working with numerals and mathematical symbols and formulas, and have difficulty understanding written procedures for solving math problems, such as "borrowing" or "carrying" in addition or subtraction. She may be able to understand math that is represented symbolically, but struggle with word problems; she may know that $3 + 2 = 5$, but be unable to work out a problem like "If Mary has 3 cookies and Tim has 2, how many cookies are there in all?"

 Essential

Your child will learn math concepts better using manipulatives and hands-on activities. Encourage him to use small objects, such as beans or his fingers, to aid in calculation. Using play money and making change may aid with understanding of addition and subtraction. Use strategies to help demonstrate patterns and relationships involved in mathematics, rather than relying on rote memorization.

Even if your child seems to have strong mathematical ability, she may use unorthodox approaches to arrive at a solution, or be unable to explain the process she uses in words. Your child may seem to know the answer to some problems immediately, but be very slow to work out pencil and paper answers. This also is a reflection of the underlying language problems, and occurs when a child relies on her stronger visual spatial reasoning skills to picture the problem and solution, rather than using orderly manipulation of numbers. Ironically, these skills may enable your child to excel later on with higher mathematics, such as trigonometry or calculus, but can hold her back during early years when emphasis is on simple arithmetic and rote memorization of math facts.

"Clumsy Child Syndrome"

Dyspraxia is difficulty with thinking out, planning, and executing sensory/motor tasks. It is sometimes called "clumsy child syndrome." Your child with dyspraxia may have difficulty coordinating small-motor functions, such as learning to tie her shoes or button her clothes. There may be difficulties with balance and large-motor coordination, such as difficulty learning to ride a bicycle or catching a ball. Your child may seem particularly clumsy or accident-prone, always breaking, tripping over, or bumping into things.

Some of these issues may also be related to cerebellar or vestibular problems. The cerebellum is a section at the rear of the brain, behind and below the cerebrum. The cerebellum is largely involved in coordination and in bodily, kinesthetic memory, which is involved in learning a new physical skill such as roller-skating. There is some research indicating the cerebellum tends to be smaller and more symmetric in children with dyslexia, who also show evidence of reduced activation of the cerebellum in small-motor tasks, such as learning and practicing a sequence of finger movements.

The vestibular system is governed by the inner ear. Its purpose is to keep tabs on the position and motion of a person's head in space. A vestibular disorder can result in dizziness, unsteadiness or imbalance when walking, vertigo, and nausea.

A child with verbal dyspraxia may have difficulty coordinating speech, which may result in stammering or garbled speech. Essentially, the brain is not sending the correct signals to the muscles to produce coherent speech. Verbal dyspraxia is extremely frustrating, because the child knows in her mind what she wants to say, but the sounds do not come out of her mouth correctly when she tries to speak. This is different from word retrieval issues commonly associated with dyslexia, which occur when the child has an idea of what she wants to say but cannot think of the correct word. With dyspraxia, the child has the word in mind, but can't seem to get her lips and tongue to cooperate.

Attention Deficit Hyperactivity Disorder

ADHD may be diagnosed with or without hyperactivity; generally the diagnosis will specify whether the child fits either the Inattentive or Hyperactive/Impulsive type. Both patterns of attention deficits are very common among children with dyslexia. However, it is common for children with dyslexia to be misdiagnosed as having ADHD because of the overlap of symptoms and behaviors associated with dyslexia.

 Fact

Your child with dyslexia is twice as likely as other children to have ADHD; about 15 percent of students with reading problems are also diagnosed with ADHD. Conversely, a child with ADHD is twice as likely to have difficulties with reading; about 36 percent of children with ADHD also have dyslexia.

It is not clear why it is so common for children to have both ADHD and reading problems. Of course, the ADHD child will find it difficult to learn if she cannot focus attention in a classroom, but it is more likely that there is a common set of learning traits to both conditions. Some educators believe that, like dyslexia, ADHD stems from a predominantly right-brained learning style. Like dyslexia, ADHD is often seen in highly creative individuals and is common in gifted children. In many ways, the symptoms of ADHD may be the result of an overactive mind and an unharnessed imagination.

Inattention-Type Attention Deficits

Because there is so much overlap between symptoms of attention deficits and dyslexia, it is important to understand how ADHD is diagnosed. The criteria for diagnosis in the *Diagnostic and Statistical Manual of Mental Disorders* specify that a child can be diagnosed with ADHD (inattention type) if she has six or more of the following symptoms:

1. Fails to pay close attention to details or makes careless mistakes in schoolwork, work, or other activities.
2. Has difficulty holding attention in tasks or play activities.
3. Does not seem to listen when spoken to directly.
4. Does not follow through on instructions and fails to finish schoolwork or household chores.
5. Has difficulty organizing tasks and activities.
6. Avoids or dislikes tasks that require sustained mental effort (such as schoolwork or homework).
7. Loses things necessary for tasks or activities (e.g., toys, school assignments, pencils, books, or tools).
8. Is easily distracted by extraneous stimuli.
9. Is forgetful in daily activities.

However, each of the above symptoms is also a common characteristic of dyslexia. Your child's academic and language processing difficulties will make it very difficult for her to sustain attention, follow instructions, or complete schoolwork. Be careful before accepting a diagnosis of "inattentive" type ADHD; a mistaken diagnosis can sometimes lead to delays in getting help or special tutoring to address reading problems. Studies show that medications commonly prescribed for ADHD do not help children learn academic skills.

Fact

Although it is estimated that 15–20 percent of school children have dyslexia, only 5 percent are ever identified. The remaining 10–15 percent have a hidden disability, but it is possible that many of these children are mislabeled as having ADHD or some other behavioral or psychological problem.

Hyperactivity-Impulsivity Type

The second type of ADHD, hyperactivity-impulsivity type, is more distinct from dyslexia. This may be diagnosed when the child has six or more of the following symptoms:

1. Fidgets with or taps hands or feet, or squirms in seat.
2. Does not stay in seat in classroom or in other situations in which remaining seated is expected.
3. Runs around or climbs excessively in situations in which it is inappropriate.
4. Has difficulty playing or engaging in leisure activities quietly.
5. Is often "on the go" or acts as if "driven by a motor."
6. Talks excessively.
7. Blurts out answers before questions have been completed.
8. Has difficulty waiting his turn (e.g., while waiting in line).
9. Interrupts or intrudes on others (e.g., butts into conversations or games).

Some of these behaviors could also be a result of the learning problems associated with dyslexia. A child who feels frustrated or confused in a classroom will have a hard time sitting still or obeying rules. Again, it is important for you to consider the context surrounding the observed behavior.

Avoiding a Misdiagnosis

For attention deficit disorder to be properly diagnosed, the symptoms must be present in two or more settings, such as both school and home. These additional criteria help to sort out ADHD from school problems, as children whose difficulties are only manifested in the classroom environment simply do not have ADHD. Many children are highly active but function normally at home or at play, where they can engage in a reasonable amount of physical activity and have freedom to choose which tasks to focus their energy on.

 Alert

Symptoms of ADHD can also be a result of physical health problems, such as vitamin deficiencies or exposure to toxins, such as lead or mercury. Some children have food allergies or sensitivities that affect their behavior, including reactions to food additives and sweets or sodas.

The National Institute of Mental Health cautions that the behaviors associated with ADHD may merely reflect a child's response to a defeating classroom situation. Such symptoms can stem from feelings of frustration in a child who has a learning disability or who is emotionally immature, or from boredom in a child who finds the classwork tedious and unchallenging. A child with true ADHD will exhibit difficulty concentrating and completing tasks even in situations when it is clear that the child wants to participate fully, or will show signs of impulsivity and hyperactivity outside of the restricted environment of a school classroom.

Nonverbal Learning Disabilities (NLD)

Nonverbal Learning Disabilities are essentially the opposite of dyslexia. The child with NLD has early speech and vocabulary development, strong rote memory skills, attention to detail, early reading skills development, and excellent spelling skills. The learning disability is found when these strengths are accompanied by significant weaknesses in motor skills, spatial reasoning ability, or social awareness. Children with NLD have difficulty processing information that is not language based, either spoken or in writing. They have difficulty interpreting facial expressions or body language. They have a good memory for detail, but cannot understand the "big picture" or relate the details to form overall concepts.

Although NLD is very different from dyslexia, the symptoms can be confused. For example, an NLD child may have difficulty with balance and coordination, poor handwriting, and difficulty with reading comprehension. These are all symptoms that can exist with dyslexia as well; the main difference is that the NLD child's reading problems stem from difficulties appreciating the ideas and concepts represented by the words, whereas the child with dyslexia can easily grasp complex concepts, but has difficulty making sense of the words used to convey the ideas.

Cognitive and Intellectual Delays

Dyslexia is not related to low IQ or mental retardation of any kind. Historically, dyslexia has always been defined as existing only among children with normal or above-normal intelligence. Children with low intellectual abilities will have difficulties that are generalized to all academic areas, as well as problems with day-to-day functioning at home. In cases of moderate to severe mental retardation, parents usually will be well aware of their child's limitations long before he is ready to attend school.

Reading Problems in Children with Low Intelligence

Children who have IQs considered to be merely below average or who are borderline mentally retarded may also have reading problems. Although these children may not fit the traditional profile of dyslexia, their poor reading ability can stem from the same underlying problems. Unfortunately, it is not always easy to get a clear diagnosis.

Historically, many educators relied on a "discrepancy" test to diagnose dyslexia, looking for a significant gap between actual reading ability and the expected ability as determined from aptitude or IQ testing. However, recent research does not support this model. There is only a moderate correlation between IQ and reading ability, far less than the correlation between reading and early language development, such as phonological awareness, which is now considered closely related to dyslexia. In other words, IQ cannot reliably be used as a measure to predict reading skill.

 Alert

Your child's "potential" cannot be measured with an IQ test. Research has shown that children with visual-spatial learning styles, including dyslexia, tend to be "late bloomers." Your child will become more capable over time as higher brain functions develop and he is able to better relate new learning to existing knowledge and experience.

Measurement of IQ can also be suspect in a child with dyslexia, as the tests of intelligence rely largely on the same sort of skills that are impaired in children with dyslexia, such as language interpretation and short-term memory. Many children perform lower on IQ tests because of their dyslexia. It is very common to see such children score much higher on IQ tests as they grow older, especially if they receive effective remediation for their dyslexia. Over time, they simply acquire the skills needed to understand the test.

Getting Help at School

The practice of comparing IQ scores to reading ability can leave many children who have reading disabilities unable to qualify for services, such as additional tutoring or accommodations from their school district. If your child scores poorly on an IQ test, he may have exactly the same reading deficits as any other child with dyslexia, but be denied extra help and expected to function in the same classrooms with other children. He may be labeled as a "garden variety poor reader" or "low achiever." In essence, he may be punished because he is not considered smart enough to have dyslexia.

Most educators now favor abandoning the discrepancy model and identifying dyslexia based on the characteristic pattern of weaknesses, rather than using an artificial standard of the perceived potential of the child. If your child has low IQ scores but does not seem to be cognitively impaired in areas other than those usually associated with dyslexia, he will need the same extra help and will benefit from many of the same kinds of educational programs as any other child who is struggling to learn to read.

Mood Disorders

Some children with dyslexia also have emotional or psychiatric problems. In some cases, the problems are caused or exacerbated by the stress or frustration experienced in connection with dyslexia and academic problems. In other cases, behavior that is a response to dyslexia may give rise to a mistaken diagnosis. Finally, of course, many children with dyslexia also suffer from additional mental or emotional problems. Even if not directly related to the dyslexia, these issues can make it more difficult to help a child with academic issues, particularly if the psychiatric problems lead the child to become unmotivated or resistant to teaching.

Depression

A child may be diagnosed with depression if he exhibits a depressed or irritable mood for most of the day, for more days than not, over a sustained period of time. His mood may be accompanied by disruptions in patterns of eating or sleeping, low energy or fatigue, low self-esteem, poor concentration, difficulty making decisions, or feelings of hopelessness.

All children have feelings of sadness or frustration from time to time, but depression is diagnosed when such symptoms are continual and persistent. Depression can be treated with counseling or medications; however, if the underlying reason for depression is the child's despair over poor academic performance, it is crucial that the school situation also be addressed.

Disruptive Mood Dysregulation Disorder

If your child frequently has severe temper outbursts, accompanied with rage or aggression, he may be diagnosed with DMDD, a new category defined by the *DSM-5*. This diagnosis might apply if your child is at least six years old, has extreme temper outbursts averaging three or more times a week, and displays a persistently angry or irritable mood at most other times. Unfortunately, it is also very common for children with dyslexia to seem persistently angry and to habitually throw tantrums over routine homework assignments or daily attendance. For your child, the demands of school may seem unbearable, and an angry rage can be a cry for help.

Bipolar Disorder

Bipolar disorder, formerly known as manic depression, is marked by extreme changes in mood, energy, thinking, and behavior. The child will alternate between periods of mania and depression. During manic episodes, a child may be extremely irritable and prone to destructive outbursts. Alternatively, he may exhibit extreme elation and high energy. While depressed, the child will be extremely sad or irritable and have low energy. There may be physical complaints, such as headaches, muscle aches, stomachaches or tiredness, talk of or efforts to run away from home, unexplained crying, or extreme sensitivity to rejection or failure.

Children with bipolar disorder can experience multiple cycles between manic and depressive moods within the same day, moving from giddy, silly highs to morose and gloomy lows. Any indication of suicidal thoughts, such as a child's talk of wanting to die or wishing that he had never been born, should be taken very seriously, as even very young children may attempt suicide during depressive periods. Bipolar disorder tends to run in families, but children with dyslexia are no more at risk than any other children.

 Fact

Bipolar disorder can be mistaken for ADHD. However, stimulant medications (such as Ritalin) that are commonly prescribed for ADHD can induce or worsen the manic symptoms of bipolar disorder. That can also happen with medications commonly prescribed for depression. If you observe such symptoms when your child is taking medication, you should contact your physician immediately.

Behavioral Disorders

A child may be diagnosed with Conduct Disorder when there is a pattern of repetitive behavior where the rights of others or the major age-appropriate social norms are violated. For example, the child may frequently bully, threaten, or intimidate others; may destroy property; or may frequently lie or steal.

Oppositional Defiant Disorder (ODD) is diagnosed when there is an enduring pattern of uncooperative, defiant, and hostile behavior toward authority figures that does not involve major antisocial violations, is not accounted for by the child's developmental stage, and results in significant functional impairment. The child may frequently lose his temper, argue with adults, or actively defy rules or refuse to carry out requests from adults. He may deliberately try to annoy others or blame others for his own mistakes or misbehavior or seem angry and resentful. It can be difficult to distinguish behavior associated with ODD from behavior that is a normal but inappropriate response to feelings of frustration and anger stemming from academic difficulties and frequent criticism encountered at school. As with other behavioral issues, it is important for parents and teachers to recognize and address learning problems as a first step toward addressing behavioral issues.

Autistic Spectrum Disorders (ASD)

Autistic Spectrum Disorders include problems with nonverbal communication, socialization, and empathy. Children with ASD have difficulty understanding what other people are saying, need assistance to play with other children, enjoy routines, and find unfamiliar situations difficult. Symptoms can range from very mild to profound social and cognitive delays. The disorder is not associated with dyslexia, but it can coexist with dyslexia. Many children with autistic spectrum disorder also have difficulties learning to read and write.

Autism

Autism is a complex developmental disability that typically appears during the first three years of life. A child with autism processes and responds to information in unique ways. Although some can function at a relatively high level, many children with autism have serious cognitive impairments, and some never gain the ability to speak. A child with autism may seem closed off and shut down, or locked into repetitive behaviors and rigid patterns of thinking. He may avoid eye contact and resist physical contact, such as hugging, or may have frequent tantrums or remain fixated on a single item or activity, such as spinning objects. It's possible that his sensitivity to pain could be higher or lower than typical.

The severity of autism can be extremely variable. Children with mild to moderate symptoms are considered "high-functioning." Two children may share the diagnosis of autism, but behave very differently and have very different skills and abilities.

Fact

Autism is about three to four times more common in boys. However, girls with the disorder tend to have more severe symptoms and greater cognitive impairment. Although autism is frequently accompanied by mental delays, about one out of ten children with autism are savants with exceptional talents in narrowly constrained areas, such as drawing ability or playing the piano.

Asperger Syndrome

Asperger syndrome is similar to autism, but milder in form. Children with Asperger syndrome have normal or above-average intelligence. They usually do not have language delays, but often have unusual speech patterns; they may speak formalistically or without inflection, or speak in a rhythmic nature or with a high-pitched tone. They tend to interpret language very literally, often have a very literal understanding of language, and have difficulty understanding irony or verbal humor.

Children with Asperger syndrome usually want to fit in and have interaction with others, but they tend to be socially awkward and have difficulty understanding conventional social rules or the give and take of normal conversation. They are often obsessively interested in particular subjects and may become proficient at knowing obscure categories of information, such as memorizing baseball statistics or bus routes. They may enjoy collecting things, such as rocks or bottle caps. Although a diagnosis of Asperger syndrome does not include reading problems, the condition is frequently accompanied by symptoms of dyslexia.

Semantic Pragmatic Disorder (SPD)

Semantic Pragmatic Disorder is a communication disorder characterized by difficulties with social interaction, communication, and imagination. Autistic features are mild and concentrated in the areas of social use and understanding of language and communication.

Children with SPD are unable to process all the given information from certain situations, often focusing on details without understanding the big picture. The condition is usually first identified because of marked delays and difficulty with speech and language development.

Hyperlexia

Children with hyperlexia demonstrate an early and intense fascination with letters, numbers, patterns, and logos, and a self-taught, precocious ability to read, spell, write, or compute, usually before the age of five. At the same time, they have significant difficulty understanding and using oral language and with socializing and interacting appropriately with other people.

 Essential

It is possible for a child to learn to read early without having hyperlexia; many intellectually gifted children easily acquire reading skills as early as age three or four. Occasionally, a child with dyslexia will also be an early reader; dyslexia may be diagnosed later if the child has problems with advanced reading skills, writing, or spelling.

Although the early acquisition of reading ability makes hyperlexia seem very different from dyslexia, both conditions are rooted in difficulties with understanding and using language. A child with hyperlexia is often highly intelligent, learning best from visually presented information. The difference is that the child with hyperlexia can easily manipulate and understand written symbols for language and concepts, but has problems with oral language. Your child with dyslexia has difficulty with symbols but will be able to communicate well verbally and understand the concepts that language represents.

CHAPTER 5

Brain Research and Dyslexia

To understand what it means to have dyslexia, and what you can do to help your child build strong reading skills, it helps to know about brain research. Scientists can now use sophisticated equipment to study the human brain. They can create an image of the brain's internal wiring to measure electrical impulses, chemical changes, or cerebral blood while research subjects perform specific tasks. The brain is a complex system, and each research project sheds light on only a small part of the processes of learning, reading, and dyslexia. Though research cannot provide all the answers, each new study does provide an intriguing and helpful look into another piece of the puzzle.

Reading Changes the Brain

Parents who understand the dyslexic brain are better able to cope with the condition, but because dyslexia is, by definition, a disability impacting the ability to learn to read, it is sometimes difficult to sort out which brain differences may be innate causes of dyslexia, and which are a result of reading deficits. The process of learning and practicing any new skill will lead to physical changes in the brain. Simply put, if you've learned something new, then your brain has changed to allow that knowledge to be stored and retrieved.

When new knowledge is combined with a new skill or set of habits, then changes to both brain structure and function can be significant, as new neural connections are formed and strengthened with practice. The brain's ability to change and grow through life is called *neuroplasticity*.

 Essential

Learning new skills can alter your child's physical brain structure. Researchers have found that certain areas of the brain grew larger when they taught their subjects to juggle. When the jugglers stopped practicing and their brains were measured again, the brain expansion seen earlier was reduced.

Researchers have observed some of the changes promoted by reading by studying the brains of growing children at various ages and levels of reading proficiency. Other scientists have looked at the brains of individuals who learned to read only as adults, comparing them to similar adults who had never been taught to read. Brain scans showed that the late-reading adults experienced significant changes in brain structure, including the growth of new white matter connections between right and left-brain hemispheres.

The malleability of the brain presents a challenge in researching the causes of dyslexia. It is easy to compare a group of subjects with dyslexia to normal readers, but it is hard to know whether differences in their brain development patterns are related to their dyslexia, or a reflection of their weaker reading skills.

However, knowing that the brain changes with new skills also means that differences observed in the brains of children and adults with dyslexia are not barriers to achievement. While your child's dyslexia may stem from differences in brain growth and function, your child is also capable of learning to use his brain in new ways.

Physical Brain Differences Associated with Dyslexia

Researchers can learn about dyslexia by looking for physical differences in the brains of individuals with dyslexia, as well as by comparing the mental activity of people with dyslexia with that of people who have no reading problems. There are very real differences in brain structure that contribute to the learning difficulties that accompany dyslexia; however, there is also considerable variation from one individual to another, and this is important to bear in mind when thinking about your own child. Each brain is different; not all individuals with dyslexia process information exactly the same way.

Physical differences in brain structure documented in some studies have not been found in others, perhaps because of differences in the criteria for selection of the research participants with dyslexia. Further, some physical differences that have been tied to dyslexia in some individuals may also be seen in others who do not have dyslexia. For example, a study may show that a particular variation in brain development may exist among all research groups, but appear at a significantly higher rate among those who have dyslexia. Thus, it is likely that these differences are contributing factors but not direct causes of dyslexia.

These physical differences do not mean that there is anything wrong with your child's brain. In fact, the structural variations tied to dyslexia are often part of an overall pattern that is also connected to intellectual strengths.

Differences in Brain Symmetry

The left and right hemispheres of the brain are specialized for different tasks. For most people, a triangular area of the left-brain hemisphere associated with language processing is significantly larger than the corresponding region in the right hemisphere. That area, called the planum temporale (PT), is larger in the left hemisphere in about 75 percent of the brains studied. The remainder is either right lateralized, with the PT being larger in the right hemisphere, or symmetrical, with the PT being the same size in both hemispheres.

 Fact

After Albert Einstein died, his brain was preserved for research. Einstein's brain had a very unusual pattern of symmetries and asymmetries, not seen in other subjects. The PT (planum temporale) area of his brain could not be properly measured, because he was missing part of his sylvian fissure, which is a long groove in the brain that also forms a boundary of the PT.

Several research studies provide strong evidence that individuals with dyslexia are more likely to have an atypical symmetry pattern, usually with the PT being the same size in both hemispheres. However, other studies have found no difference; one research group reported an opposite pattern, with the men with dyslexia they studied having an exaggerated leftward asymmetry. A different researcher reported that only subjects with a pure phonological dyslexia subtype showed the symmetrical pattern.

The different results may be due to differences in methodology among the various studies, particularly with respect to selection criteria for the subjects with dyslexia and comparison groups. It is also possible that this difference in brain anatomy is correlated with specific types of reading difficulties or levels of severity. These differences may also be connected to creative or spatial talents often associated with dyslexia, supporting the greater facility of the right hemisphere for holistic and spatial reasoning tasks.

Researchers have also found evidence of similar variations in the cerebellum, the large area at the base of the brain that regulates coordination, balance, and movement. The cerebellum is also involved in the process of automatizing learned skills, including facility with language. In most people, the cerebellum is also asymmetrical, but in a reverse pattern: the right side of the cerebellum is usually larger than the left. However, in many individuals with dyslexia, the cerebellum is more symmetrical, with the right side being smaller in volume. Differences in cerebellar structure might explain why it is harder for a child with dyslexia to transition from mere decoding to automatic, fluent reading.

Your Child's Vision: The Magnocellular System

Research suggests that individuals with dyslexia may have a different pattern of brain-cell growth related to vision. Perceptual input from the eyes is processed in the visual cortex, an area at the rear of the brain that contains two types of specialized neurons. Very large neurons, called magnocells, are specialized for detecting movement or making visual distinctions in low light, low contrast settings. Smaller neurons in the same region, called parvocells, have a slower and more sustained response to visual stimuli, and are specialized for analyzing color, shape, and other surface properties of objects.

 Essential

Children with dyslexia perform better than others on tests of their ability to recognize letters presented at the outer edges of a line of text. Accurate reading is supported by the ability to hone in on the letters at the center of the visual field, but the dyslexic visual pattern would be beneficial in settings where a broader perspective is advantageous.

Individuals with dyslexia appear to have fewer magnocellular neurons. Subjects with dyslexia have less sensitivity to motion coherence—the ability to discern that a random group of dots are moving in unison when viewed against a larger field of dots—a task that recruits the magnocellular system. They also tend to have a slower flicker fusion rate, which is the rate at which rapidly flashing visual lights are perceived as merging. Brain studies using fMRI (functional magnetic resonance imaging) have also shown reduced activity during these tasks in the area of the brain where magnocellular activity takes place.

Although words on a page do not move, the eyes must move across lines of text in order to decipher the letters on a page. Only the small optical center of the eye, called the fovea, has a sharp enough focus to make out individual letters, and this area can take in only about six to eight letters at a time. To read a line of text, the eyes will make repeated short rapid movements called saccades, alternating with fixations on separate words or letter clusters. Generally, a reader is not conscious of these eye movements, as the brain seamlessly weaves the perceptions of each separate fixation together.

Weaker magnocellular function might explain why many children with dyslexia report a sense that the letters are jumping around on the page. A magnocellular deficit could impede the ability of the brain to coordinate the eye movements needed to discern the text on the page.

However, dyslexia is probably also characterized by greater development of the parvocellular system associated with larger forms and colors. Greater dependence on parvocellular vision processing might explain the visual and artistic talents that often accompany dyslexia.

Response Time and Filtering Information

Scientists have discovered that the brains of children with dyslexia take a fraction of a second longer to respond to certain stimuli than the brains of children who read well; this pattern persists through adulthood. The delayed response time is seen both in tests of listening to the sounds of language and responding to visually presented symbols. These delays could explain why individuals with dyslexia tend to read more slowly.

Because of the problem with timing, children with dyslexia may not hear the sounds and rhythms of language in the same way that others do. That may explain why they have difficulty breaking down words into component sounds or blending sounds into words.

Other research shows that people with dyslexia have more difficulty filtering out environmental distractions and focusing attention on significant information. That may make it more difficult for them to learn how to form mental categories to distinguish important from irrelevant sensory input—for example, to sort out letters from other marks on a page, or to recognize which sounds of language are significant.

Pathways to Word Recognition

Brain scan research can also shed light on how normal readers make sense of words in print, as compared to readers with dyslexia when performing the same tasks. Researchers know that the mental steps to word recognition may differ, depending on whether the word is already familiar to the reader, and whether it is phonetically regular. Because of the irregularity of English spelling, the brain must have at least two separate pathways for processing words, relying either on visual memory or on applying a learned set of phonetic rules. Under the "dual route" model of reading, skilled readers would rely heavily on simply matching the visual letter string to their stored memory of whole words. With unfamiliar words, the phonological route would be used: the letters are matched to their corresponding sounds. That route can also used for decoding and pronouncing nonwords such as *glip* or *heem*. Beginning readers would rely mostly on the phonological route, but invoke the visual route as they learned to remember words with irregular spelling.

Visual Word Form Recognition

Researchers have discovered that the part of the brain that most people use to quickly recognize letter sequences and words does not seem to activate in the same way in the brains of adults and older children with dyslexia. In most people, an area in the left visual cortex of the brain activates almost immediately upon seeing any sequence of letters. The activity is very brief, and ends within about half a second after the word or letter sequence is first seen. Scientists call this part of the brain "the visual word-form area" (VWFA).

 Essential

Skilled readers recognize most words by sight even before becoming consciously aware of looking at a word. That is why silent reading is faster than oral reading. Sounding-out and speaking words is a slower mental process, and requires involvement of brain areas involved in speech production.

People with dyslexia simply do not seem to engage that area of the brain when presented with words or letter patterns. Part of the problem may be timing; in most readers, the visual word form area activation is completed in the fraction of a second before the brain begins to activate in research subjects with dyslexia.

The visual word form area may function as an important sorting mechanism, allowing the brain to quickly respond to familiar words or letter strings, and direct unfamiliar words to other left hemispheric areas for further processing. An inability to use this brain area may explain why children with dyslexia have difficulty remembering and recognizing familiar words.

The Phonological Route

Research also shows that the brain pathway for processing phonetic information also does not work efficiently for individuals with dyslexia. When typically developing readers encounter a new word, they activate a left hemispheric brain area overlapping with the angular gyrus and neighboring areas of the temporal and parietal lobes. This part of the brain maps letters to their component sounds. This activation pattern can be observed by using fMRI brain scans of subjects who are asked to perform tasks that force them to rely on phonetic decoding strategies, typically by asking them to make a judgment about the sound of an invented pseudo-word, such as *glip* or *blurk*.

When children or adults with dyslexia are asked to perform these tasks, the brain studies show under-activation of this critical area. On the other hand, the brain scans also show higher activation of other brain areas, such as the left frontal region involved in speech production.

Because these studies involve evaluation of a reading task, it is hard to know whether the different pattern of brain use is inherent to dyslexia, or whether it simply reflects the weaker reading skills of the subjects with dyslexia. To overcome that problem, researchers have also studied the brains of younger, normally developing readers who have the same reading ability level as the study group with dyslexia. That research indicates that areas of reduced brain activity are tied to dyslexia, whereas the areas of increased activity are tied to reading ability.

In other words, a child with dyslexia probably struggles with applying phonetic rules to learn to read because that part of her brain is not fully engaging when she tries to decipher words. Over time, she will learn to recruit other brain areas to accomplish the same task. The engagement of left frontal areas may reflect a shift to a habit of subvocalization, mouthing the sounds of the letters as they are read. Use of other frontal or right-brain regions suggest that the reader has learned to rely on other problem-solving strategies, such as focusing more on context.

Right-Brain Pathways

Scientists studying the process of learning to read in typical children have observed changes in patterns of brain activity as children gain reading proficiency. Very young children have high levels of activity in both the right and left-brain hemispheres when looking at letters and words. As children gain the ability to recognize familiar words and letter patterns on sight, the right-brain activity subsides, and a strong pattern of left hemispheric activity is observed.

The left hemisphere is important to reading because it contains pathways and regions that are specialized for attending to and understanding the sounds of language. For most readers, this part of the brain becomes specialized for connecting letters to the sounds they represent, and for connecting and blending the individual sounds in a series of letters to form a word.

Adults and children with dyslexia have more right-brain and frontal-brain activity than good readers when performing certain reading tasks. A new technology, Diffusion Tensor Imaging (DTI), can be used to map the long, white matter fiber connections that transmit information in the brain. This research has shown very different patterns of brain wiring, with some individuals with dyslexia showing the development of far more robust and extensive fiber networks in the right hemisphere.

The child or adult who is using right-brain processes to try to decipher text is probably getting mixed signals, and will understandably find reading to be a difficult and confusing task. On the other hand, the evidence from these studies helps to explain why the reading problems associated with dyslexia tend to go hand-in-hand with creativity, artistic ability, and strong spatial reasoning skills, as these are abilities associated with the right hemisphere.

How Brain Activity Influences Reading Skills

When scientists study brain activity of children and adults with reading difficulties, they do not always know whether the differences they see reflect a structural difference in the brain or whether they are seeing functional patterns that could be changed with teaching or learning. Since studies show that poor readers do not seem to use the left-brain areas for phonetic processing in the same way as good readers, scientists are interested in learning whether specific types of teaching or training can change brain use patterns.

A Different Pattern for Dyslexia

Many studies show that children and adults with dyslexia can experience changes in patterns of brain activity after receiving training for specific reading skills. For example, when children receive training to increase their sensitivity to phonetics, their brain activity begins to look more like the brains of ordinary readers, at least when performing tasks such as identifying rhymes while listening to or reading words. However, it is not clear whether such changes in brain activity actually promote overall improved reading skills, or carry over to contexts other than the specific tasks that have been studied.

 Fact

According to Dr. Sally Shaywitz, children with dyslexia need to be able to sound out words to decode them accurately. They also need to know the meaning of the word to help decode and comprehend the printed message. Both the sounds and the meanings of words must be taught.

Also, some studies have shown paradoxical results: Sometimes the research subjects with dyslexia who are the best readers also show the greatest differences from the norm in brain activity. One study evaluated brain activity of young adults whose progress had been followed from early childhood, when their weak reading skills were first apparent. Some of these young people had grown up to become capable readers, while others remained very poor readers. Surprisingly, the improved readers had a very different pattern of brain use, while the poor readers had brain patterns more closely resembling those of typical readers without dyslexia. When doing reading tasks involving making judgments about word meaning, the improved readers bypassed the left hemispheric region used for phonetic decoding, instead relying on right-brain pathways, as well as frontal activity in both hemispheres.

In another study, scientists with the National Institute of Mental Health measured blood flow in the brain to correlate brain use patterns with reading ability in young adults with and without dyslexia. After testing their subjects for reading ability, brain activity was measured while the subjects were reading sentences aloud. The researchers found that there was an inverse relationship of brain use, dyslexia, and reading ability. Among the group with dyslexia, increased right-brain activity correlated directly with improved reading ability. That was the opposite pattern for the group without dyslexia, whose reading ability was associated with increased left hemispheric activity.

More recently, researchers used fMRI and DTI to follow teenagers with dyslexia for more than two years to learn what brain structure and activation patterns best predicted subsequent reading gains. They found that the children who had the strongest white matter connections in the right hemisphere and greatest right-brain activation during a phonological rhyming task also experienced the greatest improvement in reading ability over time. This pattern was not seen in a comparison group of typical children without dyslexia.

These studies suggest that in order for a person with dyslexia to become a capable reader, he must also learn to use different brain pathways, perhaps because his innate brain structure makes it inefficient to use the left hemispheric pathways typically associated with good reading.

Phonological Training and Brain Activity

Some researchers have wondered whether it is possible to train individuals with dyslexia to use left hemispheric brain regions more efficiently, and thus develop a reading pattern more like typical readers. Using brain scans conducted before and after intensive, short-term training to improve phonetic skills, researchers have indeed observed that children and adults with dyslexia show increased levels of left-brain activity after receiving such training. However, the scans also show that such training results in higher activation of other brain regions not normally involved in phonological processing. These regions include parts of the right side of the brain that are associated with image-based thinking, intuitive thought processes, and problem-solving skills.

Thus, the research seems to suggest that while training may help children and adults with dyslexia recruit their left-brain word processing areas more effectively, the person with dyslexia is still predominantly a right-brained thinker. While most children can become good readers by learning to rely mostly on left-brain thinking processes, a child with dyslexia will need to learn to harness his natural right-brain mental strengths to build reading skills.

Fact

The more your child knows about a word, the more likely he is to recognize it in print. Even if your child struggles to decipher text on a page, you can help lay the foundation for better reading by encouraging him to develop a stronger vocabulary and understanding of the meanings of words.

This research may explain why it takes longer for children with dyslexia to learn to read. The process of developing and coordinating right-brain thinking with the skill set needed for reading is complex and can take many years to develop. This research also helps explain why children with dyslexia always learn best with multisensory strategies—approaches that integrate auditory, visual, and kinesthetic learning tools, and thus probably activate more brain regions simultaneously.

What Brain Research
Means for Your Child

As a parent, you should keep in mind that scientists still have much to learn. Each brain is unique, and even studies that report generalized findings may include some subjects with dyslexia whose brain activity did not fit the pattern that is described. Gender differences can play a part: Studies also show that many girls use their brains differently for some tasks from boys. Many of the studies of brain structure and function in dyslexia have looked at only boys and men; the findings may not apply to your daughter with dyslexia.

In any case, your child is not a research subject, but a unique person whose style of thinking and learning is as individualized as her facial features or her fingerprints. Brain research is useful because it helps to understand why some children struggle with tasks that seem easy for others, and it helps educators to develop more effective methods of instruction. The most important finding of brain research is simply the knowledge that there may be many different ways to learn. Your child with dyslexia will need to discover her own best path to learning over the years as she grows to adulthood.

CHAPTER 6

Learning to Read

Although children with dyslexia usually have marked difficulty learning to read, the process of reading development in all children includes similar elements. To become a good reader, your child will need to first learn decoding and word recognition skills, and then develop fluency and comprehension skills. The specialized help he will need may vary over the years, depending on his age, reading level, and specific areas of difficulty. Understanding what makes a good reader will help you understand what programs or reading methods are best for your child.

Stages of Reading Development

Some children naturally progress from preschool through primary years and beyond, easily learning to read from minimal instruction and gaining improved skills naturally through exposure to print and practice with reading. However, a child with dyslexia will not be able to learn so easily. Your child will need assistance and instruction tailored to his needs and specific areas of difficulty. Your child's needs will change over time, depending on his age and reading level. You will be able to better understand what methods and programs are right for him if you understand the basic stages of reading development.

Stage 0: Reading Readiness/Prereading (Birth–6)

Educator and researcher Jeanne Chall described six stages of reading development from preschool through college, as well as the ages that most children reach each stage. Five of those stages are discussed here. At the earliest stage, children first gain control of language. They begin to realize that words are made up of a series of sounds and start to recognize rhyme and alliteration. If exposed to print, preschoolers also learn to recognize the alphabet and begin to learn the sounds associated with letters. They may begin to recognize a few words, relying largely on contextual information provided by pictures and highly predictable language.

Stage 1: Initial Reading, or Decoding Stage (Ages 6–7)

Beginning readers learn to decode by sounding out words. They understand that letters and letter combinations represent sounds, and use that knowledge to blend together simple words, such as *cat* or *top*. This phase often is the first major barrier for a child with dyslexia. While your child will probably be able to understand that individual letters represent discrete sounds, he may find it extremely difficult to put the sounds together to spell words, and almost impossible to decode words by breaking down the component sounds.

Stage 2: Confirmation, Fluency, Ungluing from Print (Ages 7–8)

Once primary level students have become adept at decoding, they begin to develop fluency and additional strategies to gain meaning from print. They are ready to read without sounding everything out. They begin to recognize whole words by their visual appearance and letter sequence (orthographic knowledge). They recognize familiar patterns, reach automaticity in word recognition, and gain fluency as they practice reading familiar texts.

Your child will need extra help to develop the strategies that lead to fluency. Your child's ability to recognize whole words may be hampered by visual-perceptual problems; if so, he may need therapy to address these problems, as well as specific instructions and methods to build the orthographic skills. At this phase, children with dyslexia often begin to fall seriously behind, as the skills they need are often not explicitly taught. Although a child needs to "unglue" from print in order to progress, remedial instruction or tutoring often remains focused on the Stage 1 phonetic strategies.

 Alert

Because of dyslexia, your child may reach each of these stages at a later-than-typical age. Keep in mind that your child will need to move through each stage at his own pace. Use the information to guide you, but focus on your child's actual level within the progression, not on what the grade or age level is for other children.

Stage 3: Reading to Learn (Ages 8–14)

Readers in this stage have mastered the "code" and can easily sound out unfamiliar words and read with fluency. Now they must use reading as a tool for acquiring new knowledge. At this stage, word meaning, prior knowledge, and strategic knowledge become more important.

Your child will need help to develop the ability to understand sentences, paragraphs, and chapters as he reads. Reading instruction should include study of word morphology, roots, and prefixes, as well as a number of strategies to aid comprehension.

Stage 4: Multiple Viewpoints (Ages 14–18)

Older students move beyond reading for specific information, and are now exposed to multiple viewpoints about topics. They are able to analyze what they read, deal with layers of facts and concepts, and react critically to the different viewpoints they encounter.

 **Essential**

About 40 percent of children with reading difficulties have problems that are not apparent until they reach fourth grade. These children often do not have significant difficulties with tasks, such as letter and word recognition, or phonetic decoding. Instead, they are unable to transition from the decoding state to become fluent readers or they have difficulty understanding what they read.

Ironically, when your child finally reaches the phase where reading involves more complex thinking and analysis, he is ready to shine. Your child's whole-to-part learning style is geared for the demands of dealing with shifting viewpoint and contrasting information. He may still have difficulty with some of the mechanics of reading, but his mind is well suited to sharing and manipulation of ideas. He will be well prepared to move on to the final, fifth stage of reading—college level and beyond. Fortunately, if you can successfully guide your child past the early stage barriers to this phase, he will be able to excel at understanding and integrating advanced reading material.

Phonemic Awareness

In order to begin to read, a child needs to develop phonemic awareness. A phoneme is the smallest unit of sound that differentiates words in a given language. There are forty-four phonemes in the English language, represented by the twenty-six letters of our alphabet. Phonemic awareness is the ability to recognize and isolate the individual phonemes in a word. For example, the word *sent* has four phonemes—the sounds represented by each of its letters. An individual with good phonemic awareness is able to differentiate among and manipulate the four sounds. Phonemes are not the same as letters: the word *toad* has only three phonemes, though it has four letters; the "oa" is a digraph that represents a single sound, the long vowel ō.

Fact

> Although the terms are often confused, *phonemic* awareness is not the same as *phonological* awareness. "Phonological" awareness means sensitivity to all the sounds of oral language, such as the ability to recognize and create rhymes or alliteration. "Phonemic" awareness is the ability to recognize and manipulate the smaller units of sound that correspond to the written symbols of language.

Children do not develop phonemic awareness without exposure to print, as this skill cannot be gained merely by listening to sounds of words. It is not necessary to break up words into separate sounds to hear or to speak them; to the ear, a single-syllable word seems like one continuous bundle of sound. Children begin to gain phonemic awareness when they learn that letters represent sounds. Most children will begin to gain this skill as preschoolers when their parents, older siblings, and other caregivers point out the relationship between sounds and letters. Once children begin to learn to read, their early attempts at decoding reinforce their rudimentary skills, and the level of phonemic awareness increases. Thus, phonemic awareness is a learned skill, reinforced and strengthened through reading practice.

 Essential

> You can help your young child develop phonemic awareness skills at home drawing his attention to letters and their sounds, and playing games involving manipulation of sounds, such as pig Latin, and by teaching rhyming games and songs involving substituting letter sounds, such as the "Name Game."

Most children with dyslexia will score poorly on tests designed to measure phonemic awareness, and they will have corresponding difficulty using phonetic strategies to decode words. Their reading delays prevent them from building skills through reading experience, and they will tend to fall further behind their peers as time goes on. For this reason, programs to help children with reading difficulties often include specific training in phonemic awareness. These programs may be helpful to very young children to help them with beginning reading skills.

Morphological Awareness

Morphological awareness means the ability to recognize the parts of words and word segments that convey meaning. A morpheme is the smallest element of a word that can change a word's meaning. It can be a single letter—for example, the *s* at the end of a noun, such as *cat*, which converts the singular to plural: (*cat/cats*); or the *a* at the beginning of a word, such as *atypical*, which is a prefix conveying the meaning "not."

Understanding the morphological structure of words is crucial to developing reading fluency. At around third grade, during the Stage 2 level of reading, morphological awareness becomes more important to decoding than phonemic awareness. At this point, students need to increase their reading speed, and letter-by-letter decoding is inefficient. Students who are good readers will naturally acquire a good basic sight vocabulary of familiar words, and will easily be able to transfer what they know to decoding new words using morphological analysis. Morphology is the key to decoding polysyllabic words—for example, the word *decode* is a combination of the prefix *de–* and the familiar root *code*.

 Alert

Don't get stuck! Phonics programs are designed for beginning readers. When your child is able to read at about second-grade level, it is time to introduce additional strategies. The National Reading Panel found that phonics instruction is most effective at the kindergarten and first-grade level. After second grade, phonics tutoring did not help most students, and had only a moderate effect for students with learning disabilities.

Your child will probably need extra help to gain an understanding of morphology. It is important to begin to introduce these concepts to him at the age at which other children are gaining these skills, even if he is still struggling with phonetic decoding. Otherwise, he will not have the tools needed to progress beyond a second- or third-grade reading level.

Orthographic Knowledge

Orthography is the set of rules that dictates how to write correctly in a given language. In some languages, such as Spanish, those rules are essentially the same as the phonetic rules. English probably has the most inconsistent writing system in the world. The variability of English spelling creates a major barrier for your child. Studies show that dyslexia exists in all countries and all languages, but children with dyslexia in countries with phonetically regular languages have far less difficulty learning to read.

 Essential

Good English spellers rely heavily on their knowledge of morphology and visual memory of words. They will recognize a misspelled word on sight simply because it doesn't look right, and they will find it easy to learn and correctly use homophones.

Studies show that good readers also rely more on their orthographic knowledge as they grow older. In fact, older children and adults often do not score as well as younger children on tests of phonemic awareness, as their knowledge of orthography supplants their phonological assumptions. For example, skilled readers are slower to recognize rhymes in word pairs with inconsistent spelling like *ghost/roast* or *sauce/boss*, and are likely to report hearing an additional /t/ sound in *pitch*, but not in *rich*.

Your child's reading and spelling, as well as reading fluency, will improve tremendously as his orthographic knowledge improves; unfortunately, this is another area where dyslexia stands in the way. Even if your child tries to visualize what the word ought to look like, he probably does not have a stable memory for letters and letter patterns—after all, he may habitually reverse or transpose letters, and his memory of the correct spelling will tend to be obscured by his memory of all the times he spelled the word wrong. Your child will need special help to learn to correctly remember the visual appearance and letter sequence of words.

Automaticity and Fluency

Automaticity in reading is the ability to identify words fast, accurately, and effortlessly. It is the result of full mastery of the reader's sight vocabulary, so that known words are recognized at a level that requires no conscious thought. Beginning readers recognize very few words instantly. Through repeated exposure to the same words, they increase the number of words that they can easily recognize. It is particularly important that developing readers learn to recognize words that occur very frequently in print. The twenty-five most common words make up about one-third of all reading material, so automatic recognition of those words has a tremendous impact on reading speed and comprehension. Examples of high-frequency words are *the, and, to, you, he, it, of.*

 Question

What is the Dolch Word List?
The Dolch sight words are the 220 most frequently found words in print. These words are usually learned in first and second grade; students who learn these words have a good foundation for beginning reading. Many of these words cannot be sounded out because they do not follow decoding rules, so they must be memorized.

Fluency is the ability to read connected text rapidly, smoothly, and without conscious effort. Fluent readers are sensitive to the rhythm and flow of language, so they can read with expression, and their reading speed and comprehension is enhanced by the ability to anticipate what comes next in text. Many people with dyslexia are able to become accurate readers, but are not able to gain automaticity or fluency. They are able to keep up in high school and college through hard work and determination, but their reading remains labored and slow. However, you can help your child build fluency by providing appropriate support and instruction geared to building automatic reading skills. Support with higher-end reading skills is as important to your child as learning the basics.

Comprehension

The ultimate goal of reading is good comprehension. To achieve good comprehension, readers need more than basic skills. They need sufficient background information and vocabulary to foster an understanding of what they read. They also need to develop an array of good strategies to aid with comprehension. These strategies will include familiarity with the organization and structure of written language, different forms of writing, literary devices, such as metaphor and allusion, and development of an ability to read critically.

Your child may have problems with comprehension because of his difficulties understanding and processing language. He may not understand what some words mean, and if he reads too slowly it may cause him to lose track of meaning before he reaches the end of a sentence. If he frequently confuses or omits small words like prepositions, the meaning of a passage can be dramatically altered.

Again, your child will need specific strategies to overcome confusion and to aid in comprehension. Most of the strategies your child needs are no different from what ideally should be taught to other students, but your child may miss the opportunity to learn if his reading instruction has focused primarily on his weak basic skills.

You can help improve your child's reading comprehension by encouraging him to use his imagination to visualize what is happening as he reads. Teach him to stop at the end of a sentence or paragraph and make a mental picture depicting what he has read. This will improve his memory of the text as well as his understanding.

Phonics Versus Whole Language

Over the past several decades, there has been a cultural war over two ideologically distinct methods of teaching reading—phonics and whole language. A phonics-based approach focuses instruction on learning to connect letters and letter combinations with their corresponding sound, and provides students with specific strategies for decoding by sounding out familiar words. The teacher relies on direct instruction, using a well-developed and highly structured curriculum with carefully planned, sequential lessons.

Whole language instruction provides a literature-rich environment and emphasizes comprehension skills. Reading and writing is incorporated throughout the day in the context of lessons in other subjects. There is emphasis on both oral and silent reading and reading authentic literature. Lessons may be fluid and theme-based, rather than tied to a set curriculum.

 Alert

"Whole language" is not the same as whole-word teaching, which was the hallmark of the "look-say" method popular in the mid-twentieth century. With "look-say," children learned new words through repeated exposure and repetition in "Dick and Jane"-style basal readers.

Pros and Cons

Dr. Maria Carbo, founder of the National Reading Styles Institute, points out that neither phonics nor whole language will reach all children. She notes that phonics programs are good for children who have analytic learning styles and benefit from systematic teaching. Whole language programs are more suited to children who have strong visual, tactile, and global learning styles, who do best in an environment emphasizing hands-on learning and peer interactions.

Your child with dyslexia doesn't fit into either of these molds. His overall learning style might thrive in the enriched atmosphere of a whole language classroom; but he won't be able to absorb the tools and strategies needed for reading merely through exposure. On the other hand, as much as he needs specific help and direction, the sequential teaching of phonics is geared to his weakest learning pathway.

Benefits of Both Methods

The debate over phonics versus whole language makes about as much sense as arguing over whether you should feed your child only meat or only vegetables. Good reading requires that students have a variety of skills. The research is unequivocal: Students learn best when they are taught with programs encompassing both phonics and whole language. Students taught only phonics tend to have better decoding skills, but weaker comprehension skills. Students taught with whole language tend to have stronger comprehension skills, but weaker decoding skills.

 Fact

According to Dr. Reid Lyon of the National Institute of Child Health and Human Development, the focus should not be on phonics or whole language, but on "how components of reading instruction are integrated into a comprehensive approach that varies with the individual child."

Just as you need to provide your child with a balanced diet, he must also have balanced reading instruction. In fact, your child needs more than phonics or whole language; he needs instruction that covers all of the elements that are part of reading. He needs to be taught to focus on how a word sounds, how it looks, and what it means. He needs practice to develop reading automaticity and fluency. And he needs an array of strategies to support comprehension, build motivation, and to keep him engaged.

Different Needs of Students with Dyslexia

Your child with dyslexia will probably need some sort of special intervention or tutoring to learn to read well. Even if your child is in a classroom with an excellent reading and language program, her dyslexia will stand in the way of her learning. She will not learn well in a group setting because her language processing issues will cause her to miss much of what the teacher says. The standard worksheets used in class will not help her learn, because she does not do well with paper-and-pencil tasks. Her low tolerance for frustration and high distractibility will make it hard to focus sustained attention on learning, especially with tasks that are difficult for her.

To become a reader, your child will need tutoring or therapy that replicates the instruction in the classroom in a way suited to her unique learning needs, or she will need a different approach and set of reading strategies more suited to her learning style. However, whatever the method, there are some common elements that should be part of any reading program for a child with dyslexia.

Individualized Instruction

Your child needs instruction that is tailored to her unique needs. Ideally, your child needs to have plenty of time working one-on-one with a well-qualified teacher, tutor, or therapist. She needs help from an adult who keeps her engaged and is focused. The one-on-one attention does not need to be continuous, but it needs to be regular, frequent, and sustained.

If a one-on-one program is not feasible, look for as small a group setting as possible. The larger the group, the less attention your child will get. Videos or computer software are not an acceptable substitute for attention from a skilled professional. If your child is being taught in a resource or special education classroom, the teacher should have at least one aide who can assist with classroom supervision.

 Essential

If your child's resource or special education teacher seems stressed or overworked, volunteer! You can offer to help correct homework or prepare materials. If you are free during the school day, offer to help supervise some children doing group work while the teacher is working more intensively with others.

Multisensory Teaching

Your child needs a method that engages her visual, auditory, and kinesthetic learning modes. She needs to physically participate in her learning. She needs to see and to hear and to speak. It is important that the senses associated with your child's dominant learning style are engaged for the most effective learning.

Age-Appropriate Instruction

Your child needs a method that is appropriate for her age, for her actual level of reading development, and also for the expected level of reading development for children in her grade. Age-appropriate means that the program will not attempt to force learning of concepts that are too difficult or at a pace too fast for a very young child, and it means that the method will not be too boring or limiting for an older child.

Teaching must also be geared to her expected grade level, so that a foundation is laid and more advanced concepts introduced to help her catch up. For example, a sixth grader who reads at second-grade level may need help both with improved whole-word recognition skills of basic sight words (Stage 2, "Confirmation, Fluency, Ungluing from Print"), and strategies to improve vocabulary and understanding of word meaning (Stage 3, "Reading to Learn"). Even though she is not yet ready to read sixth-grade material on her own, she can access age-appropriate literature with the aid of audio books or computer software. A good mix of teaching strategies will help your child keep pace and catch up on as many fronts as possible.

Instruction That Builds Motivation

Your child needs a method or an environment that will be interesting and engaging for her, and will allow her to experience success. This is accomplished by breaking down lessons and expectations into manageable segments, and setting realistic, achievable goals. If your child cannot learn ten new spelling words this week, perhaps she can learn five. The child who meets a goal of five words feels proud; the child who learns four out of five feels encouraged because she has almost reached her goal. But the child who learns the same five words when she is required to learn ten feels like a failure.

 **Question**

What is "learned helplessness"?
Learned helplessness is a psychological reaction to repeated frustration and failure. Research shows that continual exposure to academic failure contributes to withdrawal, unwillingness to approach new tasks, and a lack of persistence.

The child who only experiences frustration and failure will quickly give up. She will begin to think of herself as inept and stupid and will become fearful of facing new challenges. But a child who feels capable of learning will, over time, become more and more willing to devote sustained effort to accomplishing her goals. She discovers through experience that her hard work can pay off, so she is willing to keep on trying.

CHAPTER 7

Specialized Reading Instruction

M ost children with dyslexia will struggle to learn to read. Many schools have implemented strong phonics-based early reading instruction for primary level students. Although these reading programs may provide a good foundation, children with dyslexia usually need more specialized intervention. Your child's school may offer specialized teaching for struggling readers, and if you are fortunate, your child will do well with school services. However, if your child continues to struggle, you will want to learn more about the array of available approaches for reading instruction.

Evidence-Based Instruction

In the year 2000, the National Reading Panel (NRP) issued a comprehensive report summarizing its review of several hundred research studies related to strategies for teaching reading. They identified five essential components for reading instruction: phonemic awareness, phonics, fluency, vocabulary, and comprehension. Instructional practices based on the NRP findings are often described with adjectives such as "research-based," "scientific," "evidence-based," or "best practices." The Panel's findings were incorporated in the provisions of the No Child Left Behind Act of 2001 (NCLB), and applied widely in schools throughout the nation. Unfortunately, student reading achievement did not significantly improve. A three-year study tracking thousands of students at schools that fully implemented the NRP recommendations reported that less than 40 percent of the students were reading at or above grade level at the end of third grade. While the quality of teacher training and reading instruction was enhanced, many students still needed more help. What was "best" for some clearly was not enough to meet the needs of all students.

When primary level students begin to fall behind, many schools will provide extra support, often based on the NRP principles. Unfortunately, the research relied on for the NRP report did not involve students who had been diagnosed with dyslexia. Because dyslexia is defined in part by early reading failure, it is difficult to draw conclusions about the value of a particular teaching approach without a way to differentiate among the students who were part of the research sample. Research has not yet provided the answers as to which approaches are best for students with dyslexia.

 Question

Where can I learn about the latest educational research?
The best resource is What Works Clearinghouse (WWC), an initiative of the U.S. Department of Education's Institute of Education Sciences. Its website at http://ies.ed.gov/ncee/wwc contains detailed reports evaluating many different teaching approaches used in U.S. schools. Look for measures of reading achievement for students with learning disabilities. If a program has even minimal research support, you can also check its "improvement index" and "effectiveness rating."

The WWC has continued to monitor and report on research into reading instruction. Unfortunately, although the WWC has identified dozens of reading instructional programs supported by empirical research, the studies do not provide enough information to support the use of these programs for dyslexia or other learning disabilities.

To overcome this limitation, the WWC created a separate research protocol to review studies in which at least half of study participants were known to have a learning disability. However, the quality of the available research is poor. As of 2012, the WWC had identified only two instructional programs with potential to help students with dyslexia. In each case the findings were based on a single study with mixed results; the students had improved on at least one measure but were weaker than comparison groups in another. A third phonics-based program, also with only a single qualified research study, seemed to have no impact on the children's reading achievement. Other programs simply did not have adequate research support to enable the WWC to draw any conclusions about whether or not they are effective.

The lack of good research does not mean that the programs are ineffective. Rather, it reflects the many practical and ethical barriers to conducting empirical, group-based studies on a population of students with varying individual needs. For each study that the WWC accepted, they rejected dozens that failed to meet basic requirements for empirical research, such as failure to include a control or comparison group.

Early Preventive Intervention

If your child appears to be struggling in kindergarten or first grade, his school may offer an early intervention program. These programs are geared to children who are "at risk" of reading failure. Most children served by these programs do not have learning disabilities, but do have below-average scores on early screening tests. For many, reading problems may be the result of social or cultural factors, such as lack of proficiency in the English language or limited exposure to books and reading before they begin school.

However, there is no reliable way of sorting out the child who is "at-risk" from one who has dyslexia at the age when early intervention begins. Educators and parents agree that it is important to try to reach children early, even though children with dyslexia are likely to need more specialized support. Early intervention is usually the first line of defense; even if it may not be enough to help your child, it is usually a better option than doing nothing with a wait-and-see approach.

Response to Intervention

Many schools now use Response to Intervention (RTI) as part of the process of identifying children with dyslexia or other learning differences, together with providing early support for all children who seem to be struggling with early reading instruction. RTI begins with screening of all students to identify those performing at the lowest level. Students then receive gradually intensified support, moving from special tutoring and small group instruction to more targeted, individualized interventions as needed. The process includes systematic monitoring of each student's progress. If your child is assigned to RTI and does not show improvement, he might then be qualified for special education services under the Individuals with Disabilities Education Act (IDEA).

RTI allows schools to begin delivering services to students early, without requiring formal evaluation and diagnosis of learning disabilities. This avoids a lapse of time during which struggling children would otherwise fall further behind.

 Fact

Forty percent of America's children have difficulty learning to read. More than 90 percent of these children can learn to read at average levels when taught with appropriate programs in the primary grades. The key to successful intervention is to provide support to primary-grade students before they fall behind.

However, RTI can also delay full evaluation, and it cannot provide the comprehensive information about your child's learning needs that might be gained with formalized testing.

Ideally, RTI will provide children with high quality reading instruction, using methods that appear to be most effective for typically developing readers. However, 25–40 percent of those children will need more specialized services. Most children with dyslexia probably fall within that "nonresponse" group; that is, they will later qualify for special education precisely because they could not overcome their reading problems with RTI.

Classroom Phonics Curricula

Many schools have adopted excellent text series that provide a strong emphasis on phonics instruction for general use with all children in the classroom, such as *Open Court Reading*, published by SRA/McGraw-Hill, and the *Houghton Mifflin Reading* series. The textbook publishers also provide extra materials or books geared for small group use with struggling readers. One supplemental curriculum supported by strong research is *Ladders to Literacy*, which provides activities to develop phonological and print awareness, and oral language skills.

Any phonics-based program should provide your child with guidance for understanding the sounds of language, connecting letters to sounds, and segmenting (breaking apart) and blending (putting together) individual sounds to make words. However, the context, sequence, and pace of instruction vary with different teaching systems.

Specialized Tutoring

Your child with dyslexia is likely to need more intensive support than can be provided in the classroom. Your child's school may provide small group instruction or individualized tutoring with a specially trained teacher, or may be able to offer a specific intervention program. Some early intervention programs have significant research support for use with "at-risk" children. These include the following:

Reading Recovery

Reading Recovery is a short-term program of one-on-one tutoring for struggling first graders, geared to rapidly bringing students up to grade level. Children who have fallen behind receive daily lessons with a specially trained teacher for a period of twelve to twenty weeks. The lessons focus on phonics as well as problem-solving strategies and reading comprehension, and are individualized for each child, building on strengths and responding to the child's growing abilities. As soon as the student is able to read independently at his grade level, he is passed from the program and another student takes his place.

 Alert

Reading Recovery is designed as a way of helping children catch up, but is not geared to children with dyslexia. Children who do not progress should always be referred for further testing and intervention. In no case should the instruction continue beyond twenty weeks.

Reading Recovery is not designed to help children with learning disabilities, but rather to provide an effective, early way to distinguish them from children whose reading difficulties can be addressed through short-term tutoring. About 60 to 80 percent of students do become capable readers with this program, reducing the overall number of children needing further services. Even if your child is not successful with this program, the individualized instruction may help target her areas of difficulty.

Sound Partners

Sound Partners provides individualized explicit instruction to below-average readers in grades K–3. The curriculum is designed for use by tutors with minimal training and experience. Scripted lessons focus on letter-sound correspondences, phoneme blending, decoding phonetically regular words, and reading irregular high-frequency words. The tutoring may be provided as a pull-out from the regular classroom or in an afterschool setting.

School-Wide Innovations

An alternate approach to reaching children early on is to provide innovative training or teaching methods to all children in primary grades. This avoids the need to identify students who are at-risk or to implement multiple programs; instead, changes are made that reach all students in all classrooms.

Success for All

Success for All is a school-wide reform program that provides students in lower elementary school grades with intensive instruction in language arts to build early reading skills. It includes a systematic reading program that emphasizes storytelling, and integrates phonics with meaning-based instruction. One-on-one tutoring is provided to children who are reading below grade level. The program emphasizes cooperative and fast-paced learning to keep students engaged. It has been implemented in 1,000 schools nationwide, in forty-seven states. Research studies involving almost 4,000 students have shown the program to be effective in increasing reading achievement.

 Essential

Young children who can focus their attention and persist with a task have a 50 percent greater chance of getting a bachelor's degree by age twenty-five. These behavioral factors are more predictive of long-term success than your child's performance on tests of reading skill levels at age seven. Fortunately, these skills can be reinforced at home and at school through programs that focus on self-regulation skills.

Davis Learning Strategies

Davis Learning Strategies (DLS) is an innovative approach providing teachers with techniques geared to visual and kinesthetic learners in primary level classrooms, as a supplement to the regular classroom curriculum. Teachers learn strategies to help children develop attention-focusing and self-awareness skills. Students use clay modeling to learn alphabet letters and basic sight words. DLS functions both as an intervention program for at-risk learners and as an enrichment program that builds on the creative learning process for able students. Teachers report the program is easy to implement and say that the self-regulation skills reduce disruptive behavior in the classroom and enhance the ability of all children to focus on classwork.

Orton-Gillingham Tutoring

The Orton-Gillingham (O-G) approach is the most well-established method for individualized tutoring. This is not a single program, but a model for teaching developed in the 1930s by Dr. Samuel Orton and psychologist Anna Gillingham. Dr. Orton contributed the idea of multisensory learning, adapting some ideas from the work of psychologist Grace Fernald, who used tracing and writing practice so that physical movements would reinforce the child's memory of the shapes of letters and words. Psychologist Anna Gillingham added a systemized approach for teaching the entire structure of written English through intensive studies of letters and their corresponding sounds.

 Question

What is a phonogram?
A phonogram is a letter or set of two to four letters representing a single voiced sound within a word. Anna Gillingham identified seventy-two phonograms: a, b, c, d, e, f, g, h, i, j, k, l, m, n, o, p, qu, r, s, t, u, v, w, x, y, z, sh, ee, th, ay, ai, ow, ou, aw, au, ew, ui, oy, oi, oo, ch, ng, ea, ar, ck, ed, or, wh, oa, oe, er, ir, ur, wor, ear, our, ey, ei, eigh, ie, igh, kn, gn, wr, ph, dge, tch, ti, si, ci, ough, and gu.

Elements of Orton-Gillingham Teaching

The O-G approach begins with the teacher presenting the most common consonants and vowels, one or two at a time. Each letter is taught using multisensory methods, so that the child links how the letter looks with how it sounds and how it feels to form the letter. Some tutors have the child trace the letter in sand, write it in the air using large motions, or run a finger over fine sandpaper or textured carpet. After a child has learned the individual letters, the teacher moves on to consonant blends and letter combinations. Advanced students will study the rules of English language, syllable patterns, and how to use roots, prefixes, and suffixes to study words.

There are many different reading and tutoring methods that incorporate the basic principles of the O-G approach. Each method has differences in specific techniques and manner of presentation, but all are characterized by the following elements:

- **Multisensory teaching:** Instruction involves interaction between what the student is seeing, hearing, and feeling in forming speech and writing. Language elements are reinforced by having the student listen, speak, read, and write.
- **Phonics-based:** Instruction focuses on teaching individual sounds of letters or letter combinations rather than teaching whole words or word families.
- **Sequential:** Concepts are taught in a specifically designed order, beginning with the easiest and most basic and moving on to more difficult material.
- **Structured, systematic, and cumulative:** Lessons are organized with specific patterns and activities, following a familiar routine. Each new lesson includes review of previously learned material, and concepts are reinforced through practice or repetition.

Keep in mind that the criteria above are only used to determine whether a program fits within the definition of "Orton-Gillingham."

There are other valid and emerging reading approaches that use different philosophies or strategies. You will want to find the program that seems like the best match for your child's personality, learning style, and current needs.

Finding a Tutor

Many teachers and tutors have training in O-G methods and can provide help to your child. Your child's school may provide tutoring without charge, or you may choose to hire a private tutor. You should ask your tutor whether she has specific training or certification, the name of the program or organization where she received her training, and the number of hours of specialized training. Because of lack of standardization, a tutor's qualifications may range from merely having watched a training video for a few hours, to having completed a short course of one or two days, to holding an advanced college degree and completing hundreds of hours of coursework and practice. Although there are no "official" standards for teacher training in O-G methods, there are several reputable organizations that provide comprehensive professional training. These include the nonprofit Academy of Orton-Gillingham Practitioners and Educators (*www.ortonacademy.org*), and the Academic Language Therapy Association (*www.altaread .org*). Both have rigorous standards and require college degrees for certification.

O-G tutoring is also available free of charge in many states through 32nd Degree Masonic Learning Centers, a charity of the Scottish Rite Masons. More than 5,000 school children have received up to two years of one-on-one tutoring through their centers, which also provide free training to teachers.

Effectiveness of O-G Teaching

Because O-G is so well-known, many educators assume that it has been proven over time to be effective for dyslexia. However, most support is anecdotal—despite widespread use of such methods for more than seventy years, the WWC reported in 2010 that it was unable to find any research studies meeting its criteria, and thus could not draw any conclusions as to whether or not the approach is effective. In an informal survey, the Masonic Learning Centers tracked more than 200 students from 33 learning centers over two years. They reported that the children improved with their ability to decode nonsense words (a good test of phonetic knowledge) and with reading comprehension, but remained below average on tests of their ability to recognize real words in print.

The O-G emphasis on phonetic decoding is geared mostly to beginning level readers. Because most children with dyslexia have difficulty with processing the sounds of language, an O-G teacher is working to build your child's skills in his weakest areas. Even with multisensory teaching, a good deal of drill, repetition, and practice are needed to cement the knowledge. You can reasonably expect to see steady progress with your young child, but it is unlikely that he will progress by leaps and bounds. Although progress rates are extremely variable, you will probably be told to expect about eighteen months of growth in reading ability for every twelve months of instruction, and to expect tutoring to continue for two to three years.

 Essential

Tutoring can be hard work for your child, but with a good teacher it can also be fun. Your child will do best with reading instruction that builds both skill and the desire to read increasingly complex materials. Look for a teacher who provides encouragement and finds ways to create successful reading experiences for your child.

Keep in mind that no one approach can meet every child's needs. Because O-G is highly regarded, parents are sometimes discouraged from seeking other help if their child does not seem to benefit from the lessons. It is important to support your child's teacher and her efforts to help your child. However, if your child seems to be making little or no progress after several months of tutoring, you may want to begin exploring other reading programs.

Phonics-Based Dyslexia Teaching

There is a complex and ever-growing array of "brand name" curricula and tutoring programs for dyslexia. Most are grounded on intensive study of phonics, but the method of instruction may vary. Many, but not all, incorporate the key elements of O-G tutoring. Some include instruction geared to building other reading skills, such as vocabulary development, sight word recognition, oral reading fluency, and reading comprehension. Some are offered in public or private schools, and some are systems that have been developed primarily for home use. Tutoring is also commonly available through private learning centers or afterschool programs.

 **Question**

Can an afterschool tutoring center help my child?
Franchised learning centers, such as Sylvan Learning, Kumon, or Huntington, are generally not equipped to help children with dyslexia. Local or privately owned centers may offer a wider variety of services or programs, including a variety of specialized programs. Be sure to ask about the qualifications and training of their tutors.

Classroom or Group Learning

Many programs designed for classroom or small group use have incorporated the basic O-G methodology, as well as additional techniques to support reading development. Some of the programs most commonly used in the United States are profiled here:

The Herman Method

Named for teacher Renee Herman, this approach starts each student at his point of deficit and sequentially teaches mastery of up to twenty skill levels through fifth-grade level. Students are taught in small groups of up to three students, and are not given reading material until they have mastered all necessary underlying skills. Visual and tactile exercises are used to support learning the appearance and sound of letters. In addition to decoding, children learn strategies for sight words, contextual clues, and dictionary skills, with consistent emphasis on comprehension.

Slingerland Approach

Beth Slingerland was a teacher who studied with Samuel Orton; her classroom teaching approach has been widely implemented at private schools geared to teaching children with dyslexia. Reading is taught sequentially, proceeding from single letters and symbols to one-syllable words, and then to longer words. Multisensory approaches are emphasized throughout, with each step of instruction incorporating auditory, visual, and kinesthetic channels. The Slingerland method includes teaching visual strategies for recognition of phonetically irregular words, and also provides explicit, systematic instruction in the development of vocabulary and reading comprehension.

Spalding Method

Romalda Spalding, author of *The Writing Road to Reading*, studied with Samuel Orton and developed her own variation of the O-G method, influenced in part by the ideas of Maria Montessori. The method closely integrates handwriting practice with phonics instruction based on fifty-four phonograms. The phonograms are combined into words and written in a spelling notebook compiled by the student during dictation. Students also learn writing composition, beginning with oral sentences using words in their notebooks, and moving on to writing sentences and paragraphs. This method also emphasizes early exposure to high-quality children's literature, which is incorporated into the teaching curriculum through oral reading and discussion.

Wilson Reading System

Wilson is a twelve-step program geared to students in grade two and above. Small group instruction includes many aspects of O-G teaching, including multisensory and systematic instruction, but is modified to meet the needs of older students. Wilson includes a unique sound tapping system to help the student learn to differentiate phonemes and uses a simplified method of syllable division. It uses extensive, controlled text reading material, including words suited to older students, to correspond with the skills taught. Fluency is emphasized throughout the program, which also focuses on oral expressive language development through vocabulary instruction, and building comprehension through visualization techniques.

Essential

The full Wilson Reading System program takes one to three years to complete. Research has shown that students achieved the highest gain in word attack skills, which are measured by testing of reading lists of nonsense words. Gains in passage comprehension were more moderate.

Individual Tutoring

Your child will learn best with a program involving individual, one-on-one tutoring, which allows the tutor to focus directly on your child's needs and to ensure that your child is fully engaged throughout each lesson. Some systems have been developed for home use or use by tutors with minimal training. These systems usually provide books or videos with clear, step-by-step instructions or lesson plans for the tutor.

Barton Reading and Spelling System

The Barton approach is adapted from O-G, using ten levels of highly scripted lessons, along with different sets of colored letter tiles to be used with each level. The first level focuses on phonemic awareness; subsequent levels move from study of consonants and short vowels, through prefixes and suffixes, spelling rules, and understanding Greek and Latin roots. Susan Barton, the developer, designed her system to be easy for parents, homeschoolers, and volunteer tutors to use without formal training. Like other O-G based programs, it relies on systematic and sequential learning of alphabetic rules and English spelling conventions. If your child receives tutoring twice a week, you can expect that it will take three to five months to complete each level, or two to three years to complete all ten levels.

Phono-Graphix

Phono-Graphix is an alternative phonetic approach that is faster-paced than O-G-based programs and encourages children to apply concepts quickly to reading real text. The method was developed by Carmen and Geoffrey McGuinness, authors of the book *Reading Reflex*. Children are taught that letters are pictures of sounds, that some sound pictures have more than one letter, and that some sound pictures represent more than one sound. Starting with eight sound pictures—six consonants and two vowels— the student immediately begins building and reading words. Manipulatives are used in a variety of games and exercises, along with a whiteboard and markers. During writing practice, the child says the sound of each letter as he writes each word.

A key aspect of Phono-Graphix is avoidance of drills. Rather than requiring that the child fully master every letter sound before progressing, the concepts are reinforced through the child's practice and experience with reading words in context, with immediate correction of errors by the teacher or tutor. Because of its relative simplicity and faster pace, many parents prefer to start with this approach, especially if working on their own with their child.

Developing Advanced Reading Skills

As your child grows, he will need workable strategies aimed at building reading accuracy, fluency, and comprehension skills. He will need to learn to read material containing complex words with irregular spelling patterns. Simple phonetic decoding will no longer be enough; a child who relies too heavily on sounding out words phonetically may become bogged down, habitually reading in a slow, labored, and halting manner. Your child will also need to read smoothly and efficiently. If he hesitates and stumbles while reading, his slow pace will undermine comprehension—by the time he works his way to the end of a sentence, he will have forgotten what was at the beginning.

 Fact

Guided oral reading is a learning strategy to build reading fluency. The student repeatedly reads the same passage or short story under the guidance of a tutor, with a student partner, or using a computer or tape recorder. The readings can be both silent and aloud, and may be timed to help build speed.

Some school reading programs focus primarily on strategies to develop these higher-level reading skills. These programs may be introduced as a supplement to phonics-based classroom teaching in the early years, or used with older children who have already developed an ability to use phonics, or who are beyond the age when intense phonetic instruction is likely to help.

Failure Free Reading

Failure Free Reading is a computer-assisted program for developing vocabulary, fluency, word recognition, and comprehension skills. It is geared to students in grades one through twelve who are in the bottom 15 percent for reading achievement. The program provides reading practice through repeated exposure to text, predictable sentence structure, and simple story concepts.

Great Leaps Reading

Great Leaps is for children of all ages, intended to bring the student to an independent, fourth- or fifth-grade reading level. Students work one-on-one in short five- to ten-minute practice sessions. The child completes several timed one-minute readings, with the goal of having no more than two errors per reading. The teacher provides correction of errors through immediate feedback and modeling. As soon as the child meets the goal with one passage, he "leaps" to a passage written on a slightly more difficult level.

Read Naturally

Read Naturally is a fluency-development program that relies on either audiotapes or computer software. The program uses repeated reading of text to develop oral reading fluency, teacher modeling of story reading, and daily monitoring of student progress. Students work at a reading level appropriate for their achievement level and progress through the program independently.

REWARDS

REWARDS is an acronym for Reading Excellence: Word Attack and Rate Development Strategies. It is a short-term intervention, geared to children in grades four through twelve, with twenty lessons that can be completed in four to five weeks. Students are taught to use and combine several alternative strategies to analyze word structure and segment words into parts, including phonetic blending strategies and recognizing affixes.

The Three-Part Model of Reading

Some leading dyslexia researchers now advocate a teaching approach based on comprehensive study of whole words and word patterns. Students learn to focus on multiple aspects of each word, such as the visual sequence and pattern of letters, common letter patterns signifying word meaning, word definitions and derivations, in addition to the letter-sound correspondence and the sounds of the whole words. This approach helps students build strong mental connections that will aid in recognizing and understanding real words in print.

The Connectionist or Triangle Model of Reading

Studies show that the brain makes sense of printed words through at least three connected systems for evaluating the visual appearance, sound, and meaning of each word. All three systems engage for all words, but different networks dominate depending on the type of word or the form of written representation. This is called the connectionist model of reading; it may also be called the "triangle" model.

 Essential

One of the most powerful predictors of reading comprehension ability is the speed and accuracy of reading single words. In addition to being able to quickly recognize words in print, students must also know the meaning.

Teaching based on this model uses an integrated approach, using methods that provide an opportunity to explore the phonological, orthographic, and semantic properties of selected words within the same lesson. This teaching also tends to be highly interactive, focusing on motivating and engaging the student. Rather than trying to learn sets of rules in isolation, students are able to draw inferences and recognize patterns through the study of selected words and concepts.

Dr. Virginia Berninger of the University of Washington reported impressive gains with a short-term, thirty-hour experimental program geared to fifth graders with dyslexia using high-interest materials to teach words using visual, auditory, and morphological strategies. Students focused on learning what each word looks like, how it sounds, and what it means. According to Dr. Berninger, learning all three elements of the word together builds brain connections that foster a "jump-start" in reading.

RAVE-O

Dr. Maryanne Wolf, a prominent dyslexia researcher at Tufts University, developed a complete classroom curriculum for grades one through five called RAVE-O, an acronym for Retrieval, Automaticity, Vocabulary Elaboration, Orthography. RAVE-O is based on the idea that the more a child knows about a word, the faster the word is decoded, retrieved, and comprehended.

Students learn a selected set of core words using a variety of activities and games that emphasize different skills, such as visual recognition of common patterns, or using cards with pictures to depict multiple word meanings. Each of the core words has multiple meanings, and instruction begins with an exploration of the different meanings. For example, the word *bat* could be used as a noun to refer to a stick used to hit a baseball, or to a small winged mammal; it is also a verb that means to hit or swat. Students also explore word spelling using cards or manipulative blocks to build words using onsets and rimes, to combine different beginning consonants with common letter strings, such as *bat, cat, mat* or *bin, tin, fin.*

Games and reading material keyed to the lessons are used to build speed and accuracy of each underlying skill. A recent randomized controlled study of second- and third-grade students in three cities showed that the students receiving instruction supplemented with RAVE-O performed substantially better on tests of word decoding and oral reading fluency and comprehension than students in a comparison group receiving only phonics-based instruction.

CHAPTER 8

Comprehensive Dyslexia Therapy Programs

A comprehensive dyslexia therapy combines reading instruction or practice with specialized techniques to address underlying cognitive, sensory, or perceptual differences. These programs are less likely to be available in schools, because they are considered therapeutic rather than educational, and are usually given in a one-on-one setting. These treatments cannot cure dyslexia, but they may eliminate or minimize many of the learning barriers. You will need to carefully evaluate your child's needs and the focus of any treatment program in order to decide which one is the best fit.

Choosing a Program

Each program profiled in this chapter has been available to the public for at least ten years, and is currently available at multiple locations. Because of the complexity of dyslexia, educators and therapists have diverse views as how to best help children. In addition to the programs described here, many gifted individuals are working on their own, using their own methodology or combining ideas they have learned from others, with varying degrees of success. Thus, you may also consider working with an individual provider working independently in your community, or choose to try a newly developed approach. However, keep in mind that, at times, new programs for dyslexia have been announced and promoted with claims of a miracle cure—and within a few years, the new program has disappeared from view, leaving many disappointed families in its wake. A program's persistence over time and widespread use is one sign that it is probably beneficial for many children.

Types of Programs

Most dyslexia therapies incorporate techniques to resolve particular sensory, perceptual, or cognitive barriers. The therapy may be based on a particular diagnosis or set of symptoms identified through program-specific screening, or may be promoted as being potentially effective for all children with dyslexia. Some issues that may be addressed include the following:

- Attention focus
- Cognitive skills, such as short-term memory
- Auditory discrimination
- Visual perception and processing
- Balance and coordination

It is common for children with dyslexia to have difficulties in several of these domains. No single program or approach can be effective for all children. You will want to carefully consider your child's individual needs when weighing the options that are available to you.

 Essential

Your child's age and level of functioning are important factors to consider. Your teenager may do better with a flexible approach that allows him to actively participate in choosing the direction of the program. Your younger child may benefit from a more structured approach and may be less resistant to programs that rely heavily on repetition to build skills.

Program Characteristics

Four programs described in this chapter were developed by private educators looking for new ways to help children with dyslexia or other learning differences. They learned from clinical experience, applying their own ideas and working with many students, refining and extending their approaches over time. Eventually they gained enough experience to formalize the delivery of their programs, publishing their work or training others in their techniques. Three of these programs are available in the form of one-on-one therapy from licensed providers or learning centers; a fourth is designed primarily for home use.

Two programs rely primarily on computer software with activities geared to build specific skills or enhance perception. The software is available primarily in a supervised clinical or school setting, so that a teacher or therapist can also guide and monitor progress. These approaches were originally derived from theoretical research about dyslexia, which inspired and guided the software development. Short-term pilot studies were conducted before the software was made commercially available.

The programs described vary in approach, but each can cite either direct or indirect scientific research to support the theory or methods they employ. The research does not mean that the program will work for your child, nor does it provide answers as to which method can produce the best results in general. Rather, research information will help add to your understanding of each program and the likely results of therapy.

Questions to Ask

When considering a program, you should start by determining what specific problems or symptoms will be treated, the amount of time needed to be committed to the program, and the expected outcome of the treatment. Of course, cost may be a factor as well.

Some considerations include the following:

- **Duration of program and time commitment.** Find out how long you can expect your child to continue with the program, and how much time is required on a daily or weekly basis. Ask whether there are specific activities or practice that must be done at home during the program or after its completion. Consider whether you and your child are willing and able to make the required commitment.

- **Expected outcomes.** Ask about the expected or usual outcome of the program for children the same age and with similar difficulties as your child. No one can guarantee success in all cases, but most providers can give you a general sense of typical or average results. Ask what kinds of children do best with the particular therapy, and what issues may cause children to have difficulty. In addition to helping you decide on a program, this information will later guide you in assessing your child's progress and deciding whether to continue with any approach requiring a long-term commitment.

- **Method of delivery.** Your child will learn best working individually with a well-trained therapist or tutor who can attend to her needs and take action to keep her engaged and motivated. However, such services can be costly; programs that rely on small-group instruction, or use technology, such as videos or computer software, may be more affordable. Find out how your child's individual progress will be supervised and monitored if the program does not follow a model of consistent one-on-one work with the provider.

- **Qualifications of therapist.** Find out what sort of background and training the therapist who will be working with your child has in connection with the program being offered. If your child will be at a learning center with many staff members, ask whether your child will be working with the same person at each visit and what sort of training and supervision is given to the support staff.

- **Program reputation and references.** Learn what you can about the reputation of the program you are considering, and ask the therapist you will be working with for references. Most qualified professionals will have a list of former clients who are willing to talk about their experiences.

 Fact

You may be able to find parents with experience with particular therapies on Internet discussion boards and mailing lists. This is a valuable source of information, but try to get feedback from a number of different sources. Make sure the person giving you information is relying on personal knowledge or experience, rather than rumor.

Davis Dyslexia Correction

Davis Dyslexia Correction is a distinctive approach that can produce rapid and dramatic gains in reading confidence and fluency. Developed by a man with severe dyslexia, the program combines mental training to control mental focus and stabilize perceptions with a hands-on, exploratory approach to build meaning-based, whole-word recognition skills. Geared to children age eight and over, the program bypasses teaching of phonetic coding or blending strategies, and instead is tailored to the creative, visually oriented thinking style that typically accompanies dyslexia. A modified program is also available to allow parents to begin working on foundational reading skills with younger children, ages five to seven.

Program Delivery

The formal program is available from independent facilitators who have undergone extensive training and practice to qualify for licensing by the Davis association. The facilitator will work one-on-one with your child for five consecutive full days, providing support training for you or a tutor of your choice on the final day of the program.

During the initial program week, the facilitator guides your child to recognize and resolve specific learning barriers, and ensures that your child has learned and is able to apply a specific set of learning tools. After the facilitated program, your child will need to regularly practice reading exercises and complete a program of clay modeling for word mastery.

Description of Program

The developer of the program, Ronald Davis, is a former engineer who experimented with mental exercises in an effort to overcome his own severe dyslexia. At age thirty-eight, he discovered a technique that eliminated his perceptual distortions, enabling him to easily read a complete novel for the first time in his life. Davis realized that he could teach the same basic technique to others, but that the mental training was merely a first step toward resolving the reading problems of dyslexia.

 Fact

Developed in 1981, the Davis methods were used in a clinical setting with more than 1,000 students before a program of professional training was created in 1995. Because the reading techniques are easily transferred to different languages, the program has been adopted widely and is now offered in more than forty-five countries and thirty languages.

Davis observed that the perceptual symptoms of dyslexia are tied to an escalating cycle of confusion, triggered when a child encounters words or symbols that she does not understand. Your child's frustration leads to disorientation, causing her perceptions to become even less accurate and more error-prone, and so the confusion gets worse. In order to treat dyslexia, according to Davis, it is necessary to correct both the perceptions and the underlying source of confusion.

To eliminate disorientation, the facilitator will teach a simple stress release technique along with an orientation procedure, so your child can learn to calm herself and restore her perceptions to a state of equilibrium. The Davis mental tools are taught quickly and are easy for a child to learn and practice. The program also incorporates simple exercises with tossed Koosh balls to improve balance and hand-eye coordination as well as reinforce the orientation training.

When your child can reorient herself at will, she will be able to hear the sounds of words and see letters in print accurately. That sets the stage for an error-free learning environment, geared to eliminating the sources of confusion in letters and words. Davis uses clay modeling as the primary learning tool. After first modeling the alphabet in clay, your child uses a dictionary to look up pronunciations and meanings of small, abstract words such as *for* or *in*. Your child continues to use clay to form the letters of each word, and to construct a model depicting its meaning. Davis calls these "trigger words" because it is difficult to picture their meaning and they tend to cause disorientation. The Davis list of more than 200 trigger words closely parallels the Dolch sight word list—frequently encountered words that must be recognized automatically in order to gain reading fluency.

Your child will also learn specific techniques for daily reading practice. These include Davis Spell Reading, which builds visual tracking, sequencing, and whole-word recognition skills; and Picture-at-Punctuation, an approach using visualization to build comprehension skills.

Program Outcomes

The Davis program can produce profound short-term gains. Data collected from 360 clients at one center shows that word recognition skills jumped by three to six grade levels during the initial program week among children age ten and over. An Italian research study published in 2003 found that children who received Davis-based orientation training experienced gains in reading speed that were double to triple the rates of children receiving any of seven other treatments evaluated. However, your child will need to continue with clay modeling of words, and practice the Davis exercises at home in order to maintain progress.

 Essential

Davis methods are gaining support from a growing body of independent research. A complete bibliography, links, and research summaries can be found at the Davis website at *www.dyslexia.com/ science*. The clay word mastery approach fits well with the connectionist model of reading instruction now advocated by some leading dyslexia researchers.

A Davis provider will screen carefully to evaluate your child's learning profile, level of maturity, and motivation. Because the program emphasizes mental strategies for self-awareness and control, it is not recommended for children using medications such as Ritalin to regulate attention level or behavior.

The basic strategies of the Davis program are detailed in Ron Davis's book *The Gift of Dyslexia*. You can purchase a home kit if you feel comfortable with the ideas in the book and your ability to work with your own child. Because of the self-guided nature of the clay modeling, your child will be able to work with minimal supervision once the basic techniques are learned.

Dyslexia Institutes of America

Dyslexia Institutes of America (DIA) is a franchised learning center geared specifically to tutoring children with dyslexia. The centers use a core program called Jett PHORCE, which stands for "Phonological and Orthographic Remediation with Cognitive Extensions." This two-part therapy was developed in 1997 by Dr. Elaine Jett, an educator and reading expert with experience operating and developing curriculum for Sylvan Learning Centers. The program combines therapy focused on cognitive skill development, including auditory and visual memory, visual-motor integration, and visual perception, with structured phonological-based teaching and a sight-word program.

Each child is given an individualized therapy plan based on initial diagnostic testing. Your child would attend the clinic for a once-weekly, two-hour individual session. The therapist will give you a written record of each session and a home therapy packet with learning exercises to practice at home for twenty to thirty minutes each day.

Your child's progress is evaluated once a month, with retesting every six months. During the first six months of therapy, the emphasis is on improving memory. After cognitive skills have improved, the therapy focus shifts to developing phonological skills. Therapy may continue for eighteen months to three years.

Prior to launching the first centers in 2002, Dr. Jett conducted an internal statistical review of program outcomes for seventy students. Average scores showed growth in all areas tested except for auditory and phonological memory. DIA does not claim to have independent research support for its approach; the specific techniques and curriculum are published in training manuals only available to franchisees for use at their centers.

Lindamood-Bell Learning Processes

Lindamood-Bell Learning Processes (LMB) is a set of separate programs of intensive therapy and practice to address different types of underlying weaknesses associated with reading difficulties. The reading programs include the following:

- **Lindamood Phoneme Sequencing (LiPS).** LiPS builds phonemic awareness skills by developing awareness of the mouth actions that produce speech sounds. The process uses Socratic questioning, mirrors, mouth pictures, and descriptive labels, such as "lip popper" for the sound *p* to help your child connect the sounds of words with the process of producing each sound in speech.

- **Seeing Stars (Symbol Imagery for Fluency, Orthography, Sight Words, and Spelling).** Seeing Stars is aimed primarily at developing your child's visual memory for printed words. The program focuses on your child's ability to mentally visualize the identity, number, and sequence of letters for the sounds within words. This strategy may help your child build word recognition, fluency, and spelling skills.

- **Visualizing and Verbalizing for Language Comprehension and Thinking (V/V).** The V/V program is geared toward building reading comprehension by stimulating concept imagery, defined as the ability to create "an imaged gestalt—a whole." The clinician will work with your child to enhance his ability to create mental images related to language and reading, and to describe his images in words. The clinician uses a systematic series of questions, such as asking about color, size, shape, or movement, to stimulate detailed and vivid imagery.

- **Talkies.** Geared to younger children, Talkies can help your child consciously create and access mental representations and stimulate his awareness of the imagery-language connections. It is designed as a primer program leading into V/V, for children with more serious expressive language delays or difficulties. Program goals include increasing oral vocabulary and improving language comprehension.

History of Program

Patricia Lindamood was a speech-language pathologist and audiologist who studied the relationship of phonemic awareness to reading development. In 1969, she and her linguist husband Charles Lindamood developed a program called Auditory Discrimination in Depth, a precursor to the current LiPS program. In 1986, they partnered with Nanci Bell, an experienced teacher interested in the role of visual imagery in language comprehension, and opened a learning center in California. The Lindamoods' daughter, Phyllis Lindamood, helped develop the workbooks and manuals used with the program, and now carries on her parents' work.

 Fact

There are now forty-eight permanent LMB centers throughout the United States, and two in London and Sydney, all owned by the company founders. LMB also operates seasonal centers in many locations, staffed by tutors hired for the summer. LMB tutors are called clinicians and receive seven to ten days of training before beginning to work with students.

LMB publishes annual reports based on data collected from children completing programs at their learning centers. A report issued at the end of 2011 showed significant gains among 470 children diagnosed with dyslexia, but the children still tested below average range on the measured skills. Children whose average scores were below the fifteenth percentile when they began the program increased their skill levels by twenty to thirty percentile points on tests of symbol imagery, word attack (the ability to decode nonsense words), and phonemic awareness. The children also had modest gains in word recognition, spelling, and paragraph reading accuracy.

More than a third of students receiving LMB services did not report a specific diagnosis, and students reporting a diagnosis of ADHD or Central Auditory Processing Disorder generally began with scores in the thirtieth percentile range and ended with scores well above average, as high as the sixty-eighth percentile. In general, the reported statistics suggest that you can reasonably expect about a twenty- to thirty-point improvement in percentile score for the specific skills taught in the program you select.

Program Delivery

Lindamood-Bell is an intensive program requiring a substantial commitment of time. The recommended intensive format for each program involves one-on-one therapy four hours a day for four to six weeks. The intensive format may be the key to success for some children who have failed to progress in other contexts; you might consider removing your child from school or homeschooling during the period that he is enrolled at the LMB center. It may also be possible to enroll your child for a less intensive schedule of one hour a day over four to six months.

If you work through an authorized center, the program can also be very expensive, especially if you enroll your child in more than one series. However, LMB also works in partnership with many schools, providing workshops for teachers and certifying qualified teacher consultants, so LMB-based tutoring may also be available at your child's school. LMB also offers parent workshops and sells kits and support materials through its partner company, Gander Publishing.

Audiblox

Audiblox is designed for parents to use at home, working from a kit and instruction manual. It provides cognitive skills training using manipulatives, such as small colored blocks, and also includes an exercise for reading development. The program was developed in the 1980s by Dr. Jan Strydom, a South African educator, initially as a way to prepare his preschool-age daughter for reading instruction. He later applied the same techniques successfully with older children with learning differences.

Audiblox rests on the assumption that children with dyslexia struggle because of underlying cognitive or sensory deficiencies, such as weaknesses in memory or processing speed. Activities increase in difficulty as your child's skills improve, and will be repeated and practiced until each skill becomes automatic. For example, you might work with your child to develop visual memory and pattern recognition by asking your child to remember and reconstruct block patterns of increasing difficulty and complexity.

 **Essential**

Audiblox may be a good choice if you have been told that your child is too young to be diagnosed or receive specialized tutoring. The home kit comes with ninety-six colored blocks; cards printed with colored patterns and letters; a DVD demonstrating the various exercises; and an instruction book detailing activities to address specific learning problems.

The kit manual details suggested activities for seven different program sequences, including ways to correct letter reversals and to address handwriting and spelling problems, as well as the standard program geared to dyslexia. Older versions of the kit came with word cards and reading material geared to building sight recognition skills, but those materials are no longer included. Currently the kit includes instructions for a single reading exercise geared to teaching phoneme/grapheme relationships.

Although it can be adapted for children of all ages, Audiblox can be started with children as young as age three. The instruction manual suggests that your school-age child practice the exercises for about three hours a week; with improvements expected after six weeks to three months of sustained practice. The program should be continued until all foundational skills become automatic and your child is reading above grade level; you should expect to work for a period of one to three years to reach that point.

The program may also be available from private tutors and learning centers, although the company does not currently train or certify instructors in the United States. The program is popular with many homeschoolers, although some report frustration with the repetitive nature of the exercises.

Cellfield Intervention

Cellfield is a twelve-week program of computer training sessions geared to children with reading difficulties, ages eight and over. During each one-hour computer session, your child completes ten exercises. Some involve phonological processing; others involve tasks such as finding hidden or altered text moving on screen, or correctly choosing among homophones. The language and reading tasks are sandwiched between engaging visual puzzles to keep your child motivated to continue. Your child participates in ten sessions during the first two weeks, with the goal of building new brain connections to overcome deficiencies in visual and phonetic discrimination. After completion of the first phase, your child then attends a once-weekly session for a period of ten weeks, with software activities geared to build reading fluency.

The program was developed by Dimitri Caplygin, who believed he could design a computer program that would simultaneously address both the phonological and visual perceptual deficits described in dyslexia research, and patented the software in 1999. The first clinic opened in Queensland, Australia, in 2002, and the program is now available through licensed learning centers in many other countries, including the United States, Canada, the United Kingdom, South Africa, and New Zealand.

Some research has confirmed significant reading improvement among students completing the Cellfield program, but a recent report by a prominent scientist found that children still remained behind age level on tests of word identification and passage comprehension. Data also shows that older children had greater gains with this approach than did younger children. These findings suggest that the program may provide an important boost to your child's skills, but you can probably expect to continue with some form of tutoring or school support after completion.

Fast ForWord Language and Reading Series

Fast ForWord is a set of specially developed computer games designed to build language and cognitive skills and to provide reading practice. Students play computer games five days a week, in sessions from thirty to ninety minutes long, continuing from four to sixteen weeks depending on duration of daily practice. The games in the "Language" package involve matching spoken words to pictures and differentiating among sounds to improve phonological processing, sequencing skills, and auditory memory. The software tracks student progress; your child would continue until he either attains the highest level of mastery built into the software, or reaches a plateau in development. Students average one to two grade levels of improvement in reading skills as measured by the software over a period of eight to twelve weeks.

A more advanced software package, "Language to Reading," includes games to associate sounds to letters, build visual tracking skills, and improve word analysis skills. Another series of six "Reading" software packages begins with prereading skills connecting sounds to letters and continues to advanced passage reading and comprehension skills.

History of Program

Dr. Paula Tallal, a neuroscientist who began studying auditory processing difficulties and dyslexia in the 1970s, theorized that intensive training could remedy the difficulties that children with dyslexia have in distinguishing rapidly changing sounds of language. She enlisted the help of Dr. Michael Merzenich, a neuroscientist known for his research into brain plasticity, to create a computer program to stretch out the sounds of language, and gradually increase the rate of speech as the child's ability to identify sounds improves with practice. Together they launched a private corporation called Scientific Learning to produce and market the

Fast ForWord software. Later the company added more software packages geared to building other cognitive skills, such as attention focus and memory.

 Fact

The first version of Fast ForWord language software was introduced in 1997. Within ten years, more than 570,000 students in more than 3,700 U.S. schools had used the software. An online version called BrainPro is available for home use with children age six and older.

Research Support

Fast ForWord has been extensively researched, including both privately commissioned research and independent, published research. A comprehensive database and bibliography is available on the Scientific Learning website, and there are dozens of school reports documenting measured levels of improvement in reading skills among children and teenagers.

However, the overall evidence is mixed; some studies show gains in phonological skills, but do not show similar gains in overall reading ability. An fMRI brain scan study of children with dyslexia showed changes in brain function associated with improved performance on a phonetic exercise. However, only half of the children experienced overall reading improvement, and the measured changes in brain function did not correlate with overall level of reading development.

A recent, independent meta-analysis of data from six random-assignment controlled studies involving hundreds of students also failed to show any statistically significant impact on word or passage reading skills. However, those random-assignment studies included a wide range of students of different ages, some with severe language deficits, and some who were included merely on the basis of below-average reading scores; none had been identified as having dyslexia.

It is likely that the popularity of the software among educators has led to overuse. It is easy for a school to try the software with any group of students who have difficulty with reading, whether or not those students have the listening or cognitive impairments that the Fast ForWord software is designed to address. The extensive time spent at the computer could help some children, but deprive others of time that would be better spent with personalized tutoring or another program better suited to their needs.

When a teacher or therapist works with a student using Fast ForWord, the software will report and track that student's performance. Outside the context of research, it makes sense to encourage students who are engaged and doing well with the program to continue, and to look for alternatives or make adjustments for students who do not seem to be progressing. If your child's school offers this program, be sure to ask for progress to be monitored carefully.

CHAPTER 9

Beyond Reading—Therapies for Sensory and Perceptual Challenges

Children with dyslexia may also have other learning or sensory problems, particularly attention deficits, auditory and visual processing problems, and motor coordination issues. Your child may benefit from a therapeutic program targeted to one or more of these separate issues rather than to reading. You might explore using one or more of these approaches either in conjunction with other tutoring or therapy for your child, or as a foundation to address specific problems before beginning instruction targeted to academic skill areas.

Speech, Language, and Occupational Therapy

Because dyslexia stems from a language-processing difference, it is often accompanied by problems with oral language as well. Your child may also have problems with small motor coordination that increase his difficulty with writing or other school tasks. He may also have sensory issues which make it more difficult for him to function at home and at play, as well as at school. These issues can be addressed with specific therapy targeted to your child's difficulties.

Speech and Language Therapy

Your child may have difficulties with articulation, such as an inability to pronounce certain sounds, or a tendency to mix up syllables or garble words when speaking. He may also stutter or stammer, speak in a halting manner, or seem to stumble over or forget common words during speech. These symptoms may first become apparent in early childhood, long before your child is ready to start formal schooling or learn to read.

 Essential

Your child's school may provide speech therapy even before dyslexia is suspected. A young child's speech difficulties often come to light early when the teacher has difficulty understanding the child, or the child's communications barriers make it difficult for her to participate in class.

A speech language pathologist (SLP) can help your child to overcome these difficulties. SLPs are highly trained professionals who have earned a master's degree and qualify for state licensing. The SLP can facilitate your child's language development with therapy involving playing and talking, modeling correct pronunciation, and using skill-building repetition exercises. The therapist can also help your child learn to form sounds by demonstrating placement of the tongue and lips and drawing attention to the different sounds of language.

Occupational Therapy

Occupational therapists (OTs) help children who have difficulties with tasks requiring small and large motor coordination. They are highly trained professionals who have earned a master's degree and passed a national certification exam, as well as meeting specific requirements for licensing in their states. An OT can help your child overcome practical challenges, such as difficulty using scissors, pens, pencil and paper, self-care such as tying shoelaces, or with hand-eye coordination needed to catch a ball or copy from a blackboard. An OT can also work with your child to help overcome problems with handwriting.

If your child has an Individual Education Program (IEP), the school may provide OT services as needed to meet your child's educational goals. The school-based therapy will be limited to your child's functioning within the educational environment and his ability to perform tasks or participate in activities required of him at school, such as improving handwriting or learning to work with scissors. The OT may also suggest modifications to the classroom environment or the use of assistive technology, such as a keyboard, to help your child achieve success.

Sensory Integration Therapy

Sensory Integration (SI) therapy is a specialized form of occupational therapy to help your child integrate and manage sensory input. It is based on the work of Anna Jean Ayres, an occupational therapist and educational psychologist, who observed that many learning and behavior problems stem from difficulties children experience in responding and reacting to stimuli, such as noises, light, touch, and movement.

 Alert

Up to 70 percent of young children identified as having learning problems also have sensory integration problems. If your child complains that she cannot concentrate on reading or schoolwork because of distractions in the classroom, or says that bright lights or glare from the paper interferes with her ability to focus on print, she may have sensory integration issues.

Sensory integration influences your child's development of motor and speech skills, emotional stability, attention, and behavior. The most distinctive symptom of a sensory integration problem is over or under-sensitivity to touch, movement, sights, or sounds.

Your child may recoil from being touched, or avoid textures, certain types of clothing, or foods. He may be so sensitive to gentle touching that routine self-care, such as a haircut, becomes difficult. He may exhibit fearful or aggressive reactions to ordinary movement of other children in play, or be easily frightened by loud noises. On the other hand, your child may seem to crave enhanced sensory experiences. He may seek out intense physical experiences, such as body whirling, falling, and crashing into objects. He may seem oblivious to pain or danger.

Symptoms of sensory integration dysfunction can overlap with symptoms of dyslexia. These symptoms include unusually high or low activity levels, problems with balance and coordination, problems with handwriting, poor organization, difficulty following directions, and low self-esteem. If your child has these problems, you may find SI therapy useful in helping him overcome behavioral or motor control issues that are problems at home or at play.

SI therapy is given by a specially trained occupational therapist or physical therapist. The therapy helps your child overcome his aversions and become more tolerant of his environment through exposure to stimuli through play and physical activities. Therapy is highly individualized and child-directed. The therapist will allow your child to select among activities and tailor the program to your child's response. Techniques may include deep brushing for sensory integration; swings for vestibular input (a sense of movement and balance); contact with various textures, bounce pads, scooter boards, or weighted vests and other clothing.

Auditory Integration or Sound Therapy

Several closely-related therapies use acoustically modified recordings of classical music or sounds of nature to improve or enhance listening skills. These may help a child who is hypersensitive to noise, has difficulty filtering meaningful sounds from background environmental noises, or has difficulty hearing sounds at certain frequencies. Even though it is not specifically targeted at recognizing phonemes in words, this training may improve your child's ability to attend to and distinguish the sounds of language.

The different therapies all derive from the work of a French otolaryngologist (ear, nose, and throat doctor) named Alfred Tomatis, whose ideas stemmed from his work with opera singers during the 1950s. Dr. Tomatis designed a listening device, which he called the Electronic Ear, which filters recorded music allowing only certain frequencies to be played. With the therapy, your child would listen to Mozart and Gregorian chants programmed to switch constantly between low or high frequency channels, exercising her ability to attend to and discern different sound frequencies. This may help your child learn to tune in to the high frequency sounds that carry the consonants of language, while suppressing low frequency sounds that interfere with that perception.

Based on strong anecdotal reports of benefits for children with an array of learning barriers, Dr. Tomatis's work was embraced by other professionals. Some who studied under him developed their own programs, making changes to the content of the recordings, equipment used, or the duration of listening practice.

Some auditory training approaches now available include the following:

- Tomatis Method, based on Dr. Tomatis's original work
- Listening Fitness (LiFT), a Tomatis-based program using an alternative portable audio device
- The Listening Program (TLP), also built on the work of Tomatis but using its own digitally recorded music
- Berard Auditory Integration Training (AIT), a briefer form of therapy developed in the 1960s by Dr. Guy Berard, another French physician
- Samonas Sound Therapy, developed in the 1990s by Ingo Steinbach, a German sound engineer, incorporating elements of both the Tomatis and Berard approaches

The various forms of listening therapy are now widely used or recommended by many audiologists and speech therapists. However, in 2004, the American Speech-Language-Hearing Association cautioned that this form of listening therapy has not yet met scientific standards for efficacy to justify its practice.

Vision Processing or Sensitivity

Your child's ability to read begins with the task of focusing on letters on the page. Disturbances in vision or the way that her brain processes visual information will impede her ability to learn. Dyslexia is not a result of vision problems, but vision issues can stand in the way of progress for many children with dyslexia.

Vision Therapy

Vision processing difficulties can impair your child's ability to focus on print, as well as her ability to shift focus from one word to the next. Your child may experience blurred vision, eye strain, headaches, or double vision when reading. She may frequently lose her place, omit words, close one eye, or show difficulty sustaining reading for long.

 Fact

It is possible for your child to have 20/20 vision but still have undetected vision problems that impact her ability to read. If you suspect a hidden vision problem, look for a board-certified developmental optometrist, using the website for the College of Optometrists in Vision Development at *www.covd.org.*

These vision problems are correctable, sometimes with specialized lenses or prisms or with specific exercises and practice geared to help your child learn to use her eyes effectively. Some visual skills that may affect reading include the following:

- The ability to quickly locate and inspect a series of stationary objects, such as moving from word to word while reading (fixation)
- The ability to clearly see and understand objects at near distances, such as print on a page (near vision acuity)
- The ability to shift focus from near to far quickly, such as looking from a chalkboard to a book (accommodation)
- The ability to keep both eyes aligned on a book or other near-point work (eye teaming, binocularity, and convergence)

Different exercises can be tailored to various problems; for example, your child may practice shifting focus from a near to far object and back with one eye covered, and then repeat the exercise with the other eye covered. If needed, the doctor will develop an individualized program for your child. Treatment may be from several weeks to several months depending upon the condition. Some insurance plans may cover vision training.

Colored Lenses or Filters for Dyslexia

Many children are better able to focus on print when using colored overlays. Psychologist Helen Irlen, author of *Reading by the Colors*, coined the term Scotopic Sensitivity Syndrome after she found that she could help many children improve reading fluency with colored filters. She used that term to distinguish their reading problems from dyslexia. Some symptoms of Scotopic Sensitivity Syndrome are discomfort working under bright or fluorescent lights, problems reading print on white or high gloss paper, or perceiving print as shifting or blurring.

If you choose to have your child evaluated at an Irlen Center, your child will be screened to determine whether reading improves with use of a colored overlay. If this seems to help, your child will work with a diagnostician using a wide array of colored filters to determine the precise color that seems to work best for your child.

 **Essential**

Keep in mind that colored lenses can only address a particular problem with vision. They may help your child comfortably focus his eyes on a page, but cannot address other symptoms of dyslexia.

An alternative product is called ChromaGen, the name for prescription colored lenses available only through optometrists who have been certified by the manufacturer. The eye doctor would evaluate each of your child's eyes separately, and the colored lenses can be combined with prescription lenses if your child already wears glasses.

You may be able to achieve some of the benefits of this approach simply by buying colored overlays from an educational supply website, or an art or theatrical supply store.

Brain Training

Another approach to addressing learning problems is to train children to use their brains more efficiently. Rather than specific tutoring geared to areas of academic weakness, training is done through games that are geared to build particular thought processes or cognitive skills, such as attention focus or working memory. This differs from tutoring because the programs do not teach academic skills, such as word reading or arithmetic, but instead try to build the brain's agility with underlying abilities, such as the ability to accurately remember a series of sounds or symbols.

Cognitive Skills Training

Cognitive skills training programs use repetitive tasks, exercises, or puzzles of gradually increasing difficulty to build discrete mental skills. The skills addressed may include processing speed, listening skills, visual discrimination ability, short-term memory, and logical thinking.

Individualized, personal training is available at LearningRx centers or with private tutoring from a Processing and Cognitive Enhancement (PACE) therapist. An optometrist named Ken Gibson developed these programs. PACE was developed first, and it is available as a twelve-week program from private tutors who have been trained and qualified to provide the program as part of their own practices. LearningRx is a learning center franchise with multiple centers throughout the United States.

You can also choose from among a growing number of software packages that offer cognitive skills training. One product designed for children is BrainWare Safari, an Internet-based computer game package with twenty activities to bolster attention, memory, logical thinking, visual and auditory processing, and sensory integration. Other products, such as BrainHQ from Posit Science and Lumosity, have been developed with adult users in mind, but may include activities appropriate for older children and teenagers.

Neurofeedback

Neurofeedback, also known as brain-wave training or EEG Biofeedback, is a technique to enable your child to become aware of and learn to regulate his own brain-wave activity. The training uses a computer game programmed to respond to the production of specific brain waves, as measured by electronic sensors placed on the earlobes or scalp. One approach, initially developed for children with ADHD, encourages the increased production of brain waves associated with concentration and mental focus. When the targeted brain waves are produced, your child can guide an animated character to achieve a goal, and win the game. One software package, called Play Attention, combines brain-wave training with games for cognitive skills development, using a bicycle helmet lined with sensors to monitor attention focus.

To help with dyslexia, therapists are also experimenting with games to encourage the production of a left hemispheric brain wave state involved in reading, using a more sophisticated measuring tool called a quantitative electroencephalogram (QEEG), which can map the source of brain wave production by using a head cap with many electronic sensors.

 Fact

> Neurofeedback may seem like science fiction, but it is not difficult to learn to use the mind in new ways. Researchers have even been successful in training cats and monkeys to control their brain waves, and use the applications to help severely disabled persons, such as quadriplegics, use their minds to control electronic devices, such as prosthetic limbs, or to work with computers.

Movement, Rhythm, and Balance

A variety of programs claim to address learning problems or enhance learning abilities through a systematic program of physical exercises. Your child will regularly practice specific physical movements, perhaps coordinating movements with a musical or spoken rhythmic beat. The theories supporting each approach are varied. Some are premised on the notion that coordinated physical movements can strengthen the connection between left and right hemispheres. Others are based on the idea that dyslexia is caused by weaknesses in cerebellar function or the vestibular system, and will be improved with exercises that promote a sense of balance. Still others expect that rhythmic movements will speed up or optimize your child's mental processing.

Brain Gym

Brain Gym is a series of twenty-six exercises designed to help learners improve coordination of their brains and bodies. It consists of simple movements similar to natural movements, such as crawling, which are part of early childhood development. The program's goal is to improve your child's sense of balance and ability to focus, as well as to relieve stress. Many of the movements can be done while a child is seated, and the exercises can be easily incorporated into a classroom setting. It is not usually used as a specific therapy for learning disabilities, but rather as an approach to enhance the learning process for all children; however, it can be helpful to children with attention focus problems and learning disabilities. This program provides a simple and easy to learn approach that could boost your child's overall readiness to learn.

Balance Training

Learning Breakthrough uses balance-training exercises to improve small and large motor coordination, and cross-lateral movements. Your child can work with a therapist, or you can purchase a home kit containing a special balance board set on rockers called a Belgau Balance Board, as well as beanbags and other tools to support the training. The program is based on the work of educator Frank Belgau, and was originally called Balametrics.

An alternative approach, the Dore Program, is very similar but begins with an assessment at a learning center to design an individualized program of home exercises. After the assessment, your child would be given a home kit containing a wobble board, beanbags, gym ball, and eye chart. Your child would practice ten-minute sets of exercises twice a day, returning occasionally to a Dore center to monitor progress. The exercises would continue for nine to eighteen months, depending on rate of progress. The Dore program was first established in the United Kingdom in 2002, and was initially promoted as a cure for dyslexia, with centers rapidly opening in many parts of the world. In 2008, most Dore centers in the United States, the United Kingdom, and Australia were shut down because of financial difficulties. However, the program has now been re-established, with U.S. centers opened in Mississippi and Texas. Dore now claims only that the program will improve your child's response to other appropriate teaching methods by strengthening brain connections in the cerebellum.

Interactive Metronome

Interactive Metronome (IM) uses movement to improve your child's sense of rhythm and timing. Your child performs repetitive hand or foot exercises in time with a computer-generated beat. He wears headsets to listen to guide tones, and uses his hands and feet to tap in time to the rhythm. A touch pad or wireless sensors attached to bands on his wrists or ankles send signals back to the computer. If your child taps before the beat, he hears an auditory guide tone in the left side of his head; if his movement comes after the beat, the tone comes from the right. When your child is able to match his movements to the beat, a reward tone is heard simultaneously through both ears. The computer records reaction time in milliseconds and provides a score; the goal is to reduce the time interval to optimum levels.

 Essential

Research shows that children with dyslexia have difficulty detecting beats in sounds with a strong rhythm. Awareness of beats may influence the way young children assimilate speech patterns and affect their ability to break down the sounds of words. One dyslexia researcher reported that classroom music lessons help build phonologic and spelling skills.

By learning to keep the beat, your child becomes better able to sustain focus, disregard distractions, and stay on task for longer periods of time. This program is done under the guidance of an educator or health care professional with specialized training, and takes about three to five weeks to complete, with weekly sessions lasting three to five hours.

NeuroNet Therapy

NeuroNet is a system of rhythmic movement exercises designed to foster learning readiness, including both large motor tasks. Your child would work with a therapist who may also provide you with software needed to practice the exercises at home. NeuroNet's *Early Learning Program* helps children ages three to five to reach developmental milestones in hearing, balance, and communication. *Integrated Rhythms* is for school-age children with learning difficulties; exercises incorporate rhythmic movement, listening, and talking, and drawing and writing tasks. A separate program for school-age children, *Tools for Learning*, provides exercises to automate auditory processing skills and build auditory memory, together with exercises to develop handwriting speed and accuracy. All exercises are coordinated to a beat or rhythmic verbal cues set by the therapist or software. NeuroNet therapists are state-licensed health professionals who have received additional training and certification in the specific programs they offer.

Diet and Nutrition

Your child's ability to sustain attention and learn may also be influenced by her diet and nutrition, as well as possible sensitivities to particular foods. A variety of nutritional supplements containing essential nutrients have been marketed as a potential cure for dyslexia or ADHD. Those claims are unfounded, but it is possible that your child's energy level and ability to stay focused on tasks may improve if you ensure that her diet provides an adequate source of nutrients important to the developing brain.

Essential Fatty Acids

A dietary deficiency of long-chain polyunsaturated fatty acids (LCPs) or essential fatty acids (EFAs) may play a part in attention deficits or learning disabilities. To understand which nutrients your child needs and what supplements may be best, it helps to know what all the abbreviations for various chemical names mean. Here is a list of the most important:

- **EFA:** Essential fatty acids (fats which cannot be manufactured by the body and must come from the diet)
- **LCP:** Long-chain polyunsaturated fatty acids (necessary nutrients that are described by their chemical composition)
- **LA:** Linoleic acid (an omega-6 fatty acid found in many vegetable oils)
- **ALA:** Alpha-linoleic acid (an omega-3 fatty acid found in vegetable oils and dark-green leafy vegetables)
- **DHA:** Docosahexaenoic acid (an omega-3 fatty acid needed for brain function, found in oily fish)
- **EPA:** Eicosapentaenoic acid (an omega-3 fatty acid needed for cardiovascular function, found in oily fish)

LCPs are the "good fats" that your child needs to help growth and learning. These are needed for visual functioning in the retina of the eye, in the synapses of the brain, in nerve tissues, and in the adrenals for regulating stress. They are called "long-chain" polyunsaturated fatty acids because they are made up of molecules that consist of chains of twenty or more carbon atoms. ALA, DHA, and EPA are three types of LCPs needed by the body, but only ALA is deemed "essential," because the body can produce DHA and EPA on its own.

The two essential fatty acids are ALA (alpha-linoleic acid) and LA (linoleic acid). ALA falls into a group of fatty acids known as omega-3s. Many children do not get enough of this important nutrient in their diets, and children with dyslexia or ADHD may be more likely to have deficiencies even if their diets are adequate. It is possible that children who are unusually active or under a lot of stress may simply "burn through" fats and other important nutrients at a higher than average rate. In addition to potential benefits for learning, adding ALA to your child's diet may improve stamina, mood, and ability to handle stress.

Fact

An Oxford University researcher conducted a trial with forty-one children with reading problems. Half were given fish oil supplements, a good source of omega-3 fatty acids, and the others were given a placebo. After six months, the children receiving the fish oil supplements were able to concentrate better and had reduced anxiety levels.

The best source of ALA is flax or flaxseed oil. It is also found in smaller quantities in walnuts, cold-pressed canola oil, wheat germ, and dark-green leafy vegetables.

ALA is also vital to the production of two LCPs, DHA (docosahexaenoic acid) and EPA (eicosapentaenoic acid). DHA is crucial to brain function; the brain is about 60 percent fat by weight, and DHA is the most abundant fat. The fat in the brain is contained in cell membranes of neurons and in the protective myelin sheath that covers them. The highest concentration of DHA is in the forebrain, the brain area used for concentration and higher-order thinking. DHA is also needed by the rods in the retina of the eye for normal ability to adapt to see in the dark and to adapt to bright lights. A deficiency in these fats can impair the ability of the brain cells to communicate and may affect overall brain development.

Although your child's body can manufacture DHA on its own, it requires an abundant supply of ALA as well as other nutrients, vitamins C, B_6, B_3, zinc, and magnesium. DHA can also be obtained through the diet; the best source is oily cold-water fish like salmon, trout, sardines, herring, tuna, and eel.

 Alert

Although fish is an excellent source of omega-3 fatty acids, some types of fish have dangerously high levels of mercury and should not be fed to your child. In general, it is best to choose smaller fish that are low on the food chain.

Because of the clear benefits of adding EFAs to the diet, supplements are readily available. The most readily available and inexpensive source of ALA is flaxseed oil. DHA and EPA can be obtained through fish oil capsules. Several commercial formulations, such as Efalex and ProEFA, are marketed as being helpful for children with learning difficulties. Although these supplements may boost your child's performance, they are not a cure for any learning disability.

The Feingold Diet

Dr. Benjamin Feingold, a pediatrician and allergist, believed that hyperactivity and related learning problems in children were influenced by sensitivities to certain natural food substances as well as to artificial food additives. He developed a program to test for such sensitivities through a diet that eliminates all synthetic colorings and flavorings, certain preservatives, and salicylates (chemicals similar to aspirin that are found in a wide variety of foods).

The Feingold program consists of two stages. During the first stage, the chemical compounds found in certain food additives and the salicylate compounds found in certain foods are avoided. You would avoid feeding your child foods with artificial coloring and flavoring, preservatives, and fruits and nuts such as almonds, apples, berries, cherries, grapes, oranges, plums, and tomatoes. During the second stage, the salicylates are tested by adding them back into the diet one at a time to determine which can be tolerated.

The Feingold program is controversial, in part because research findings are mixed, and in part because it is difficult to follow. At best, this program may help about 20 percent of children who appear to be sensitive to the foods targeted by this diet; it is not difficult to see why there is skepticism over a diet that only helps a small fraction of children. However, if you suspect your child is one of the small numbers who will be helped, you may find it worthwhile to try this approach. Because the goal of the program is to test for food sensitivities, it does not need to be followed long-term if it does not seem to be helping.

Medications to Control Dyslexic Symptoms

Dr. Harold Levinson is a psychiatrist and the author of several books about dyslexia, including *Smart but Feeling Dumb* and *The Upside-Down Kids*. Dr. Levinson believes that dyslexia stems from a disturbance in the inner ear, which is critical for maintaining balance. He theorizes that this disturbance causes the brain to receive scrambled signals, producing symptoms commonly associated with dyslexia. Dr. Levinson treats these symptoms with a combination of anti-motion sickness antihistamines and medications commonly used to regulate attention, such as Ritalin.

Although Dr. Levinson has written a number of popular books describing his approach, his theories are unorthodox and have not been accepted by other medical professionals. Most educators and therapists do not feel that prescription medications should be used to treat dyslexia, and all medications can produce unwanted side effects in some individuals. Talk to your child's regular pediatrician before considering this approach.

CHAPTER 10

Choosing a School

You may decide that your child is not well-suited to a traditional, public school environment. Perhaps you are concerned about large classes, overburdened teachers, or lack of funding for support services. If another family member has dyslexia, you may start thinking about school choice even when your child is still a toddler or preschool age. If your child already is in school and struggling, you may be seeking an alternative placement. This chapter explores a variety of alternative approaches you may consider in choosing the best educational path for your child.

Charter, Alternative, or Magnet Schools

Many public school districts offer parents excellent choices in addition to the regular schools. These may be labeled as charter or alternative; in general such schools receive public funding and must meet some guidelines of your district, but they are allowed to use different curricula and strategies for teaching. The philosophies and programs of these schools cover a wide spectrum. Some may be highly structured and offer a challenging academic curriculum; others may be innovative and focus on creating a hands-on, child-centered environment. Some may be parent co-ops, encouraging a high level of parental involvement in the classroom and outside activities.

 **Question**

What is a charter school?
A charter school is a publicly funded school that is typically governed by a group or organization under a contract with the state, which exempts it from selected rules and regulations. In 2009, there were more than 5,000 public charter schools in the forty states that allowed them.

Your district may also have magnet schools. Magnet schools generally are schools with a special focus, such as arts, or science and technology. You are more likely to find magnet schools at the middle school or high school level. Some are open to all students in the district, whereas others may require that the child demonstrate a special aptitude or talent.

In considering a school, focus on your child's personality and his strengths. Of course you will want to consider what services each school offers for children with dyslexia and whether the curriculum used will fit your child's needs. But it is a mistake to focus exclusively on your child's areas of weakness. Ideally, you want to select a school where your child will be happy, will be able to make friends, and will enjoy participating in school activities beyond the classroom.

As with choosing a specific program for dyslexia, there is no one best answer for choosing a school. Part of your choice will be based on your own preferences and expectations for your child, and part will be based on your child's wants and needs. It is important for you and your child to visit a prospective school, rather than rely merely on the school's local reputation or factors such as standardized test scores. The "best" school in the district may not be best for your child. Instead, it may be a place where your child simply encounters demands that he cannot possibly live up to, whereas a school with a lesser reputation may be a place where he can shine and receive more individualized attention and support from his teachers.

Private Schools

There are many good reasons to choose a private school for your child. You may feel that a private school can better meet her unique learning needs, or you may prefer private education in general. There is a wide range of choices and types of programs and many ways that private schools can help meet your child's needs.

However, in choosing a private school for a child with dyslexia, there are a few things to keep in mind. Unlike public schools, private schools are under no legal obligation to provide special educational services for your child. Teachers at a private school with a strong academic program may be unwilling to make special accommodations for your struggling child. If your child is unable to keep up with the work, you may be asked to withdraw your child. You may still be eligible for services via the public school district, but you may find it impractical to arrange for your child to receive those services while attending the private school.

 Alert

You naturally want the best for your child. However, even if your child is exceptionally bright, you should avoid placing him in an academically demanding private school unless it is clear that the school will be sensitive to his learning needs and provide extra support where needed. Your child will do better in the long run if he learns in a nurturing environment where he can experience success.

Some of the social and emotional issues that accompany dyslexia may manifest as classroom behavioral issues. Your child might be a physically active, kinesthetic learner, always on the move—but to a teacher, she may seem like a troublemaker who refuses to stay in her seat and obey the teacher. Unlike the public school, a private school is not legally obligated to retain students whose behavior is disruptive. Whereas in public school you could arrange via an IEP for specific classroom modifications to address your child's unique learning needs, in a private setting your child may simply be subjected to repeated discipline and eventually asked to leave the school.

Of course, many private schools are very sensitive to the needs of children with learning differences. In fact, a private school may offer exactly the supportive environment your child needs. Some things to look for in a private school include the following:

- **Small classes.** Many private schools offer smaller classes and a higher teacher-to-student ratio than public schools. Your child with dyslexia will do better in a smaller group setting, where the teacher has more time to focus attention on her needs.
- **Flexible educational approach.** It is important that the school administrator and teachers show a flexible attitude and a willingness to consider individual needs. Your child can do well in almost any environment if the adults who work with her are willing to adjust their expectations and modify teaching when appropriate.
- **Enrichment and special-interest programs.** A private school may offer enrichment or special instruction in areas of high interest to your child, including many where your child shows a strong aptitude or talent. This may include instruction in the arts or music, athletic programs, or enrichment activities geared to gifted students.

When choosing a school, be sure to ask whether there are other students with dyslexia or learning disabilities enrolled, and what type of support can be given to such students.

Montessori Schools

Montessori is a child-centered, individualized approach to learning following the philosophy of Maria Montessori, an Italian physician and educator. In the early part of the twentieth century, Dr. Montessori developed a set of hands-on, self-correcting materials to assist children with severe learning disabilities. At the time, the children were labeled as mentally defective and relegated to asylums, considered wholly uneducable. Yet Dr. Montessori was able to teach these children to read; in only two years, her pupils were able to pass standardized tests given by the public schools for their age level. Dr. Montessori had invented the first "multisensory" approach to teaching; the handicapped children that she worked with would likely be diagnosed with dyslexia, high-functioning autism, or related learning disabilities by today's standards.

 Fact

Maria Montessori believed that children experience sensitive periods in their development, during which they seek certain stimuli with immense intensity, to the exclusion of all others. These are transitory periods in which they develop specific mental functions, such as the following: movement, language, order, refinement of the senses, and social awareness. If a child's need for specific stimuli is not met during the sensitive period, learning will be more difficult later on.

Soon after this success, Dr. Montessori was asked to open and administer a day care center for working class children in the slum district of Rome. She found that the children age two to five were fascinated by educational devices she had developed for use with older, disabled children. She allowed the preschool-age youngsters to explore the materials, following the same progressive approach she had developed for teaching the asylum children. By age four, most of the pupils in her "Children's House" were reading, writing, and performing four-digit mathematics calculations.

The Montessori approach is based on providing children with access to specially developed materials that allow each child to discover basic concepts on his own, through self-guided work, and to use knowledge gained to move on to progressively more advanced concepts. Classes are typically large, with twenty to thirty students and two to three teachers per room. Children work individually with materials that are kept on low, open shelves; the teachers are trained to observe each child carefully and introduce new materials when the child appears ready to move on.

Children are introduced to the letters of the alphabet by learning the sounds of each letter and by running their fingers over sandpaper cutouts of the letters. They prepare for writing by tracing insets or stencils of simple shapes, like circles and triangles, until they have the manual dexterity to manage letters as well. Most will learn to write before they can read, encouraged by the teacher to piece together letter blocks or cutouts on their own to form words. This phonetic approach begins at age two; a child is never pushed or prodded by the teacher, but simply allowed to progress at his own individual pace, under the watchful eye of the teacher.

Children in a Montessori environment are kept in mixed-age groups, such as ages two to five or six to nine. This allows younger children to learn from observation of their older peers, and also provides a classroom that will be well stocked with materials appropriate for many different ability levels. At the elementary and middle school level, Montessori continues to be highly individualized, allowing each child to work at his own level, but there is more focus on group work as older children are better able to work and learn cooperatively with their peers.

If you are fortunate enough to recognize your child's unique learning style when he is still a toddler, you may find the Montessori classroom to be a place where he will flourish and build a strong foundation for learning. Many of the skills and concepts that are emphasized in remedial programs for dyslexia are included as a natural part of the Montessori child's world. For example, your child will be learning to recognize letters and associate them with their sounds long before the typical age when "early intervention" to teach phonemic awareness begins for children in traditional schools.

However, if your child is older, it may be difficult for him to integrate into a Montessori environment. The Montessori classroom has its own set of norms and rules. It is an orderly, clean, and quiet environment that depends on the cooperation of children who have grown up with the concepts of self-care and responsibility inherent in the approach. An elementary school-age child may have a hard time fitting in, especially if he has come to rely on the teacher-directed instructional methods used in traditional classroom settings.

Even if your child has been in a Montessori environment since preschool, he may not be able to successfully become a reader without extra support and intervention. The individualized, child-led approach of the Montessori method will serve your child well in most cases, but it may not give him all he needs to learn to read. You may need to supplement your child's schooling with specialized tutoring or programs to help him fill some of the gaps left by the self-guided approach of his school.

Waldorf Schools

A Waldorf school follows the philosophy of Rudolf Steiner, who felt that schools should cater to the needs of children and encourage creativity and free thinking. A key element of Waldorf schooling is a strong emphasis on arts and music, with formal reading instruction delayed until second- or third-grade level. During the early years, emphasis is placed on developing oral language skills through storytelling.

During the elementary years, the students have a single class teacher who stays with them from year to year. In early grades, all subjects are introduced via artistic media. All children learn to play the recorder and to knit; children also spend time gardening and usually study two foreign languages. Math instruction relies on developing a conceptual understanding. Textbooks are avoided, but children maintain their own workbooks for each subject, recording their experiences and what they have learned. No grades are given at the elementary level; instead, the teacher writes a detailed evaluation of each child at the end of each school year.

 Alert

Because your child will not be expected to read until about age nine, it is unlikely that dyslexia will be detected in the early years. This is a mixed blessing: while your child will develop and learn in a supportive environment, it will be harder for you to know when extra help is warranted.

A Waldorf school can provide a safe and nurturing environment for your child with dyslexia, where the child grows and learns in a supportive, family-like atmosphere. The emphasis on art projects and imaginative play provides a realm where your child can flourish emotionally and learn through the sensory pathways that best fit his learning style.

On the other hand, few Waldorf teachers will be prepared to help your child if he does not naturally transition into reading at age nine or ten. The teachers are not trained in methods for dyslexia, and the practice of having your child with the same teacher can backfire if that particular teacher is not skilled at guiding children toward reading proficiency.

Democratic Schools

Some children do best if they are allowed to be the captains of their own ships, charting their own paths by exploring their interests and pursuing their passions. If you favor this approach, you may want to choose a private school following a "democratic" philosophy, such as the Sudbury Valley model, where students of all ages determine what they will do, as well as when, how, and where they will do it.

The theory behind the Sudbury approach is simply that all children are curious, have an innate desire to learn, and that the most effective learning takes place when it is compelled by the intrinsic motivation of the learner. This approach can provide significant emotional benefits for a child with dyslexia, as the child will naturally tend to utilize his strengths and talents, and, over time, will gain confidence in his own ability to seek and explore new information. It can also provide a welcome respite for a child who has come to feel demoralized and discouraged in a conventional school setting.

On the other hand, your child will naturally tend to avoid tasks that are difficult unless they clearly lead to a desired goal. A child with good reading skills can use books to learn about almost anything, but the child with dyslexia who is unable to read is unlikely to use books as a source of knowledge. With modern technology, your child may be able to do well relying on information gained from Internet videos or interactive learning sites. All may seem to be well when a bright and active nine-year-old has not yet mastered the basics of reading, but the situation may be very different when the child is fifteen and still unable to read. At the very least, a child with dyslexia needs access to a good teacher or tutor when he is ready and asks for help on his own. As with other alternative approaches, if you choose the Sudbury model, you should be prepared to supplement your child's education with private tutoring or outside services if necessary.

Specialized Schools for Dyslexia

There are now many excellent private schools geared to students with dyslexia—in fact, far too many to list or describe in this book. However, a brief profile of some of the schools will help you get a sense of what you might look for. Most schools offer remedial teaching based on traditional Orton-Gillingham principles as well as providing a full academic curriculum; some offer more innovative or emerging teaching strategies for dyslexia. Some schools focus primarily on helping their students gain sufficient proficiency in reading and other academic skills to re-enter mainstream schools. Others provide a comprehensive and high-quality education with the expectation that they will retain students through completion of their educational program.

Most schools offer day programs. Some offer both boarding and day programs, and a few offer only boarding programs. Because of the higher cost of providing specialized services, the tuitions charged can be quite hefty. However, some schools are able to offer financial assistance to some of their students. Additionally, parents are sometimes able to arrange for tuition subsidies from their child's public school district or through a state program to assist children with learning disabilities.

Assets School

The Assets School in Honolulu, Hawaii, is a combined K–12 day school for gifted children and/or children with dyslexia. The curriculum is individualized and matched to meet each child's specific needs. Faculty is specially trained to provide acceleration, remediation, and enrichment. The school provides a model for providing an environment that nurtures the strengths and gifts of children with dyslexia while at the same time providing support and specialized teaching to assist them in areas of weakness.

The Lab School of Washington

The Lab School of Washington is a K–12 day school with campuses in Washington, D.C., and Baltimore, Maryland, that offers innovative teaching to students with learning disabilities. The curriculum emphasizes hands-on experimental learning and the use of the arts to teach academic skills. Elementary education incorporates work with computers and storytelling as well as art, with a continual emphasis on project-based learning through junior and senior high school levels. More than 90 percent of Lab School students go on to college.

 **Essential**

> Many private schools also offer summer sessions that are open to children who are not enrolled during the school year. There are also many summer camp programs for children with dyslexia or related learning problems. Some focus on providing a fun environment to help build self-esteem, but others include extensive tutoring and support.

The Landmark School

Located in Massachusetts, the Landmark School offers both day and boarding programs for children in grades two to twelve. The Landmark academic program emphasizes achievement rather than grade placement levels, with a primary emphasis on development of oral and written language skills at all levels. The elementary program provides a daily one-to-one tutorial for children aged seven to nine; class size is limited to a maximum of six. Middle school children up to age fourteen continue with the daily individual tutorial and receive rigorous remediation in language and other skills in classes of six to eight students. The high school program continues with the same format, but provides a full college preparatory curriculum as well as elective courses and classes in visual and performing arts.

Shelton School

The Shelton School in Dallas, Texas, serves nearly 850 students with dyslexia and similar learning differences. Founded in 1976, the school provides an individualized academic program, with the goal of remediation and return to mainstream classrooms when possible. Students from preschool through grade twelve learn in a highly structured, small class setting. The school provides a nurturing environment and a curriculum emphasizing academics and self-esteem, as well as a social skills curriculum spanning all grade levels. In addition to a full-time day program, Shelton offers a weekly, Saturday tutoring program, and a summer school.

Tax Deductions for Specialized Teaching

If your child's doctor recommends tutoring by a teacher who is specially trained and qualified to work with children with learning disabilities, you may be able to deduct part of the costs of such services as a medical expense. If the doctor recommends that your child attend a school that provides specialized services for learning disabilities, and if the principal reason for your child's attending such a school is to overcome his dyslexia, you may be able to deduct the costs of his tuition, meals, and lodging at that school.

Because these costs are treated as a medical expense, you can only deduct amounts that exceed 7.5 percent of your adjusted gross income. Tax laws are always subject to change; if you are planning to deduct expenses associated with your child's dyslexia treatment, consult IRS Publication 502 (Medical and Dental Expenses) for the current tax year.

If you have a Health Savings Account (HSA) in conjunction with an eligible high deductible health plan, or a flexible spending account (FSA) through your employer, you may also be able to use those funds to pay for special tutoring services or schooling. As with the tax deductions, you will need a doctor's recommendation for specialized teaching to support such payments.

CHAPTER 11

IDEA and the IEP Process

In the United States, public school districts are required to provide appropriate support for your child through the provisions of
the federal Individuals with Disabilities Education Act (IDEA). Your
child will qualify for services if he is determined to need specialized teaching because he has dyslexia or another specific learning
disability. Once your child qualifies for services, you will attend a
formal meeting with your child's teacher and school administrators to create a written plan for addressing his educational needs,
called an Individualized Education Program (IEP).

Qualifying for Services

Your local public school district must provide a free evaluation of
your child if there is reason to suspect a learning disability. The
evaluation process may be initiated at the request of a teacher or
school administrator familiar with your child. However, if you suspect that your child has dyslexia, you can start the process yourself
by requesting evaluation. Be sure to put your request in writing and
send it to the school principal.

How to Request an Evaluation
Federal law specifies that dyslexia is a "specific learning disability," a broader term that refers to any language-based disorder

manifested in the "imperfect ability to listen, think, speak, read, write, spell, or to do mathematical calculations." When you request an evaluation, it is best to use the phrase *specific learning disability* rather than *dyslexia*, as the law requires that your child be assessed "in all areas related to the suspected disability," and it is possible that some of your child's problems may stem from another related condition. Your letter should briefly state the reasons you suspect a learning disability, and then request full evaluation of your child. The letter should also say that you consent to evaluation under the terms of the Individuals with Disabilities Act. Be sure the letter is dated and is signed by you, and keep a copy for your records.

 Alert

The school must provide notice and obtain your consent before evaluating your child for learning disabilities. If you are opposed to such evaluation for any reason, the school is legally prohibited from proceeding with an evaluation unless it is ordered after an impartial hearing, called a "due process hearing."

The Evaluation Process

Federal law requires the school to complete an evaluation of your child within sixty days after you make the request, unless your state has set a different time frame through its own laws. The evaluation will determine whether your child has a disability that is covered under IDEA, and will also determine your child's educational needs.

The evaluation must be based on a variety of assessment tools and strategies to gather relevant information about your child's learning needs. As part of the process, your child's lack of adequate progress in a Response to Intervention (RTI) program may be considered as evidence of a learning disability. However, your child's assignment to an RTI program cannot be used as a reason to delay the IDEA evaluation, even if your child has not completed all tiers of the intervention structure.

If the evaluation shows that your child has dyslexia or a related disability, the law requires that the school also determine whether your child needs special education services. Generally, your child will be entitled to help if her academic achievement in areas such as reading, writing, or mathematics is not adequate for her age or falls below state-approved grade-level standards.

You are legally entitled to inspect and review all educational records that the school relies on in making its determination, so you will be able to see the specific results of whatever diagnostic testing is completed.

Requesting an Independent Educational Evaluation

If you are not satisfied with the results of the school's evaluation, you may request an Independent Educational Evaluation (IEE) by a qualified evaluator of your choosing. The school must provide you with information about where the independent educational evaluation may be obtained. The IEE will be done at public expense, unless the school initiates a proceeding before an impartial hearing officer to oppose the second evaluation.

 Fact

If you are confused about procedures, you can get assistance from your state's Parent Training and Information (PTI) center. Every state has at least one PTI; these are agencies funded by the U.S. Department of Education to provide training and information to parents of children with disabilities.

The school may ask you the reasons that you object to the initial determination; however, you are not required by law to give an explanation. Of course, like the initial request, you should make any request for an IEE in writing and keep copies of all correspondence.

Keep in mind that the goal of the evaluation under IDEA is to determine whether your child has a learning disability that requires special education services. You should not make the mistake of seeking further evaluation simply because you do not like the label or terminology used in your child's evaluation, as it is common for evaluators to use words other than *dyslexia* to describe the same problem.

The Individualized Education Program (IEP)

The primary mechanism for ensuring that your child's needs are met is the IEP. Your child's first IEP meeting must take place within thirty days from the time she is determined to be eligible for special education services. Your child qualifies for services if she has been found to have dyslexia or any other specific learning disability, or another type of disability listed under IDEA, and if her disability impairs school performance.

An IEP has two purposes. First, it sets reasonable learning goals for your child. Then, it outlines the services that the school district will provide and specifies where they will take place.

The IEP Meeting

As a parent, you are entitled to have input into the entire IEP decision-making process. The school must take steps to ensure that one or both parents are present at each IEP meeting and are given the opportunity to participate. That includes notifying you of the meeting early enough to enable you to attend, scheduling the meeting at a mutually agreed-upon time and place, and providing you with all necessary information about the meeting and your rights as parents. Your child may also attend the meeting if you wish.

 **Essential**

You can improve the quality and effectiveness of your child's IEP meetings by bringing a buddy. Bring your spouse or a close family member if you can. Consider pairing up with another parent of a special needs child—offer to attend her IEP meetings if she will attend yours. Don't forget your child—as he grows older, he can learn useful self-advocacy skills by being an active participant in the IEP process.

Your child's IEP will be determined by a team consisting of the following individuals:

- The parents
- At least one of your child's regular classroom teachers
- At least one special education teacher
- A school district representative who is qualified to provide or supervise special education services, knows the general education curriculum, and knows about the availability of school district resources
- A person who is qualified to interpret evaluation results, such as a school psychologist
- Any individuals who have knowledge or special expertise regarding the student, including an advocate or private tutor invited to attend by either the school or a parent
- When appropriate, the student

The school must initiate and conduct a meeting to review your child's IEP at least once every twelve months to determine whether annual goals are being achieved, and to revise the IEP as needed to address any lack of expected progress. You can ask for more frequent meetings, if you feel they are needed, to address concerns or issues that arise with your child.

Contents of the IEP

The IEP should begin with a statement of your child's present levels of educational performance and explain how your child's learning disability affects her involvement and progress in the general curriculum.

The IEP should then specify a set of objectively measurable annual goals, including benchmarks and short-term objectives. These goals should be directly related to the learning disability that qualifies your child for services. The IEP goals should focus on reducing or eliminating your child's academic problems.

IEP goals should be specific and directly related to your child's learning needs and achievement levels. For example, "Michael will increase oral reading skills to fifth-grade level as measured by the Gray Oral Reading Test" is measurable and specific; "Michael will work to improve reading fluency" is not. Make sure that goals are both reasonable in light of your child's present level of functioning and her expected grade level.

The IEP must also specify how your child's progress toward the annual goals will be measured, and regularly reported to you. You are entitled to progress reports at least as often as school report cards are issued.

Finally, the IEP must specify the services and modifications that will be provided to address each of your child's needs. The actual availability of services has no bearing on the IEP. That is, if a service is needed it must be written in the IEP; if the school district cannot directly provide the service, it must arrange for and fund the service to be provided by another agency.

The IEP must be individualized. It is not appropriate for the school to present you with a form IEP that is used for all children with similar learning issues; your child is entitled to a unique plan to meet all of her specific needs. The plan may address her nonacademic as well as academic needs. For example, if your child has social or behavioral issues that are connected to her dyslexia, the plan may specify those and provide for appropriate interventions.

Preparing for the Meeting

In order to advocate effectively for your child, you should plan and prepare in advance for the IEP meeting. If you are not ready, you are likely to find the process intimidating—you may arrive to find yourself confronting a roomful of teachers and school administrators, and find it difficult to express yourself or hold your ground.

Start by talking to your child. Ask her what is going well in school and in what areas she would like to do better. Explain the purpose of the meeting, and ask your child whether she would like to attend.

Write a short description of your child, including a list of her strengths and weaknesses. Include items such as hobbies, behavior at home, and relationship with family and friends. Focusing on your child's strengths, interests, and preferences will help develop a productive plan. Write out a list of your specific concerns and questions, and list your own recommendations or ideas for how to best meet your child's needs.

Write down some goals you would like to see your child achieve in the coming year. Be sure that you know your options. Gather information about various programs offered within your school district, as well as any privately provided programs that may be appropriate for your child. Talk with your child's teacher, the district special education administrator, and other parents. Visit your child's classroom so that you can observe her present learning environment. As much as possible, visit potential programs that might be indicated for your child before the IEP meeting.

 Essential

The IEP meeting is a time to use teamwork to help your child, and create goals for the future—not to revisit or argue over past mistakes. Try to find common ground by talking about some areas you know everyone will agree with. Avoid speaking in absolutes, such as "always" or "never." Use questions ("What if we tried . . . ?") to elicit suggestions from others at the meeting.

Use this information to develop your ideal IEP to present at the meeting. Gather all available information that supports your position and your child's ideal IEP. This can include new information, such as an evaluation by someone outside the school district or a statement from your child's pediatrician.

Ask for a written list of the people the school plans to have at your child's IEP meeting. Let your school contact person know if you plan to bring others to the meeting as well. Try to find out in advance what school staff members are likely to recommend at the meeting. It is especially important for you to know what to expect from your child's teacher, as her opinions and suggestions will usually be given great deference. If possible, meet with the teacher in advance to go over your mutual concerns—things will go better if you and the teacher present a united front.

Invite appropriate people who can support your position to speak at the IEP meeting. You might bring an experienced advocate, a professional who has worked with your child, or someone who provides services that you would like your child to receive. If a key person cannot attend, have her prepare a written statement for you to read at the meeting. It is also a good idea to bring a support person, such as a friend or another parent, who can assist you by taking notes and helping you stay focused at the meeting.

Organize your materials in advance and make photocopies of any important documents or exhibits, such as samples of your child's schoolwork, so that you can distribute these to the other people at the meeting. You may want to assemble a portfolio of your child's work, and keep a binder with all school documents, reports, and information related to the IEP process. These materials can be updated from year to year.

FAPE—Free and Appropriate Education

As a parent, you naturally want what is best for your child. You want your child to receive the best education possible; your goal is to maximize his learning potential. You may have a specific program or therapy in mind that you think your child needs. Unfortunately, the law does not require that school administrators provide the best possible interventions for your child. Rather, the law requires only that the school provide your child with a "free and appropriate education"—commonly designated as FAPE.

FAPE means that the school is required to provide individualized instruction with sufficient support services to enable your child to benefit educationally from the instruction. In other words, the school must provide the minimal level of support that is adequate to allow your child to learn. The Supreme Court has held that this standard is met with services that are reasonably calculated to enable the child to achieve passing marks and advance from grade to grade.

Many children with dyslexia are extremely bright, and often their pattern of weaknesses and strengths leaves them highly functional in many areas, even though they struggle in others. For example, your child may read very slowly, but with excellent comprehension, and he may have a strong ability to retain information learned from oral instruction and class demonstrations. Through hard work and determination, your child may be able to keep up in class and generally earn Bs and Cs in classwork. With such a child, you may find it difficult to qualify for school services, even with a diagnosis of dyslexia—the school may take the position that the dyslexia is mild and does not affect his ability to learn.

 Fact

Dyslexia is as likely to be found among gifted children as any other group, but the IDEA does not provide for services for giftedness. However, several states require IEPs for gifted students under their own laws. In those states, FAPE may be construed to include enhanced educational goals via an accelerated and enriched curriculum.

Even if your child does qualify, you may feel that the services offered are not adequate. Through formal testing or your own observations, you may realize that your child is intellectually gifted and capable of learning at an accelerated pace, if only the reading barrier were addressed. You will want to find a corrective approach to dyslexia—one that is geared to eliminating barriers and employs a fast-paced instructional methodology—but the school will probably see its obligation to be far more limited in scope. In fact, if your child does receive special education services, you may find that as soon as he progresses to what you consider to be a level of minimal proficiency, the services are withdrawn.

You can't change the law, but understanding the concept of FAPE will help you know how to frame your discussions when dealing with school authorities. Use language like *appropriate* and *adequate* when asking for services, and highlight your child's weakest skill areas. For example, if your child is earning Bs in the regular fourth-grade classroom, but standardized tests show that he is reading on a first-grade level, work toward an IEP that will specify efforts to be taken to help him learn to read at grade level. Do not let your child's strong compensation skills overshadow his need for specific remediation in areas of weakness.

A few states have enacted laws requiring specific services for dyslexia. These may entitle your child to a broader range of interventions or impact the interpretation of FAPE.

Typical Special Education Services

Usually, an IEP for a child with dyslexia will provide that the child will spend most of her time in the regular classroom, but also spend part of each day in a resource room with a special ed teacher. Class size in resource rooms is typically limited to eight to fourteen students, allowing individualized attention and small group instruction. The resource room typically serves the needs of children with a variety of learning difficulties. Your child may also spend a specified amount of time each week working with a speech and language therapist or an occupational therapist.

 Alert

Research shows that children placed in special ed often fare worse over time than their counterparts in regular classrooms, showing an overall deterioration in reading skills rather than an improvement. This may stem from practices that deprive children of exposure to grade-level language arts instruction while they are receiving remedial reading instruction.

If warranted, the IEP may specify that your child be placed in a special education classroom for all of her studies. The IDEA requires that services be given in the "least restrictive environment," meaning that your child should not be removed from the regular classroom for more time than absolutely necessary to provide supportive educational services. Full-time placement in a special ed class is rarely a good choice for children with dyslexia, as it often segregates them to learn with children with much more severe intellectual and emotional problems. If such a placement is being considered for your child, be sure to visit the special ed classroom; although rare, there are some special ed or LD classrooms with skilled and innovative teachers who are able to bring out the best in their students. Some schools may have specialized classrooms for dyslexia. While you should be wary of a full-time special ed placement, keep an open mind until you have met the teacher and seen for yourself what type of students will be in the classroom with your child.

Appeals and Due Process Hearings

If you are unhappy with the determinations that have been made at your child's IEP meeting, ask what the procedures are in your district for administrative review. Sometimes a higher-level school district administrator brings a new perspective to the issue or has the ability to authorize resources that can help resolve the issue. You may also be able to request mediation.

If you still cannot reach an agreement with your school district, your next step is to request a due process hearing. This is a proceeding before an impartial hearing officer who has the power to consider evidence presented by both the parent and school district, and then render a decision to resolve the dispute. The cost of the hearing officer is paid for by the school district. It is a good idea to seek advice from a lawyer or special ed advocate to prepare for this hearing.

Payment for Private Services under IDEA

You may feel that that the services provided by the school will not meet your child's needs. Based on your own observations and exploration of various methods, you may have decided on a specific method or program that you would like your child to receive. Unfortunately, the provisions of IDEA do not allow you to choose or specify the method of instruction as part of an IEP.

 Alert

> If you do not understand or agree with your child's IEP, you do not have to sign it. Alternatively, attorney Pete Wright suggests you preserve your objections by writing a statement on the IEP above your signature, saying "I consent to this IEP being implemented but I object to it for the reasons stated during the meeting."

As a practical matter, your child's initial IEP will probably be structured around services that are available at his school, based on available resources. The lack of resources does not excuse the school from providing FAPE to your child, but generally school officials will want to try to help your child using available staff or programs before considering other options. When warranted, school districts may pay for private services, including placement in a private school for dyslexia. In some states, partial funding may also be available from different sources. For example, if you live in Florida, you can apply for a McKay Scholarship, which is available only to students with disabilities and can be used toward private school tuition.

You may be able to convince the school to subsidize the cost of services with a strong presentation at the IEP meeting. If not, you may ultimately succeed in obtaining such help by demonstrating that your child is not receiving the promised FAPE. You will have to show that your child has either not received promised services, or that the services provided by the IEP have not been adequate to help your child attain the specific goals set by the IEP. So if your fourth grader who was reading at a first-grade level shows no significant gains after a year of services via the resource room, you might have a good case for convincing the school to try something new.

You should request the placement or service you want at your child's next scheduled IEP meeting, or you can request that an additional IEP meeting be scheduled. If the school does not grant your request and does not provide an alternative that appears to meet your child's needs, you may choose to enroll your child in the private program at your own expense. Under certain circumstances, you may later be able to obtain reimbursement from the school district for the private tuition or fees. However, to preserve your rights, you must either give the school notice of your concerns and your intent at the IEP meeting, or else give written notice of your intent at least ten business days prior to placing your child in the private setting.

You will still have to present your case for reimbursement at a due process hearing. It will be important to keep good records of your child's progress in the alternative placement, so that you will later be able to clearly demonstrate to a hearing officer that your privately funded services were effective in assisting your child to meet stated IEP goals, and that the services offered by the school did not meet FAPE requirements.

Keep in mind that you are not required to agree to an IEP or to accept the services provided by the school. You may be advised that legally you need to allow your child to remain in a classroom where he is struggling and falling further behind in order to build a case that the school program is not adequate to meet FAPE, but your child may suffer both academically and emotionally in the meantime. If you have found an alternative program or school for your child and have the financial means to pay, you may need to consider whether your child's immediate needs are more important than winning a prolonged legal battle with the school system.

CHAPTER 12

Accommodations and Modifications

Whether or not your child qualifies for special education services, your child has the right to receive accommodations or modifications necessary to provide equal access to educational services. Your child is protected by federal disability laws, and may also benefit from special legislation that applies to schools in your state. As a parent, it is important to understand what your child's rights are and how to make sure they are enforced. You can also help your child by arranging for informal modifications and adjustments as needed.

ADA and 504 Accommodations

Your child may be entitled to accommodations or classroom modifications under the Americans with Disabilities Act (ADA) or Section 504 of the Rehabilitation Act. These laws protect your child from discrimination on the basis of her learning disability. The protections are available whether or not your child has qualified for special education services under IDEA. Accommodations can help your child excel, even if she does not qualify for educational support because she is not "behind enough" and does not seem to need extra tutoring in order to keep up. If your child does qualify for services, you might prefer the ADA/504 protections if you do not agree with the educational plan and goals that would be required by her IEP.

 **Essential**

A teacher may object to revising class assignments on the grounds that it is not fair to other students. Remind the teacher that your child has a disability that makes it harder for him to do the same work as the other children. Fair doesn't mean giving every child the same thing, but giving every child what he needs. To be fair, you have to treat a child with learning differences differently.

The difference between protections under ADA/504 and the IDEA is that your child does not have to demonstrate a need for special education services in order to receive ADA/504 accommodations. With ADA/504 alone, the school will not provide specialized tutoring, but may offer accommodations, such as the use of a calculator, keyboard, or tablet PC; or modifications such as extended time on exams. You will still need to show that your child needs these services to overcome her specific disability-related limitations; however, usually the diagnosis of dyslexia will suffice.

Suggested Classroom Modifications

Modifications should be tailored to your child's specific needs, and they may vary in different settings or with different classes. Some common accommodations include the following:

- **Extra time.** Your child might need extended time on just about anything: written homework, oral tasks requiring a rapid response, or simply moving from one task to another in class.
- **Alternative assignments.** Your child might need to substitute all or part of an assignment with an alternative project or task. For example, a science project could be modified to allow your child to build a model or create a video or Power-Point demonstration in lieu of writing a paper.

- **Assistive technology.** Your child may do better on written assignments if he is allowed to use a laptop computer or keyboard to type them, rather than turn in handwritten work. In addition to common utilities like the spell checker, your child may benefit from more sophisticated software like predictive-text programs, text-to-speech utilities, dictation software, or handheld devices like an electronic spelling dictionary or calculator.
- **E-books or audio books.** Your child may find it easier to read textbooks on a tablet or e-reader. Those devices may allow your child to adjust the size of the fonts displayed for more comfortable reading, and to use built-in text-reading functions. Your child may also benefit from using audio books or specially recorded books from organizations like Learning Ally.
- **Video and multimedia support.** Rather than relying on reading textbooks, your child may be able to learn subject material better through video or multimedia presentations. High quality support materials may be available through the school library or on the Internet.
- **Changes to classroom seating arrangement.** Your child may do better if seated closer to the teacher or in an area that is shielded from distractions.
- **Modifications to curriculum.** Your child may need modifications to the expected curriculum, such as a shorter spelling list or a spelling list made up of easier words.

 Fact

Dr. Martin Kutscher, a pediatric neurologist, suggests these strategies to teachers to improve communication with a child who has difficulty following directions: Establish good eye contact, use a cue, such as tapping on the desk to bring the child back into focus, alert the child's attention with phrases such as, "This is important," and break down longer directions into simpler chunks.

Keep in mind that the ultimate goal is to maximize your child's ability to learn by eliminating learning barriers and ensuring that assignments are within his capacity to complete and to master. You do not want to make things too easy for your child, but your child will be discouraged and soon give up if every assignment ends in frustration and failure.

Assistive Technology

Modern technology is your child's best friend. Although you do not want assistive technology to take the place of learning basic skills, the ready availability of tablet devices and assorted apps means that your child's skill deficits will not be a barrier to learning in other contexts. While part of her school day should focus on learning to read independently, technology makes it easier for her to explore and learn about history, geography, science, and other subject areas.

Audio Books and Visual Aids

Your child may also be able to keep up with assigned reading and improve her own fluency and comprehension skills by listening to recorded books, or by reading e-books using a tablet device that includes a text-to-speech function. Your child can improve fluency and reading speed by reading the text silently while simultaneously listening to audio. She can also rely on listening alone to keep up with grade-level reading assignments that are beyond her own independent reading capacity.

 Essential

Your child's dyslexia should qualify him for a free membership at *www.bookshare.org*, which provides access to a large catalog of books in digital format, to enable text-to-speech capability. Alternatively, you can join the nonprofit Learning Ally at *www.learningally.org*, which distributes books that have been recorded by volunteer readers.

Your child may also supplement classroom reading by watching educational videos or films of novels and plays that are assigned reading. Multimedia content may also supplement textbooks on any number of subjects. Your highly visual child is likely to learn, retain, and understand far more from watching a documentary about the Civil War than by reading a chapter in her history book. Keep in mind that if your child does not read comfortably at grade level, audio-visual media is her primary means to access more advanced topics and subject matter.

Word Processing Programs

Use of a word processing program will eliminate mechanical barriers, such as poor penmanship and weak spelling, enabling your child to showcase her ideas through her writing. Although your child may encounter resistance to producing typewritten assignments in elementary years, by the time she reaches high school her teachers will expect all significant written work to be typed. In later years and at the college level, she is likely to bypass the printer and frequently submit work via e-mail.

There are many software programs available to help young children learn keyboarding. While typing is generally a slow process for very young children, your child with dyslexia may still find a hunt-and-peck approach more efficient than handwriting, especially if she has difficulty writing legibly. Generally, typing speed will improve when the child is about age ten to twelve.

 Alert

Help your child set automatic save options to preserve a copy of his work at frequent intervals. You should also set the program to automatically preserve a backup copy of a document each time it is saved. There is nothing more frustrating to a budding writer than losing the product of several hours' work due to a computer malfunction or keyboarding error.

In addition to learning to input text, your child should learn how to use features such as the spell checker, AutoCorrect, and automatic text completion options. These can simplify text entry and help avoid common spelling and typographical errors.

Using a word processing program also enables your child to work with her teacher to improve the quality of her writing through revisions and redrafts. Because the student is spared the laborious process of writing out a second draft by hand, the teacher is free to offer detailed comments and suggestions. Your child will become more confident about writing when she realizes that her first draft does not have to be perfect.

Another advantage to using the computer is that the child can set display options to make it easier to read material and also by choosing a preferred font.

Additional Tools for Accessibility

A wide range of software tools and apps can make it easier for your child to work with a computer or tablet device. In some cases you may want to purchase specialized software, but many features are now already included with newer devices. These may include the following:

- Speech recognition or dictation capability, allowing your child to dictate text or instructions to a computer, tablet, or smartphone
- Predictive text function, which will present full words or phrases after your child has typed the first few characters
- Text-to-speech capability, to digitally read aloud the content of any file and highlight words on the page as they are read
- Specialized recording devices, such as the Livescribe Smart-pen, which aids notetaking by creating an audio recording tied to the user's handwritten notes; or the WizCom Quick-tionary pen, which can scan and digitally read aloud lines of text on a printed page.

Accommodations on Standardized Tests

If your state uses standardized tests to determine your child's eligibility to advance to another grade or to graduate from high school, you need to plan ahead to make sure that your child will have appropriate support and modifications. If your child has an IEP, make sure that it contains goals that will meet the content requirement for such tests; your child cannot reasonably be expected to pass a test on material he has never been taught. If your child is in a resource or special ed class even for only part of the day, he may be missing instruction that is important to meet grade-level standards.

Students with dyslexia tend to have difficulties performing on standardized tests, and their scores often do not accurately reflect their level of achievement. One problem is simply that these tests are written, and your child has a disability affecting reading. Your child is likely to have more difficulty deciphering the questions and the set of answers given. He is also likely to read slowly, or need to reread questions several times. Typically, the "right" answers to a multiple-choice question depend on specific words in a question, often phrased in the negative. For example, the question may ask the child to choose the one answer that is "not" correct. Since other test questions may ask the child to choose the "best" answer, he may misread the question and assume that he is again being asked to choose the "best" correct statement, rather than the single incorrect statement. He may compensate for his poor reading speed by adopting a strategy of choosing the first correct answer that he reads, resulting in an incorrect choice if there is more than one potentially correct answer listed. If your child focuses on carefully reading each question, his slower reading speed will lead to his running out of time and leaving many questions unanswered.

Your child's intellectual strengths and his creativity may also work against him. Children with dyslexia tend to have more unusual ideas and different reasoning strategies from children who are primarily left-brained, analytical thinkers. Given a set of five responses to choose from, where the fifth choice is "none of the above," an imaginative child might think of obscure or trivial reasons why each of the first four choices is flawed. If asked to choose the "best" of several options, your child's definition of "best" may be unconventional. In a classroom setting, your child's originality may delight his teachers, who recognize some of his ideas as being ingenious. On the standardized test, his novel approach will simply be deemed an incorrect response.

 Essential

Your child may also have perceptual and motor coordination problems that work against her. She may correctly see that the correct answer is choice "d," but then mark "b" on her answer sheet. In filling in bubbles on a Scantron form, she is more likely than other students to have difficulty lining up the row of answers with the number of the question, and thus may simply mark a series of answers on the wrong lines.

Ask that your child's IEP or 504 plan provides for multiple or alternative forms of assessment in making any decisions about grade retention or advancement. Even if your child has met the educational objectives set forth in the IEP, the standardized test used by your state may not be an accurate or valid measure of his achievement. Your child should be afforded the opportunity to demonstrate progress through other means, such as teachers' assessments of classroom performance or a portfolio of his work.

 Alert

Testing accommodations will not be allowed if they would invalidate the test, making the results meaningless. For example, if a test of reading comprehension is read aloud to your child, then it doesn't measure her ability to understand what she sees in print. Instead, it tests her understanding of what she hears.

Your child's IEP or 504 plan should clearly specify the modifications and accommodations to be provided during administration of standardized tests. These may include extended time for testing or provision for oral administration of the tests. Many students have encountered unexpected barriers when they mistakenly assumed they would be allowed the same accommodations that had been provided informally in class.

Informal Modifications

You may be able to arrange modifications for your child without using the formal IEP or 504 process, simply by making a request or suggestion to the teacher. You can arrange this by meeting with the teacher, or via a telephone conversation, written note, or e-mail; or you can guide and encourage your child to make suggestions on her own.

 Essential

If your child has not yet been diagnosed with dyslexia, or does not have severe enough problems to qualify for school services, informal modifications can be the best way to tailor the school curriculum to your child's needs. If your child attends a school that follows a philosophy of individualized education, you may be able to rely solely on the informal process to arrange needed modifications.

Of course, for informal arrangements to work, you need a cooperative and supportive teacher. Many teachers will be happy to work with you and your child, and may come up with many helpful ideas of their own. Even with an IEP or 504 plan in place, you will probably find it more efficient to work out many issues as they arise through informal discussions with the teacher. Some advantages of the informal process include the following:

- **Greater flexibility.** You cannot anticipate all possible problems in an IEP. Classwork and homework assignments change over time and are likely to present new and unexpected barriers. Informal modifications can be implemented immediately, revised by trial and error, and changed, extended, or abandoned as circumstances warrant.
- **More choice and control.** You and your child will have more control of the process and are more likely to have your suggestions implemented by working with a single teacher, rather than by trying to convince a group of teachers and administrators to agree to something that must be reduced to writing at an IEP meeting.
- **Improved implementation.** No teacher likes having a committee tell her how to do her job, and busy classroom teachers may forget or ignore many specifications of an IEP. By working directly with the teacher, you will be able to arrange modifications that you know the teacher is willing and able to implement.
- **Increased self-advocacy skills.** Your child will learn continually from the informal process. When very young, she will learn that it is acceptable to ask for changes to meet her learning needs, and she will learn problem-solving and communication skills by observing how you work with the teacher. As she grows, she will be able to follow your lead and handle the task of arranging modifications on her own.
- **Wider range of modifications.** You and the teacher will be free to try new things and make revisions as needed. Changes do not need to be tied directly to your child's learning disability but can simply be implemented with the stated goal of helping your child learn or improving classroom behavior.
- **Ability to enhance the curriculum.** The modifications provided by the IEP or 504 process are geared to helping your

child overcome areas of weakness. With informal arrangements, you can use the process to also substitute or add to the curriculum to enrich your child's education or add challenge in areas of strength. This approach can improve the overall quality of your child's schooling and also increase her sense of accomplishment and self-esteem.

The drawback to relying on informal accommodations is that the teacher may later refuse or fail to implement agreed-on changes. Since you are working with individual teachers, you will have to renegotiate with each new teacher. In some cases, a school principal or other staff member who disagrees with the plan may intervene to prevent implementation of the modifications, perhaps citing concerns of fairness or discipline. You also will not have a clear record of the past history of accommodations, which can later stand in the way of arranging modifications such as extended time on standardized tests.

 Alert

If you arrange informal modifications without an IEP, try to get something in writing to record the arrangement, especially if it may affect your child's grades or likelihood of promotion at the end of the year. Make sure that the teacher or school district will not later penalize your child, and that you and your child clearly understand any possible negative consequences related to uncompleted work.

If your child qualifies for an IEP, the best approach usually is a combination of both formal and informal changes. Use the IEP or 504 process to negotiate and enforce the most important and generalized modifications or to obtain some broad standards. Use informal negotiation and discussion to deal with less-important matters or issues specific to a particular teacher and aspect of the curriculum.

Taming the Homework Dragon

Homework can often become a family battleground, with your child's efforts to complete routine assignments leading to hours of frustration that almost always end in tears or tantrums. When you try to help your child, you may find that you frequently end up arguing and resorting to threats and punishment due to your own frustration. Home life is disrupted as your child's homework demands keep him up well past his expected bedtime, and take away from time that you can relax with your spouse and your other children.

Your child's right to modifications to accommodate his dyslexia is as important at home as it is at school. You will need to set limits and stick to them, both with your child and with the teacher. The purpose of homework is to help your child learn; if it is not fulfilling that purpose, then expectations should be adjusted.

Setting Limits on Study Time

Ask your child's teacher how long she expects her students to spend on homework each night. One good rule of thumb is ten minutes for every grade in school—so a fourth grader may have forty minutes of homework, a sixth grader an hour. Your own child's teacher may expect something more or less. After the teacher explains what she feels is reasonable, tell her how much time your child is actually spending. The teacher may be stunned to learn that a routine assignment that she thought would take twenty minutes actually takes three hours to complete at your home.

Explain what aspects of the assignments cause difficulty for your child, and ask for modifications to better meet your child's abilities and eliminate sticking points. For example, some teachers may insist that children copy out the questions in a book as well as writing the answers. A modification to allow your child to provide answers only may immediately cut homework time in half.

An easy time saver is simply to reduce the number or length of assignments. If there are thirty multiplication problems on the page, perhaps your child can do ten. If the teacher wants a five-paragraph essay, perhaps your child can write two paragraphs.

Set a Time Limit

The agreed modifications should also include a time limit. Tell the teacher that you will monitor your child to make sure he puts in effort on homework; if he is unable to complete the assignment, you will send a note indicating how much time was spent. Ask the teacher to accept partially completed homework if a minimum agreed time has been spent, to give your child credit for doing his homework, and to at least give your child a passing grade.

At home, make sure that your child has a place to do his homework that is free of distractions and where all materials he needs are at hand. This should also be a place where you can observe and monitor your child to make sure he is focused on homework. If he is working with a computer, make sure you can see the screen; otherwise, your child could be playing computer games, looking at videos, or chatting online with friends when you think he is working.

Reach an agreement with your child about the total time to be spent on homework, including the time he will start and the time by which he must finish. Use a kitchen timer to keep track of how long your child has been working. If your child has a hard time sustaining attention or sitting still, break up the session with opportunities to relax, stretch, and move around; stop and restart the timer as needed to keep track of actual time worked.

When your child has worked for the agreed time, tell him that his time is up. If your child is working at a good pace without frustration and wants to continue, allow him to do so. However, do not allow your young child to work beyond the hour that is your family deadline for completing homework. Give your child a warning about ten minutes before that time, and suggest that he set his alarm early to complete work in the morning if he protests. Your child's bedtime should be age-appropriate, but it should also be firm.

 **Essential**

Sleep is essential to learning. During sleep, information learned during the day becomes integrated into long-term memory. It is counterproductive for a child to forego sleep in order to study. He may finish the assignment, but he will undermine his ability to remember and understand the content. Rest is particularly important to children with dyslexia, as their performance deteriorates markedly under conditions of stress or fatigue.

Use common sense: If your child ever becomes actively engaged in a task that has always been difficult for him, don't fight success. There may come a time when something seems to click for your child, and for the first time in his life he becomes absorbed in reading a book or excited about a poem or a story he is writing. If and when that happens, rejoice. Thomas Edison said, "Genius is 1 percent inspiration and 99 percent perspiration"—don't get in the way of the inspiration when you see it. You can reinstate the rules later on.

Set Priorities to Manage the Workload

Help your child learn to set priorities for his schoolwork. Some of your child's homework is probably easy for him; some is quite difficult. Some requires him to do things that he doesn't enjoy, but some tasks might be fun. Some of the homework is important to help your child master a particular skill or learn required material; some is mere busywork, assigned mostly for the sake of having the child do something.

Help your child learn to sort his work so that homework can be completed in the most efficient manner possible. When your child is very young, you might make the decisions for him. As he grows older, he will better be able to make these choices on his own.

Encourage your child to complete all assignments that are easy or fun whether or not they seem useful. Typically, an art project might fit this category. If the project is likely to absorb your child's interest for a long time, have him begin work on it after the more difficult work is completed.

Difficult work should be attempted only if it is educationally useful to your child. If the assignment seems to be busy work with no apparent purpose, do not force your child to complete it. Instead, ask the teacher to explain its purpose, and use that information as a guide to develop appropriate modifications. If the assignment seems to be useful for other children but doesn't help your child, look for an alternative that will achieve the same goal. For example, a teacher may ask her students to write a separate sentence for each word on a spelling list, to ensure that they know the meaning of words and give them writing practice. For your child, sentence-writing may be so overwhelming that there is no time left to study and learn the spelling. Your child might do better to focus on studying and writing the individual spelling words, and dictating sentences or writing short definitions instead.

 Fact

One bright third grader with dyslexia asked his teacher to allow him to write one sentence containing all twelve weekly spelling words, rather than a separate sentence for each word. The boy enjoyed the challenge of trying to pack all the words in the list into one or two very silly sentences, and the teacher looked forward to reading the very creative and often amusing results. What had once been frustrating was turned into a fun and challenging game.

You and your child might also find the task of managing homework easier if the teacher provides a weekly assignment sheet listing all homework to be completed by the end of the week, rather than ask for separate assignments each day. You can then plan for assignments that are likely to be more time-consuming by spreading the work out over several days.

Group Projects

From time to time, your child may be assigned to work with other children to complete a group project. While it is good for children to learn to work cooperatively, many times one or two children in a group end up doing most of the work and feel frustrated and resentful of those who cannot contribute much to the effort. Of course, your child with dyslexia is likely to be the one who bears the brunt of that resentment.

The group project is a good occasion to help your own child recognize her particular strengths and talents, and to help the other children develop a greater appreciation of those abilities. Encourage the children to assign roles and responsibilities that will build on each of their talents. For example, one group of sixth graders was assigned to prepare a class presentation on African history. Two highly verbal girls in the group immediately divided up topics and got busy researching and writing their own sections. They quickly became frustrated with the third member of their team, a boy with dyslexia who seemed to take little interest in the project. When they shared their anger with a parent, the mom asked about the boy's interests, and was told that he liked music and art. The mom then asked, "Did the people in Africa have music? What kind of instruments did they use? What kind of artwork did they create?" The group quickly recognized that music and art were indeed important aspects of understanding African history, and the boy was assigned to find books with African artwork at the library and to create music for their class presentation. He quickly became the most enthusiastic member of their team and their colorful class presentation, presented to the background beat of an African drum, was a huge success.

These same principles can be used in almost every context. Your child will benefit from discovering ways to express her talents, and her peers will realize that there is more to learning than simply reading and writing about topics. Of course the book learning is also important, but the group project should be an occasion for exploring other ways for your child to contribute.

CHAPTER 13

Working with Your Child's Teacher

With careful planning, school can be a rewarding experience for your child despite his learning barriers. You can help pave the way for a successful and enjoyable school experience by anticipating possible problems, building strong relationships with your child's teachers, setting clear expectations at home, providing consistent emotional support, and becoming an able advocate for your child. By working closely with a teacher, you can become allies in the mutual effort to help your child.

Be the Teacher's Friend

It is important that you be able to communicate your concerns to the teacher without engendering hostility. The first step toward good communication is to make an effort to understand the teacher's point of view. Remember, your child is not the only student in her class. The regular teacher may have twenty or thirty children to worry about. She must manage the classroom and structure lessons and activities. She cares about your child, but there may be other children with equally or more severe learning problems, or disruptive children who need to be monitored, limiting the amount of attention she can devote to your child.

If you have the time and your school permits it, offer to volunteer in the classroom. Even though you are concerned about your own child's welfare, use your time assisting the teacher to get to know and observe the other children and develop a sense of the classroom dynamics, as well as a typical day's schedule. When you think about accommodations for your own child, ask yourself how these will fit within the environment you observe.

Try to establish a friendly relationship with the teacher. If you cannot volunteer in the classroom, ask the teacher if there are other ways you can help or if she needs any classroom supplies. An inexpensive purchase for the classroom, such as a few reams of binder paper or extra boxes of pencils, may win the teacher's appreciation. If the teacher's first contacts with you are as an involved and helpful parent, she will be more open to suggestions about your child.

Focus on Actual Needs

Do not assume that your child will have problems in class before they arise. Parents can sometimes make the mistake of worrying too much and having too little faith in the teacher. Many teachers are keen observers and know to make changes and adjustments on their own. Some may challenge and motivate your child in ways that surprise you, and encourage your child to succeed in ways that you would not have expected.

Ask your child how things are going at school—ask him if he likes his teacher and what his favorite class activities are. If your child complains about problems, ask him to elaborate, and ask what kind of changes he would like. Your child may come up with some sensible suggestions, or he may ask for the impossible—but even the impossible requests will give you an idea of what areas need adjusting.

If your child does not have an IEP or a formal diagnosis, you may want to describe your child's problems to the teacher in terms of learning style or personality quirks: "Sam is a strong visual learner. It helps him to learn if he can see pictures or diagrams illustrating the point." Or, "Megan is a bit of a daydreamer. You may need to call her name or tap her gently on the shoulder to make sure she is paying attention before you start giving instructions."

Resist the temptation to educate the teacher by supplying her with books and long articles about dyslexia, unless she asks for such information. A very short article or bulleted list, perhaps copied from a brochure or website, is a more efficient way to get the point across.

Support the Teacher's Goals

When you first talk to the teacher about your child's needs, start by asking whether the teacher has any concerns about your child. Children with dyslexia often have problems with communication or attention focus that cause problems for teachers; the teacher may be frustrated because your child has difficulty following directions or is slow to obey instructions. It is also possible that your child is disruptive or argumentative with the teacher or has other behavior problems in class.

 Essential

Special education expert Richard Lavoie says, "The pain the learning different child causes at home and in the classroom is never greater than the pain he feels." He explains that any child would rather look bad than look dumb. Disruptive or disobedient behavior may simply be an attempt to distract attention from the embarrassment of not being able to complete an assignment.

If the teacher complains about your child's behavior, do not argue or try to defend or excuse your child's conduct. Instead, take this opportunity to point out the connection between the learning problems and behavior. You can start by suggesting strategies with the dual goal of meeting your child's needs and helping the teacher improve classroom management. Ask for more detail about the setting and circumstances that accompany behavior problems; this may be a key as to how to go about eliminating the problem.

Avoid using the diagnostic label that has been given to your child and focus instead on descriptions of precise areas of difficulty. If the teacher complains that your child ignores her directions, it will not help to simply say, "He can't follow directions because he has dyslexia." The teacher may not understand why a reading problem would affect your child's ability to participate in class or listen to her oral instructions. Don't expect the teacher to become an expert on dyslexia. Instead, say something like, "James has a problem processing the sounds of language; it takes him longer to make sense of the words and it is hard for him to remember several steps at a time." Then you can work together to think of ways to help address the problem.

You may be surprised to learn that a new teacher is unaware of your child's learning disability, or that she has not seen or read the IEP. You may want to give the teacher another copy of the IEP, with a cover page that has a summary of the major points that apply to her classroom.

Leave the Teacher in Control

Take note of the teacher's good qualities as an educator whether you observe them in the classroom or hear them from your child, and remark on ways that she has helped your child. It is always easier for a person to accept suggestions if you have started by showing that you appreciate her abilities and the things she has been doing right. Ask the teacher what she thinks of your suggestions, rather than make demands. Say, "Do you think it would help if we tried . . . ?" rather than, "I want you to . . ." or "You have to . . ." If the teacher seems resistant to implementing items that are on your child's IEP, you could point out the specific IEP modification or goal, and then ask, "What are some ways we could begin implementing this?"

If the teacher does implement some of your suggestions and it seems to help your child, be sure to let the teacher know that things are going well. Send a note or a thank-you card with a brief statement mentioning the improvement you have seen in your child.

 Alert

Most schools regularly schedule one or more teacher conferences in the year. You do not have to wait until the first teacher conference to raise your concerns; in fact, it will probably be easier to arrange modifications separately as issues come up. If modifications are already in place, the teacher conference is a good time to review them and assess how they are working. It is also an ideal time to consider new modifications.

Building Self-Advocacy Skills

Ultimately, your child will do better in school if he is able to advocate for himself. This is especially important as your child grows older, but even a kindergartner can be encouraged to speak up for himself when appropriate. Most modifications can also be arranged through informal, direct negotiation with the teacher. In a classroom, this can also take place in the course of normal communication; if your child learns to raise his hand and explain when he is having a problem, many issues may be resolved instantly.

Begin by helping your child understand his own learning style. Explain that every person is good with some things and has difficulty or needs to try harder in other areas. Use examples, mentioning some things that are hard for you or someone else he respects. Encourage your child to think about what strategies help him learn new material or what types of learning activities he enjoys.

Help your child learn how to approach his teacher and ask for specific changes or adjustments. Make sure your child knows the importance of speaking courteously and choosing an appropriate time to talk to the teacher. If your child has an IEP that lists specific modifications, make sure that your child knows what it requires, using language he can understand.

Your child may have better luck arranging modifications to assignments if he learns to offer something in exchange. For example, if the teacher has asked for a five-paragraph essay about a geography topic, your child might say, "I have dyslexia and it is hard for me to write, but I draw well. Can I write two paragraphs and draw a map?"

 Essential

One tool that many teachers are comfortable with is an independent learning contract. This is an agreement between student and teacher that specifies the work that the student needs to complete in order to earn an agreed-on grade. This creates an opportunity for extensive modifications and adjustments, but at the same time holds the student responsible for completing assigned tasks.

Help your child learn to state things positively: "I usually learn better if I . . ." He should try to avoid the appearance of making excuses for himself or trying to simply avoid work; "I can't" or "I don't want to" are not phrases that go over well with teachers.

Your child may find it helpful to volunteer to do tasks that are easy for him, such as running errands for the teacher or passing out and collecting classroom supplies, simply to demonstrate to the teacher that he is an eager participant. This will help avoid problems that arise when a teacher believes a child is lazy or uncooperative.

When your child has difficulties with a teacher at school, go over the events and conversation at home. Try to draw your child's attention to points where he might have said the wrong thing; ask him, "How could you have said things better?" Have your child try out strategies you suggest, and report back later on whether the problem has been resolved.

As your child grows older, try to encourage him to resolve issues directly with the teacher as much as possible. You can continue to offer helpful suggestions and guidance at home, if your child asks for your help. Resist the temptation to take over or contact the teacher if your child seems satisfied with the arrangement, even if you feel that expectations are set too high or too low. Your child will always have dyslexia; it's important that he develops the ability to advocate for himself and to exercise good judgment in making decisions. The skills he learns at school will later be crucial to success at college or in employment.

Assessment and Grading

Your child may be able to learn most of the material covered in class, but may still face barriers when it comes to the way that her work is assessed and grades are assigned. Traditionally, grades are assigned based on uniform criteria for all children in a class, often reflecting how a child measures up to her peers. It is a competitive process that may give little information about what the individual child has actually learned. It sets up children with learning difficulties for repeated failure, because no matter how hard they work, most are unlikely to be able to earn high marks. This system not only undermines your child's self-esteem, but also contributes to behavior problems.

Along with modifications to curriculum, suggest and encourage the teacher to use alternative forms of assessment. The best approaches will factor in your child's demonstrated effort and her level of improvement over time. The teacher can use records of past performance, such as with spelling or arithmetic, as a way of determining the level of performance that can reasonably be expected of your child. Improved performance should result in an improved grade—for example, if a child who usually gets seven correct answers out of twenty problems is able to increase performance to ten, the child's improvement should be recognized and rewarded.

Ask the teacher to mark your child's paper in a positive way, noting correct answers prominently. The teacher can score the papers by simply counting the number or percentage of right answers on homework assignments or quizzes, recording those in her grade book. If a pattern of improvement is seen, the teacher can help your child chart her progress; at the end of the term, a grade can be assigned that is consistent with the level of improvement.

 Alert

Busy teachers often ask classroom aides, student teachers, or parent volunteers to help with grading papers and exams. If you have worked out special modifications for your child, make sure that the teacher will personally mark your child's work or communicate the arrangement to whoever is helping with the grading.

The teacher can also modify grading practices to specifically exempt certain considerations for your child. For example, the teacher can agree to disregard spelling mistakes in all subjects other than spelling. Thus, your child would be graded on the content of her written essays or answers to questions, not on the mechanics of producing them.

Once the teacher has agreed on modifications for your child, it is helpful if the teacher can create a specific rubric for grading her work. A rubric is a set of written requirements that sets forth requirements to earn each passing grade. Usually it can be set out on a grid, listing the specific criteria for an A, B, C, and so forth. If the teacher generally uses a rubric for the whole class, modifications can simply be noted on your child's copy.

In addition to guaranteeing that agreed-upon modifications will be considered in assigning a grade, a well-drafted rubric will also help improve your child's performance. For example, a rubric that indicates that writing two paragraphs will earn a C, but writing three or more paragraphs will earn a B, might provide your child with the incentive to work hard to complete an extra paragraph, as she can clearly connect her extra effort to the reward of a higher grade. It also gives your child a greater sense of control and enables her to better understand how the grade relates to the work she has produced.

Dealing with a Problem Teacher

Sooner or later, you will encounter a teacher who is inflexible and unwilling to make changes or adjustments to benefit your child. Even if modifications are required under a written IEP or 504 plan, the teacher may be unwilling to implement them, resulting in conflicts when you or your child attempt to enforce the rules. There may simply be a personality conflict; for example, a teacher who places a high value on maintaining an orderly classroom may have little patience for a child whose learning difference leave him prone to a messy desk, lost paperwork, and constantly dropped pencils.

You may become aware of the problems from your child's complaints, or from your own contact with the teacher. Start by trying to get a better sense of what is going on. If possible, volunteer to help out in class or at the school so that you will have an opportunity to observe how the teacher generally interacts with students. Seek out parents of your child's classmates or parents who have experience with the teacher from previous years to learn whether other students have similar problems. Talk to other school staff members, such as a guidance counselor or the school principal, to see whether they can offer any insights.

Handling a Personality Conflict

If the problem seems to be unique to your child, keep in mind that your child's own behavior and response to the teacher may be part of the problem. There are many unintended behavioral aspects of dyslexia that teachers may wrongly attribute to insolence or disobedience. Behavior quirks, such as classroom fidgeting, a speech impediment, or regularly forgetting to turn in homework, may frustrate the teacher.

In some cases, you may be able to help by recognizing these issues and providing the teacher with information showing how the problems relate to your child's learning disability, as well as suggesting strategies to help address the issues. If the teacher won't listen to you, try to find someone else who may be able to approach the teacher in a nonthreatening manner. This may be another teacher in the school who knows and likes your child and who can offer the problem teacher some helpful hints.

Your child may not be aware of how his own behavior is affecting the teacher. If the teacher is not willing to change expectations, you cannot change your child, but you can help your child to develop greater insight. Talk to some of your child's classmates about specific incidents that your child has mentioned; the kids may be able to fill you in on missing details. Even if your child cannot change behavior that stems from his learning difference, it may help him to better understand why the teacher is becoming upset.

If you cannot resolve problems with the teacher, consider whether you and your child can live with the situation. If so, you can help your child develop better coping skills and show your child that you support him and sympathize with his predicament. Sometimes your child simply needs a sympathetic ear. If your child generally has a good attendance record, consider allowing him a few "mental health" days—days when you let him stay home from school and plan some fun activities together.

The Verbally Abusive Teacher

If your child seems very upset, or actively tries to avoid school, complaining of stomachaches or headaches or crying on the way to school, it may be a sign that the teacher is behaving in a verbally abusive manner. Although most teachers care about their students and treat them with respect, a few use emotional abuse as a means of exerting control. An abusive teacher may repeatedly threaten to tell parents of misbehavior or unsatisfactory work, reject your child or ridicule his work, allow other children to tease or harass your child, label your child as "dumb" or "stupid," or provide a continuous experience of failure by insisting that your child complete tasks that are beyond his capacity to fulfill.

 Essential

The most common and pervasive effect of verbal abuse is negative self-image. Your child may say things like, "I'm stupid," or, "Nobody likes me." Or he may simply seem withdrawn, sullen, or depressed. The organization Prevent Child Abuse America defines emotional abuse as a pattern of behavior that impairs a child's emotional development or sense of self-worth.

If you have reason to believe that a teacher is behaving in a verbally abusive manner toward your child, then you may simply need to find a way to get your child away from that teacher. These problems could arise with any child, but a child with learning differences is particularly vulnerable to suffering emotional damage from someone who treats him harshly. In some cases, you may be able to bolster your child's sense of self-worth with outside activities. Perhaps you can help foster a positive relationship with another adult authority figure such as an athletic coach.

Don't be afraid to ask the school principal to intervene. If other parents have witnessed your child being mistreated, ask if they will write a letter for you to help document it—that way, it won't simply be your word against the teacher's. The principal may be able to arrange to transfer your child to another classroom for at least part of the school day. If not—or if the principal is not helpful or supportive—you may need to consider homeschooling for the remainder of the year or transferring your child to another school.

If it is not possible to get your child away from the teacher, try to arrange counseling for your child. There are many charitable organizations and agencies that can arrange free or low-cost counseling if you cannot afford to pay for a therapist. It is not your child's fault that he is subject to abuse; counseling can help build his self-esteem and develop better coping strategies. A therapist who understands the effects of emotional abuse on children will be able to help your child recognize what is happening and help him overcome some of the ill effects.

Fortunately, you will find that situations like this are rare. Although many teachers are far from perfect, most are willing to work with you if you treat them with respect and show a willingness to understand their needs and to compromise. It is far more common for problems to arise from honest misunderstandings than from ill intent. While you and your child may continue to feel frustrated, you usually can work toward improvements that will at least make the classroom tolerable for the remainder of the school year.

CHAPTER 14

Academic Barriers

Even though your child is legally entitled to protection from discrimination and may also qualify for special education services, you will find that, over the years, she will encounter many academic barriers at school. Some will be major barriers, such as requirements that she perform successfully on standardized tests. Others will be less significant, and focus on single or short-term classroom assignments, but may nonetheless cause considerable frustration. This chapter will help you anticipate some common problems and plan for them.

Speed Contests and Rote Learning

Unfortunately, a good deal of teaching in elementary school and middle school involves rote memorization, often with an emphasis on speed. Your child's dyslexia is not merely a reading issue; it also is reflected in the speed with which he processes linguistic information or translates his thoughts into written or oral expression. Even when your child knows an answer, he is likely to freeze up, become forgetful, or make many mistakes when under pressure to answer quickly.

Typically, your child will be expected to memorize math facts and multiplication tables, usually quizzed in a format emphasizing speed, such as a "mad minute" where children are assessed based on how quickly they can solve simple math problems. Your child will be given weekly lists of ten to twenty spelling words to master; as he grows older these will be replaced by vocabulary lists, with word definitions to memorize. Your child will be expected to memorize facts, such as historical dates, state capitals, or lines of poetry or famous speeches.

Essential

Your child's teacher may not understand that assignments that call for rote memorization of isolated facts are particularly difficult for children with dyslexia. Your child will learn better when she can study subjects in depth, and can relate facts to other knowledge that explains their significance. Encourage the teacher to provide alternative assignments that will give your child an opportunity to shine.

All of these tasks rely on strong verbal and linguistic skills. Even the rote memorization of math facts is a linguistic—not a mathematical—skill. None of these tasks is particularly important to your child's ultimate educational success: Not only can your child figure out or look up this information if memory fails him, but the need to memorize many of these facts has been rendered obsolete by modern technology. This doesn't mean that these skills shouldn't be taught to those children who can easily master them—but it does mean that you should try to arrange modifications, such as alternative assignments or extended time for your child.

School Privileges and Punishments

Even if your child has an IEP or a written 504 plan, you may find that she is denied privileges or punished in subtle ways at school because of her learning problems. For example, a teacher may allow all children who have finished all their classwork free time to play games on some afternoons while other children are sent to the library or a study hall to finish their assignments. Of course, your child never gets any free play time, as her slower reading speed and labored writing make it impossible for her to complete assignments early. Similar difficulties may also lead to specific punishments, such as being held inside for recess, being denied permission to attend a school assembly, or being held after school. You may even find that your child is being punished or denied privileges by being forced to make up assignments that she missed because she was pulled out of class to work with the resource teacher.

 Alert

Your child may not tell you about the day-to-day slights and inconveniences he suffers because of his dyslexia. He may not understand that difficulties other than reading are also related to his learning differences, and he may feel embarrassed about the treatment he endures or fear your disapproval. Although frustrated, he may perceive the teacher's rules as "fair" because they are equally applied to other students, and he may be reluctant to ask for special treatment.

In some cases, your child may suffer negative consequences because of problems that are not directly related to her reading ability. Many children with dyslexia have poor organizational skills; your daughter may habitually misplace her homework or forget to write down assignments. Her language processing issues may lead her to frequently misunderstand instructions or miss "hearing" them altogether. Your child's teacher may not understand how the reading problem relates to difficulties with focusing attention, listening, following instructions, or keeping track of deadlines and paperwork. You will need to work to educate the teacher about your child's limitations, and arrange for appropriate modifications in your child's IEP or 504 plan. You might point out to the teacher that some of her rules end up singling out the same students week after week for punishment or denial of privileges, and thus are not effective as incentives to change behavior. Arrange informal modifications that will give your child a chance to rectify the problems, such as reduced volume of work, or the opportunity to work on finishing assignments over the weekend.

Helping with Organizational Skills

You should also work at home to help your child develop stronger organizational skills—an area often missed at school. Provide your child with a planner that he can use to track assignments; ask the teacher to check his planner each day or week to make sure that he has everything correctly noted. If the teacher is unwilling to assist your child this way, help your child find a classroom buddy who can help track the homework. Pick a child who is reliable, has good attendance and grades, and encourage your child to regularly check with his buddy to make sure he is on track. If your child is embarrassed to ask or has a hard time making friends, consider hiring the other child to be your child's "secretary"—for a few dollars a week, you may gain a trusted ally for your own child.

 Essential

Your child may find an electronic diary, PDA, or smartphone more to her liking. You may be able to save money by buying a used model. Your child doesn't need a device with all the latest features—she just needs something that allows her to keep track of her work.

Help your child keep organized at home as well. Use a huge wall calendar in a prominent place in your home, such as the kitchen or dining area, to track appointments and events, including homework deadlines and reminders. Create a filing system using colored folders or binders to keep track of your child's work; keep this near his regular study area, and help him learn to keep his papers filed in the appropriate "to do" or subject folder, rather than left loose in his backpack or bedroom.

Also encourage your child to keep graded papers that have been returned to him in a file or folder for each subject, so he can review the papers later when preparing for exams. Sometimes teachers make mistakes and fail to record grades from completed work; when that happens, they often will not believe the protestations of a child who claims to have turned in work when there has been a history of missed assignments.

Use incentives at home to help keep your child on track, filling the gap where he may be denied privileges at school. Set more reasonable and smaller, short-term goals for your child. Organizational skills are partly a matter of habit, and habits must be practiced repeatedly over time before they become ingrained.

Academic Honesty

At some point, your child might face an accusation of academic dishonesty. You can work to avoid that possibility by being proactive, and recognizing the temptations your child will face because of her dyslexia. One drawback of modern technology and the wide array of support materials available to your child is that it makes cheating very easy. As your child's sophistication with computers grows, she will soon discover the ease with which she can cut and paste text from Internet resources and reference materials.

Your child should not be deprived of access to resources and technology that will enable her to learn merely because of the risk that she may misuse them. Rather, it is important that you discuss with her your own expectations about intellectual honesty, as well as legal and ethical concerns. Many children simply do not know or understand that it is wrong to copy or paraphrase material from websites; others simply are overwhelmed with their workload and feel they have no choice but to take shortcuts. A child with a learning disability is far more likely to be tempted to copy others' work.

You can help by continuing to supervise your child's work and being an active participant in the writing process. Offer to proofread your child's written work, both as a way of helping your child, and so that you are aware of what her original work looks like and have an opportunity to see work that she is turning in.

 Essential

If it appears that your child has copied passages of his work from the Internet, take the time to discuss with him the importance of putting information into his own words. Most children with dyslexia are highly creative thinkers; compliment your child whenever possible on his originality of thought and encourage him to voice his own opinions in his writing.

Keep in mind that until your child overcomes all aspects of her reading disability, she will be at a disadvantage in comparison to her peers for reading and writing assignments. Many children with dyslexia do overcome most of their learning problems by the time they reach high school, but many others do not. Your child is as intelligent as her classmates and should be entitled to the same quality of education. For her, digital books, videos, and study guides are necessary tools that will afford her access to the same quality of learning as children who are stronger readers. If your seventh grader receives tutoring because she reads at a third-grade level, she cannot reasonably be expected to read *Huckleberry Finn* on her own. Her mind is ready to appreciate the rich vocabulary and complex themes presented in the book, and she will certainly learn far more by listening to an audio book and watching a movie than by trying to struggle through reading the book on her own. This alternative is far preferable to reading an abridged, limited vocabulary version of the book or being denied the educational benefit of advanced literature while consigned to reading material geared to third graders. No teacher would deny a blind student the opportunity to rely on recorded books; if your child does not have the ability to read at a level equivalent to her intellectual ability to understand, she should be entitled to use whatever forms of educational aids are available.

As a parent, it is important that you help your child learn to strike an appropriate balance between reading on her own and using technology and available media to supplement her learning. Make clear to your child that you expect her to be honest about letting you and her teachers know when she has relied on supportive material. Keep in mind that reliance on such support will help your child develop a more advanced vocabulary and thinking skills that will, in turn, allow her to develop into a better reader and writer.

Grade Retention

If your child struggles in school, it is possible that at some point a teacher or school official will recommend that he be retained, and repeat a grade. Grade retention is almost never a good idea for a child with dyslexia, as the possible negative consequences far outweigh the benefits. Dyslexia is not something that can be outgrown or cured by waiting for a child to mature; repeating the same curriculum a second time around will not help your child improve his basic skills.

What the Research Shows

Retention is far more likely to hurt your child than help him; this is especially true in the early elementary years. Dozens of research studies conducted over several decades show that students who are retained because they are performing poorly may show short-term academic improvement in the years immediately following retention, but over time they usually fall further behind. Children who are promoted despite concerns about their academic skills may still have difficulties, but, over time, their performance tends to be marginally better than their counterparts who have been retained.

Of course, statistics don't tell the whole story—some children do benefit from retention. However, researchers have found that the students who benefit usually have mastered reading skills and had been held back for other reasons, generally because of a large amount of absenteeism or a midyear transfer to a new school. In other words, a student who is a capable learner but needs to make up for missed instruction may benefit from repeating a grade; a student with learning difficulties needs a different sort of help.

The long-term effects of grade retention can be devastating. Students who are retained for a year are more likely to drop out of school, even when compared to students with equally poor performance. Retention can also be emotionally traumatizing. In one study, 84 percent of retained first graders said they felt "bad" or "sad" or "upset" about the retention and many reported being teased by their peers. In another recent study, children indicated that they believed grade retention was the worst thing that could happen to them, even worse than losing a parent or going blind.

 Fact

Studies show that grade retention increases the likelihood—by as much as 40 percent—that your child will not complete high school. If your child is retained more than once, there is an almost 100 percent likelihood that he will later drop out.

Studies of middle and high school students also demonstrate a high social cost of retention; students who are old for their grade level reported higher levels of emotional distress, substance abuse, involvement with violence, and suicidal thoughts. No matter how well intentioned, holding a child back a year can send the message that he is a failure and that the teachers do not believe him capable of keeping up with his peers.

When Retention Is Appropriate

The only time you should favor retention is when you have positive answers in your own mind to the questions "What will be different in the coming year?" and "What plan is in place that will help my child learn when he repeats the same grade?" If retention will make your child eligible for services that he cannot receive with promotion—for example, if promotion means moving on to a different school site, or if there is a specialized program only available to children in certain grade levels—the prospect may be more appealing.

Retention may also be appropriate if you know your child will be placed with a specific teacher that you feel is particularly well qualified to help your child, either because of the teacher's reputation or because of specialized training she may have. Consider your child's feelings as well: In some cases, a child may prefer retention because of fears or uncertainty about his ability to perform in the next grade. While such fears should not be the sole consideration, often children have a valid basis for their concerns that should be explored.

You may also consider retention if your child is moving to a new school where the curriculum or standards are somewhat different—in that case, while the child may stay at the same grade level, he is not truly "repeating" a grade. This situation is common when children move from public to private schools, as some private schools have a more demanding curriculum. Some parents have also found it valuable to delay entrance into middle school or high school for a year, home schooling their child in the interim. Because of social ramifications, this choice should only be made when the child agrees to the plan.

Alternatives to Retention

The best alternative to retention is appropriate, specialized help for your child's learning difficulties, combined with appropriate modifications and support to enable your child to keep up in academic subjects other than reading. If your child already has an IEP, it usually makes more sense to review the IEP and reconsider the goals set and the specific educational services being provided, rather than hold your child back.

Kindergarten and Entering First Grade

If retention is suggested at the primary level because of your child's poor reading skills or apparent lack of reading readiness, you should immediately ask that your child be assessed if she has not already been diagnosed with a learning disability. Do not accept the teacher's opinion that your child is merely immature or needs an extra year. Even if the teacher turns out to be right, the apparent need for retention is a red flag that your child should be evaluated and considered for special education services.

If your child is still in kindergarten, consider both her actual age and social fit. Although the practice of holding children back to repeat a year of kindergarten is common in many districts, there is no research evidence proving that this will help. However, many of the studies reporting long-term deleterious effects of retention focus on the child being old for her grade. If your child is one of the younger children in her class, there may be no harm in repeating kindergarten, particularly if she seems socially immature or unready for the behavioral expectations of first grade.

 Essential

If your child is attending a private school in the United States, you are still entitled to request free evaluation for learning disabilities from the public school district. If your child qualifies for special education services, he will also be entitled to educational support for his dyslexia.

However, it is still important that your child be evaluated for learning disabilities. Keep in mind that some early intervention strategies—particularly phonemic awareness training—seem to lose effectiveness if delayed past the age of seven. Find out what services your school offers to first-grade students, and ask whether your child can receive the services with a repeated year that she might also get if promoted.

Beyond First Grade

At first-grade level and above, you should not agree to retention based on concerns about your child's academic skill level if your child will simply be repeating the same curriculum in the same basic setting. Your child does not need more of the same instruction; she needs a different approach. Tutoring and remedial teaching can be provided to a promoted child as easily as it can to a retained child, and your child is likely to be more motivated and engaged in school if being introduced to new material.

One alternative to retention is to place your child in a transitional classroom with an enriched curriculum designed to lead to double promotion, with the intent that after the transitional year he will catch up with his age cohorts. It is possible that even without such a classroom, an IEP could be written to effectively serve the same goals.

 Fact

The National Association of School Psychologists strongly cautions against grade retention, and recommends that struggling students be promoted along with a plan of special interventions, accommodations, and services geared to the specific academic areas where they are struggling.

In some schools, you may be able to arrange partial acceleration or retention—that is, a combined approach where your child moves on to the next grade for some or all subjects, but leaves the classroom to work with the lower grade for areas where there are specific skill deficits, usually reading or arithmetic. This should not be used in lieu of specialized remedial help, but is something to consider if it is clear that your child will not be able to keep up even with accommodations in isolated subject areas.

Some elementary schools have mixed-age, ungraded, or combined grade classrooms. Often, such schools have overlapping grades—for example, one classroom may have a grade 4/5 combination, with a grade 5/6 combination in another classroom. In such a setting, the decision to keep your child with the "lower" graded combination is not the same as retention— teachers in this environment are used to having students for more than one year and to teaching a varied curriculum. If your child has been doing well with a particular teacher in that type of environment, she may benefit from staying with that teacher another year. Conversely, if she has not been doing well, it may be time for a change, even if it seems illogical to push the child into the more difficult level.

High-Stakes Testing

High-stakes testing is the practice of using a single, standardized test to make important decisions about a student's education, usually whether the child will be promoted to the next grade or be allowed to graduate from high school. Such tests tend to work in a discriminatory fashion against students with dyslexia, both because of the content of the test and the method of assessment. At least through eighth-grade level, these tests almost always are focused largely on appraising reading and math skills; by definition, a child with dyslexia can be expected to have poor reading skills. But even after gaining skills, the timed, multiple-choice format works against students who have a history of dyslexia; many such students become capable readers and strong students but continue to perform poorly on standardized tests. Thus, the high-stakes test is a double barrier for your child.

School Pressures for Testing

Many states and individual school districts impose strict testing and grade retention policies because of political or social pressure to increase standards among their students. The practice of social promotion—promoting children to maintain age/grade level regardless of level of achievement—can lead to children being passed from one level to the next in school without learning anything. Obviously, this is not an acceptable outcome for any child. However, retention policies do nothing to improve the quality of teaching.

The federal No Child Left Behind Act passed in 2001 created additional pressures on schools to retain children who perform poorly on standardized tests. In order to measure school performance, the law mandated nationwide annual standardized testing in grades three through eight. Schools were penalized and parents gained the right to transfer their students from schools that failed to meet yearly progress goals. Unfortunately, these penalties increased the pressure on schools to raise test scores by any means necessary; one possible strategy was to hold back the students who did not test well. That tactic did not help the child, but it removed him from the testing pool of the promoted class so that he wouldn't bring scores down the following year. In recent years, that pressure has subsided as the Department of Education has granted waivers to the majority of states, releasing them from many of the pressures associated with the law in favor of setting new educational targets.

Misuses of Standardized Tests

Unfortunately, schools often misuse standardized tests to make grade-retention decisions, applying their results for purposes where they are not valid. The most common problem is using norm-referenced tests, geared to testing school performance, to also measure individual achievement. Those tests are designed to provide a good statistical sampling of how a group of students at one school score when measured against typical students. However, those tests are not valid as a measure of individual achievement. In some cases, they may contain questions about material that has not been covered in your child's school. While it may be valid to criticize the school for failing to teach content appropriate for each grade level, it is not appropriate to draw conclusions about your child's abilities based on subject areas where he may not have received adequate instruction.

 Question

What is a norm-referenced test?
A norm-referenced test compares a student's score against the scores of a group of students who have already taken the same exam, called the "norming group." Some widely used tests are the California Achievement Test (CAT); Comprehensive Test of Basic Skills (CTBS); Iowa Test of Basic Skills (ITBS) and Tests of Academic Proficiency (TAP); Metropolitan Achievement Test (MAT); and Stanford Achievement Test (SAT).

Even on subject matter that has been covered in class, the group norm-referenced test is ordinarily not designed to measure individual ability or achievement. In many cases, missing a single question can cause a major change in an individual student's percentile rank. The test designers try to choose questions that are useful to sort students along a curve. Many items that most students in a grade level would be expected to know are not tested, and questions may be deliberately designed to focus on more obscure knowledge, in order to help rank the students. Thus, there is too much left to chance—and too much material that is not included in the test—for the test to give a good picture of your child's abilities.

When the test results of many students are considered cumulatively, as is done to measure school performance, individual variation loses significance. The tests can give a good general picture of how well the students at a particular school perform in comparison to nationally expected averages. But when the same test is used to measure your child, the test is simply being misused.

Further, on a test of reading achievement, it is unfair and unreasonable to expect your child with dyslexia to score well against a norm-referenced standard. By definition, children with dyslexia will score significantly below average for reading skills—in fact, it is likely that your child only qualifies for services at your school by virtue of such low skills. The concept of "grade level reading" is by itself an expression of a norm, or average; it reflects what the typical, or midrange, student is expected to be able to achieve at each grade. It is neither reasonable nor possible to expect that every child will perform at or above average; statistics make that goal impossible.

It is a reasonable goal to expect a child with dyslexia to eventually achieve reading proficiency; many will, in fact, become excellent readers. It is not reasonable to expect your child to read the same as a "normal" child at the same age or to somehow radically increase his performance when measured against other students within a single year.

Thus, your child's reading achievement should be measured using criterion-based tests—that is, tests that measure many skill areas without referencing how your child's performance compares with others. Those test results should be used as a guide for your child's IEP or other educational planning, and not to create additional barriers.

CHAPTER 15

Teaching Reading at Home

You may want to try teaching your child to read at home. This may be a good choice if you feel that his school provides a positive learning environment, but lacks the resources to give him the specialized reading support needed. Alternatively, you may want to homeschool your child, either for a short period to help him catch up to grade level, or as a long-term alternative choice to formal schooling.

Deciding to Homeschool

Many parents feel they can best meet the needs of their children through homeschooling. If you choose to homeschool, you will be able to provide your child with the individualized attention that is so important for a child with dyslexia, and create an educational plan that fits her needs exactly. You will be able to afford your child the extra time she needs to master subjects and skills that are difficult for her, and allow her to forge ahead in her areas of strength. Your child will not face the humiliation or daily frustration of classroom failure.

However, homeschooling takes work, and it isn't the ideal situation for every family. For your child with dyslexia, you will need to consider carefully whether you can successfully take on the dual role of parent and teacher, knowing that your child may present some unique challenges.

If you did well in school as a child, and are the type of person who enjoys reading and solves problems in a logical, rational fashion, you may find that it sometimes seems as if your child with dyslexia comes from another planet. Your child's style of learning and communication may be very different from yours, and you may find that your attempts to explain new concepts in the simplest, most direct fashion you can imagine leave your child totally baffled.

 Fact

In 2007, an estimated 1.5 million students, or almost 3 percent of all students, were homeschooled in the United States. More than 70 percent of parents reported dissatisfaction with academic instruction in schools as a reason for choosing home education. Homeschooling families have a greater percentage of both gifted students as well as students with learning disabilities than the national average.

Ingredients for Success

To succeed in homeschooling your child with dyslexia, you will need to live by three rules: patience, flexibility, and fun. Patience means the willingness to give your child the time she needs to explore and master a subject, even if that means that a lesson you think should take twenty minutes ends up spread over many days or weeks.

Flexibility means the willingness to learn new things and change approaches. You may have decided to homeschool out of dissatisfaction with the reading methods or curriculum used in the local public school. Perhaps after doing your own research, you think you have figured out what type of instruction your child needs, and believe that you can do a better job than the school is doing. Armed with your knowledge and your firm commitment to help your child, you purchase the books you know she needs and get to work . . . only to find that your home-based lessons are a disaster, invariably ending in shouting and tears. Flexibility means simply that you must be ready to change course, to try new things, to back off at times, to listen to your child, and to observe her in an effort to let her interests and inclinations guide you, until you discover your own child's best learning strategies and ways to accommodate them.

Fun means that you need to always keep your sense of humor, and mix the work of learning with play. Be creative: Use games, puzzles, songs, rhymes, or physical activity. You are bound to have good days and bad days. If you can't see the light side of things, the task of helping your child on the bad days may simply overwhelm you. Your child is entitled to have a parent who provides unconditional love and support; she will not be helped by seeing disappointment or anger in your eyes when she falters or stumbles.

Have Faith in Yourself

Once you decide to homeschool, you will need to have faith in yourself. Invariably, if your child's reading is delayed, you will encounter criticism from friends, neighbors, and other family members. Some may blame you for your child's difficulties, suggesting that it is your bad teaching or overindulgence of your child that has caused her to lag behind. Others may offer well-meaning but misguided advice or suggestions. If you decide to delay reading instruction until you feel your child is developmentally ready, someone is bound to admonish you, citing the importance of early intervention. On the other hand, if you decide to start very early with a structured approach, you are sure to hear from someone that you are pushing your child too hard. You need to understand that these sorts of comments come with the territory of homeschooling, and learn to graciously ignore unwanted advice.

However, don't be afraid to seek help or advice with your child's reading problems from an outsider. If you feel that you are overwhelmed or have reached a wall trying to teach your child, it may be time to seek professional therapy or tutoring. In some communities, your child may be eligible to receive home-based services from the local school district or to participate in remedial reading programs at the school; policies vary considerably from one state to another with respect to homeschoolers. Sometimes it helps to pool resources with another homeschooler, who may be able to help your child with a fresh approach. Even a tutor with minimal experience, such as a high school student in your neighborhood, may give you and your child a welcome break from each other and help build your child's motivation.

Choosing a Curriculum

There is a wide array of educational and curriculum materials available to homeschoolers. In planning for your child, keep in mind the importance of teaching to your child's strengths through multisensory and participatory methods. It may be tempting to purchase textbooks and workbooks specifically designed for homeschoolers, but most of these materials are not designed to reach children with divergent learning styles. You will either want to supplement such materials or focus on using materials geared for children with visual or kinesthetic learning styles.

 Alert

Before you start, check to find out what the legal requirements are in your state for homeschooling. Some states have strict requirements about teaching qualifications, record keeping, curriculum standards, and/or require you to report on your child's progress using standardized tests. In other states, regulation is minimal and you will be free to pursue whatever course you choose.

When it comes to teaching reading, there are many methods, kits, and books to choose from. Homeschoolers of struggling readers report a high level of success by following the approaches outlined in the book *Reading Reflex*, by Carmen and Geoffrey McGuinness, which details the PhonoGraphix approach to teaching reading; or *The Gift of Dyslexia*, by Ron Davis, which explains the key elements of the Davis Dyslexia Correction program. The two approaches are very different, but each book provides detailed instructions for how to use and apply the methods.

Many homeschoolers like AVKO Sequential Spelling, which teaches spelling patterns through a word-family approach, such as a beginning lesson including the word set: *in, pin, sin, spin, kin,* or a word-building approach that lets a child progress from *all* to *tall, stall, install,* and *installment.* Popular programs for teaching math include RightStart Mathematics, which uses an AL Abacus to teach math concepts; and the manipulative-based Math-U-See curriculum.

 Essential

Don't allow your child's reading problem to monopolize your time at home. Even if you have decided to homeschool only for a short time to focus on building your child's reading skills, be sure that your lesson plans include plenty of opportunities to explore other areas of learning, especially those that are of high interest to your child.

If possible, try to integrate different types of skill learning with in-depth exploration of a topic or subject area, and include fun activities such as art or construction projects. Cooking projects are a great way to introduce and apply basic math concepts (counting and measuring) and to start learning about science. Literature can be enhanced with projects, play-acting, and activities geared to exploring history, geography, and science themes raised in the books.

Motivating Your Child

At its best, homeschooling is a rewarding experience for both parent and child, allowing your child the opportunity to fully explore his interests and develop his potential. You may prefer to "unschool"— to follow your child's lead, allowing him the opportunity to learn in his own way and in his own time, without trying to set external goals, rely on a predefined curriculum, or use formal instruction to teach skills. Unschooling can be a welcome break for a child who has been under stress and has lost confidence in himself because of negative school experiences, but in some cases, it can also allow a struggling reader to fall further behind. In a home where information is readily available through TV and the Internet, your child may have little inclination to put in effort to learn a skill that is elusive.

Some children simply lose interest in gaining skills without the external pressures of deadlines, assigned reading, tests, and grades that might compel a school child to put in extra effort to develop reading, writing, and spelling skills. Each child is different; some thrive in an atmosphere where they are free to follow their own inclinations, but others simply need more structure and external prodding. To be successful at homeschooling, you need to make sure that your own parenting style meshes well with your child's personality. Observe your child and his progress. Be ready to allow him to follow a different path, but at the same time be willing to add structure or increase demands if your child seems unfocused.

Building Early Literacy Skills

Before your child begins to read, she must know what the words mean, and she needs to have a sense of the grammatical structure and flow of language. Because children with dyslexia tend to be highly visual learners, they may miss integrating the finer points of language as they are growing up. Your child may seem to speak well and easily understand what you say, but most oral communication is also accompanied by gestures and other visual clues. Conversation involves an exchange of ideas often communicated in short bursts or partial sentences. Adults typically use a simplified vocabulary, with short words and active sentence structure, when talking to children. So, your child may very well grow up with very strong communication skills, but nonetheless have weak language skills. To prepare your child for reading, you will want to help boost his understanding of language and encourage development of stronger listening skills.

Read to Your Preschooler

You should begin reading to your child as early as possible, and continue the practice for as long as your child is willing to sit still and listen. When you read aloud, you help your child develop a love of literature; you model the process of reading for him and you expose him to an enriched vocabulary and more sophisticated and complex language structures. Even after your child begins to read on his own, you will be able to enhance his enjoyment of reading and improve motivation by continuing to read aloud, allowing him to share in reading some selections along the way.

Read from a variety of children's books, and include classic stories, such as *The Velveteen Rabbit*, fairy tales, picture books, and poetry. Make reading a regular part of your day, perhaps as part of a bedtime ritual. Hold your child in your lap or have him sit next to you on a couch or large chair so that you can see the book together.

 Essential

When reading a book where the print is large, point at each word as you read. This will help your child learn that reading goes from left to right and understand how the printed words correspond to the words you speak. Answer any questions your child has about the words and letters.

As you read, take the time to discuss the meanings of new words and to point out an interesting use of phrasing or elements, such as rhyme or alliteration. Encourage your child to talk about the events of the story and to predict what may happen next. Read some books written in verse to focus your child's attention on the rhythm of language as well as rhyme. Choose some books with repetitive phrases or themes; read your child's favorite books over and over again. Help make the stories come alive for your child. If you can instill a love of literature, your child's strong motivation to read will help overcome difficulties that may be the result of dyslexia.

Limit TV and Internet

Limit your young child's exposure to TV, and monitor what he watches. Unfortunately, TV does very little to help small children with language, and too many hours in front of the TV can undermine development of strong language skills. A small child is much more likely to pay attention to images on the screen and follow the action by focusing on what the actors or cartoon characters do, rather than attending to dialogue. The rapid pace and frequent scene changes, along with frequent commercial interruptions, condition your child to respond quickly to stimuli, which does little to help lengthen attention span. Since he cannot talk to the actors on the screen, your child does not get any of the feedback or practice that he might have with ordinary conversation with an adult or older child. Too much time spent looking at Internet videos or playing computer games can also undermine his development.

 Alert

Programs like *Sesame Street* are fun for a child to watch, but will not promote literacy in a child prone to dyslexia—the rapid-fire presentation of letters in isolation and in random order simply sends the wrong message about words and print. You can help your child by watching programs together and then discussing the story lines and events you see.

Teaching Prereading Skills

Help your child focus on the sounds of words through nursery rhymes and song lyrics. Introduce your child to the idea of rhyming, and encourage him in playful conversation to make up his own rhymes. Sing songs like "Down by the Bay" ("Did you ever see a moose / Kissing a goose?") and help your child invent his own lyrics. Help your child focus on smaller word segments and phonemes by playing games with the sounds of the words; teach songs like "Apples and Bananas" ("I like to eat, eat, eat, eat / apples and bananas / I like to ate, ate, ate, ate / ay-ples and bay-nay-nays").

Include songs and games that involve clapping, jumping, and other movements to music. This will help your child develop a stronger sense of the rhythm of language and may help development of skills related to right/left bodily coordination or timing that are implicated in dyslexia.

 Essential

Encourage games and activities that involve sorting and organizing items, as well as practice with order and sequence. Help your child develop an awareness of temporal sequence (beginning/middle/end), as well as spatial relationships (above/below, over/under, in/out, left/right). Your child can explore these concepts while playing with blocks, putting away toys, or helping to set the table.

When your child is very young, gently introduce the habit of visually scanning or counting objects from left to right. For example, you might line up a row of toys and hold his hand to count each one, beginning with the left side and moving toward the right. You can begin this even before the child knows the difference between left and right; the idea is to try to create a habit of always beginning from the left and moving to the right, in the hope that will make the transition to reading easier.

Learning Letters

Introduce your child to letters by teaching both the sound and the name of each letter. The letters do not need to be taught in order, but it is important that a young child associates a letter such as *K* with both its sound (kuh) and its name ("kay"). You may want to start by helping your child learn the letters in his own name, and then move on to names of other family members. Show your child how each letter relates to the sounds in the name, but do not try to drill or teach a very young child to apply that information in other contexts. For example, you might point to each letter in the name Kevin and say the sound; you might even show your child how that name contains the word *in* and later remind him of that pattern when showing him rhyming words like *bin* or *tin*. With a very young child, keep these "lessons" casual, as things that you mention when the occasion arises. You want your child to start to understand the idea that letters represent sounds and that words are composed by combining the sounds in an orderly way; formal instruction can wait until your child starts school.

Draw your child's attention to different letters on signs and in print, such as words on the front of cereal boxes. Encourage him to make his own letters by molding them with clay or Play-Doh, and supply toys such as magnetic letters that allow him to move and touch the letters.

Never push your young child to learn something he seems to have difficulty with. It is cute when a preschooler has learned to sing his ABCs, but if he doesn't have a clue as to what each letter looks like or that letters represent sounds, it is not going to help him read. Once frustration sets in, your child is not likely to learn from the experience.

Supporting the School-Age Reader

Your child with dyslexia probably has experienced great difficulty learning to read at school. Even after your child has mastered the basics, she may read slowly and laboriously, with considerable effort. If your child is receiving intensive remedial instruction at school, you should focus efforts at home on making reading a fun and pleasurable activity—this will help build and sustain motivation and build a familiarity with literature that will support development of advanced comprehension skills.

Reading with Your Child

Continue to read aloud to your child at home. When reading for pleasure, allow your struggling reader to relax and listen attentively without being expected to read. You should still encourage your child to sit next to you, so she can see the pages of the book as you read. If you are helping your child with a book that must be read for school, encourage your child to participate by taking turns reading; you can ask your child to read a sentence or a paragraph, then read several paragraphs yourself, and then let your child have another turn.

In books with a lot of dialogue, another technique for shared reading is to let your child take the role of one (or more) of the characters, reading the quoted words for that character. This is also a good opportunity to help your child focus on punctuation, such as quotation marks, commas, periods, exclamation points, and question marks. Many children with dyslexia do not understand what punctuation means, and they tend to ignore or disregard punctuation marks when reading because they are so focused on trying to decipher the letters and words. With oral reading, punctuation takes on added significance, as it provides information about when the reader should pause and the intonation that should be used.

When your child is reading aloud, do not interrupt to correct mistakes that do not change meaning, such as reading *mom* for *mother*. Frequent interruptions will cause your child to lose confidence and make comprehension more difficult. If your child stumbles over a word, simply tell him what it is. Do not try to use teaching techniques such as having him sound out words at this time. Instead, enjoy the story together, discuss the plot, and praise your child for his efforts when he reads aloud and is able to figure out some words on his own.

Teaching Reading Skills

If you are working with your child to try to teach reading or supplement instruction at school, do the "lessons" at a separate time—and with different books—from reading for pleasure or to gain experience. Oral and shared reading should be used to build fluency and comprehension skills; these simply cannot be combined successfully with teaching the mechanics of reading and decoding.

 Alert

If you are satisfied with the quality of instruction your child receives at school, do not try to supplement with lessons, drills, or practice basic skills at home unless your child's teacher asks for such support. Otherwise, you run the risk of overwhelming your child and confusing him with conflicting information.

If your child is in school but is not receiving specialized reading instruction, or if you are not happy with the methods being used, you may choose to tutor your child on your own. Make sure that your child wants to learn from you. If your child feels overwhelmed and exhausted from his efforts each day at school, she may need your loving support and a chance to relax far more than she needs more lessons.

If you are teaching your child on your own, you may want to choose a specific approach geared to struggling readers, using books or kits developed for home use. Try to choose a single method, starting with one that seems comfortable for you and easy to implement; mixing more than one approach at the beginning can simply cause greater confusion. If your child does not seem to be making progress after several weeks, or seems to reach a plateau or barrier after several months, you can then consider moving on to a different method.

If your child is in school and you are teaching at home using different techniques, explain to your child that there is more than one way to figure out words. Point out that you are going to teach or practice a different strategy from the one her teacher uses. Explain that she should use the time with you to practice the new strategy, but when she reads on her own, she should use whichever is easiest for her.

If your child has difficulty with sounding out by sequentially blending separate word sounds, such as putting the sounds of /b/, /a/, and /t/ together to make *bat*, you might try an alternate approach of teaching—onset and rimes. Focus your child's attention on the beginning sound (onset) of a word or syllable, and then teach the remaining single-syllable sound combination (rime) as a whole. For example, in the word *bat* the onset is /b/, while the rime is *at*. Knowing the *at* rime will make it easier for your child to learn *cat*, *hat*, *rat*, and so on.

 Essential

> Your child may find it helpful to hold an index card or ruler under each line of text as he reads. This will help him stay focused on the text. It is also possible to purchase a reading guide with a colored filter in the center, which is designed so that your child can move it down the page as he reads.

Observe your child to see what types of words give her the most trouble, and to see what sort of strategies she typically uses for decoding. Use common sense so that you can make practical suggestions, geared to the types of problems she is having and the type of words she is trying to read. Keep in mind that once your child is able to read at a first- or second-grade level, she will encounter more words that are phonetically irregular, and will need to learn other skills beyond simply phonetic decoding to progress. You may be able to help her improve reading skills by learning to look for familiar letter patterns, to break words down into syllables or word segments, or to recognize common roots and affixes. Teach her to look at the whole word before starting to decode; she may recognize a familiar pattern or segment toward the end of the word that will make word recognition easier.

Visualization and Reading Comprehension

One of the most effective ways to help improve reading comprehension is to encourage your child to form mental pictures of the events described in the stories she reads. This is especially useful for children with dyslexia, who tend to be highly imaginative and visually oriented. Studies consistently show that children who are encouraged to use visual imagery have improved performance on tests of comprehension and recall of materials.

Although your child may be a daydreamer who finds mental imagery natural in contexts other than reading, she may struggle to relate the words on the page to mental pictures. When she does try to visualize the story, she may get lost in her thoughts and lose track of the words on the page. She will benefit from a strategy geared to make sure that she understands and thinks about word meaning as she reads and that provides a specific scheme for visualizing. For example, the Davis Picture-at-Punctuation technique encourages students to stop to form a mental picture whenever encountering punctuation signaling the end of a clause or sentence. That allows the child to build imagery directly related to the concepts conveyed in the reading, while continuing to focus on the printed symbols on the page.

Mental imagery can also be promoted through modeling and use of open-ended questions during and after reading. You can integrate your child's own artwork with story reading, by asking her to draw a map or diagram of events, or to represent the story in cartoon form.

However, illustrations in text generally do not promote the formation of a child's own mental images. While richly illustrated text is very appropriate to build interest in young children, studies show that older children report forming fewer, not more, mental images when text is illustrated.

Games and Software to Build Reading Skills

Your child may be able to learn from educational games, toys, computer software, and tablet apps geared to building basic reading skills. Skill-building software such as the "Reader Rabbit" series is not designed to help with dyslexia, but there is no harm done as long as your child seems to enjoy working with it. The same is true for any game, whether it is one specifically designed to teach reading skills, such as The Phonics Game, or a game that incorporates word play, such as Boggle or Scrabble. Many children with dyslexia enjoy doing puzzles and may be able to gain reading and decoding practice with games and apps.

However, it is a mistake to force your child to play or work with a game that he finds frustrating. The value of presenting information in the form of a game is that your child is more receptive to learning when he is relaxed and having fun, and he may be more motivated if he stands a chance of winning the game or improving his score; but that purpose is defeated if the game makes your child feel discouraged or inadequate. You may be able to make the game more palatable by changing the rules or the way that you use the game; but if your child still balks, put the game away.

CHAPTER 16

Strategies for Spelling, Writing, and Math

Your child will probably have specific difficulties with other academic subjects. While he may receive specialized tutoring and support for reading at school, he probably will not have such support with other subjects. You will want to help him, but as with reading, his dyslexia means that he will have difficulty learning with conventional strategies. This chapter will help provide ideas and specific strategies for helping with the most common areas of difficulty—spelling, writing, and math.

Building Visual Memory for Spelling

Difficulty with spelling is the most common and persistent difficulty that accompanies dyslexia. Even after your child becomes a capable reader, his writing is likely to be riddled with spelling errors. One reason is the extreme variability of English spelling; almost every "rule" that can be taught has numerous exceptions, and many words simply are not spelled the way they sound.

Good spellers generally have strong visual memories for what words look like in print. Try to avoid study or practice techniques that expose your child to incorrectly spelled versions of the word. Many children with dyslexia have strong visual memories, but they will remember erroneous spellings as easily as correct ones, and they will have no way to remember which is right. Teachers might try to make spelling homework fun by offering a practice quiz where your child must select the correct word from a list of incorrect spellings or find the word in a puzzle where the letters are scrambled. Your child may enjoy some of these games, but for a child with dyslexia, they are counterproductive for learning correct spelling.

 Essential

When practicing spelling words at home, observe your child to see whether she does better when asked to orally spell the words as opposed to writing them. This will give you a clue as to how to best reach your child. If your child does better with oral spelling, encourage her to say the letters out loud as she practices writing her spelling words.

One technique that sometimes works for children with dyslexia is to learn how to spell a word backward as well as forward. Encourage your child to try to visualize the word in his mind; with a clear mental picture, the word can be spelled backward by "seeing" the letters in order and calling off the letters from right to left.

Word Families and Patterns

Good spellers also recognize familiar spelling patterns and understand morphological word structure including common prefixes, roots, and suffixes. It will be easier for your child to learn when words are taught in groups that share a common pattern or structure. This is better than learning "rules" in isolation, especially rules that have many exceptions. A popular program for home use that builds on common word elements is AVKO Sequential Spelling, which was developed specifically for children with dyslexia. Make sure that your child's word list for each study session includes only words reflecting the pattern being studied. Work with your child's teacher to modify school spelling lists so as to avoid confusion, and limit the number of words being studied.

Do not try to teach your child homophones, such as *their* and *there*, in the same session. Most people with dyslexia find homophones extremely confusing, and they will not be able to simply memorize the difference. It is better if the words are taught separately with words sharing a similar pattern; for example, *there* can be taught along with *here* and *where*. Make sure your child learns word meanings along with spelling; it will aid in memory to associate meanings with spelling patterns, as opposed to individual words. For example, it may be easier to remember that the "ere" sequence is associated with words signifying place (*here, there, everywhere*).

Have your child look up words with irregular patterns in the dictionary to learn about the word derivations and etymology. She will soon discover other keys to spelling—for example, that the word *their* comes from the Old Norse *theirra*. Knowing that some words with similar sounds come from different languages will help your child understand why they are spelled so differently.

Tips for the Reluctant Writer

The best way to help your child become a better writer is to separate the mechanics of writing (spelling, handwriting, punctuation, grammar) from the creative aspects. Your child's strength is in his vivid imagination, a valuable asset in a writer. Help your child learn that writing is a two-stage process; the first stage is getting the ideas on paper; correcting or editing work is the second step.

 Fact

Your child may enjoy reading books written by children's authors who also have dyslexia, such as Patricia Polacco's many richly illustrated storybooks, including *Thank You, Mr. Falker*, where she describes her own early struggles with reading; or Jeanne Betancourt's novel for young readers about a boy with dyslexia, *My Name Is Brain Brian*.

For writing the first draft of an essay or story, follow this rule: There will be no corrections or criticism for spelling or grammar. Your child should be encouraged to write things down in whatever form or order he is comfortable with. Once the ideas are in written form, you can guide your child to develop a more polished version. When your child is very young, you will give a lot of help; as he grows older, he will learn to do more for himself. Remind your child that even professional writers rely on editors to proofread and correct their work.

Mind Mapping

One good technique for getting ideas to flow is mind mapping. To do this, your child starts with a main subject, and writes down a few words or draws a picture representing the idea in the middle of a blank sheet of paper. He will then draw lines or branches radiating out from the center for each main idea he has about the subject; with each line he can write a few words or draw another picture. He can add details to each idea by again writing a few words, connecting them via a line or branch to the idea they relate to.

Once the ideas are written down in a mind map format, you can help your child develop them into written sentences, using the map as a guideline for developing the structure of his paragraph or essay.

Experiment with Different Formats

If your child seems to balk at writing anything in narrative format, encourage him to try writing poetry or verse. Introduce your child to the concept of free verse—poetry that does not have to have a particular rhythm or cadence, and does not have to rhyme. One of the advantages of writing poetry is that it frees the child from writing conventions, such as the need to use complete sentences. It also allows your child to experiment with the sounds of words and to use novel words that are evocative of a particular mood or feeling.

Your child might enjoy writing haiku, in part because it is short. Haiku traditionally has three lines consisting of seventeen syllables in total, usually arranged in lines of five, seven, and five syllables. Although the form is very brief, writing haiku will also help your child develop sensitivity to the phonetic structure of word segments.

You might also encourage your child to write a play; it is sometimes easier for the budding writer to focus only on the dialogue among the characters. Your child might enjoy presenting his play as a puppet show or using a video camera to make his own movie using his own written screenplay.

Use Artwork as Inspiration

Your child may do better with writing if you encourage him to draw a picture of his ideas or a story he wants to write, and then use words to describe what is going on in the picture. He might want to write in comic book or storyboard format, with a series of pictures and a short sentence describing each one. Alternatively, your child might draw a larger, more complex picture and then write several sentences or paragraphs describing what is going on in the picture. You might also want to encourage your child to write a story, a set of impressions, or a poem about an illustration or artwork in a book.

 Essential

You will find an intriguing set of pictures to use as writing prompts in *The Mysteries of Harris Burdick*, by Chris Van Allsburg. The book's premise is that the pictures were drawn by a man who disappeared before he could explain what the pictures were about, leaving it up to the reader's imagination to find the story behind each.

Understanding Math Concepts

Most children with dyslexia are ready to understand math concepts, but they often struggle with pencil-and-paper math as it is taught in school. The problem generally stems from difficulty understanding and manipulating math symbols, including numerals as well as symbols for operations, and with difficulty understanding and applying words commonly used to express mathematical concepts. Thus, the language-based disability that is part of dyslexia becomes a liability for learning arithmetic.

Modeling Math Concepts

When your child asks for help with arithmetic, start by finding out whether he understands the concepts underlying the problems he is working on. A child with dyslexia often has unexpected gaps in learning; sometimes even a very simple concept may be at the heart of a misunderstanding. Use three-dimensional objects to model mathematical ideas. You might use beans, coins, or small blocks to model functions such as addition, subtraction, and multiplication. You could demonstrate the concept of fractions by measuring liquid in a cup or by cutting a slice of bread into halves or quarters. Place value can be demonstrated with pennies and dimes. If your child understands the relative value of coins, they can also be used to model fractions or equivalencies.

Many arithmetic or algebraic concepts can also be modeled using geometrical shapes, and a set of pattern blocks can be useful to help your child visualize numerical relationships, such as understanding multiplication, division, and fractions. For example, your child can discover that a rectangle constructed of square blocks that is 3 blocks high and 4 blocks wide will have 12 blocks in all—the same as the problem $3 \times 4 = 12$.

Explain Words and Symbols

Make sure that your child understands all the symbols used in arithmetic problems, and also understands numerals and what they mean. While your child may understand isolated numerals, he may be confused by two-digit numbers, the meaning of 0 (*zero*), negative numbers, decimals, or commas used in numbers with four or more figures.

Be sure that your child understands all the words used in describing a problem. Your child may be confused by specific terminology—words such as *sum* or *reciprocal*. He may also confused by words that are used outside of mathematics, such as *positive* or *even*, as well as words signifying relationships, such as *from* or *than*.

 Alert

Try to avoid situations where your child must copy problems from a book, as children with dyslexia commonly make transposition errors. If your child must copy, encourage her to vocalize the numbers as she writes them—she is less likely to transpose 346 if she says "three, four, six" or "three hundred forty-six" as she writes the numbers. Your child may prefer to have you dictate the problems to her to write down, rather than trying to copy them on her own.

When your child writes out a mathematical problem, use paper with a grid or graph paper to help him keep the numbers lined up properly. If your child is working from a printed sheet of problems, have him circle operational signs, such as (+) or (−) in different colors, so that he understands what is expected with each problem. Check to make sure he has copied correctly before he begins to work out the problems.

Use Multiple Approaches

Most mathematical problems can be solved in more than one way; the more complex the math, the more likely it is that there are multiple strategies that can be applied. Often, the conventional algorithms taught in school cause unnecessary confusion. For example, your child may be stymied by the concept of "borrowing" or "regrouping" to subtract 6 from 12 on paper, but might be able to solve the same problem quickly in his head, simply by recognizing that 6 is half of 12. Many very complex arithmetic problems can be solved more efficiently by factoring or manipulating the numbers.

Encourage your child to use his knowledge of number concepts to find different approaches for calculation. Although these skills may lead your child to deviate from the approaches taught in the early years, they are the foundations of understanding algebra and higher mathematical concepts. In the long run, your child will do better in math if he is able to turn a problem on its head or restructure the problem to make it easier, such as restating the problem 15×9 as $[(15 \times 10) - 15]$ because it is easier to subtract 15 from 150 than to do double-digit multiplication.

Handling Word Problems

Word or story problems are very difficult for children with dyslexia, even when they have a strong understanding of math concepts. To start with, the problem requires reading, which is an effort for your child. Word problems also require highly accurate reading; a missed or misunderstood word can change the entire meaning of the problem. Many of the words used in story problems are also confusing; your child may understand how to "subtract" but be confused by the use of words like *less* or *from* to describe the same concept. Your child may also be confused by the use of pronouns in a story problem—the question "How many of them did he have left?" may leave your child scratching her head wondering what *them* refers to and who *he* is. Finally, your child may be confused by extraneous information in the problem used to describe the setting—the problem may be asking for a calculation of the amount of change to be given for buying movie tickets, but your child is trying to guess from the illustration in the book what movie was playing.

Help your child visualize the problem by imagining or acting out the scenario depicted. Explain that an arithmetic problem is a puzzle that always requires her to figure out a piece of missing information. Have your child read through the problem—or read it to her—and then ask her if she knows what information the problem calls for her to figure out (for example, the number of cookies that each child will get). Then, ask your child what information she will need to figure out the answer. Guide her, as needed, to look for the specific information she needs for that problem (the total number of cookies and the total number of children). Allow your child to explore the possible ways that she can figure out the answer; there may be more than one acceptable strategy.

Specialized Therapies for Math

Two providers of dyslexia treatment services have also developed specialized programs for helping with math. These programs begin by focusing on very basic math concepts, and children work with them to develop more advanced proficiency. The goal of each program is to ensure that your child has an intuitive or image-based understanding of the concepts underlying arithmetic concepts and to help your child relate the concepts to the words and symbols used to represent them.

Davis Math Mastery

The Davis Math Mastery program applies clay-modeling techniques to help your child master foundational concepts underlying mathematical relationships, such as change, cause/effect, before/after, consequence, time, sequence, and order/disorder. Clay modeling is also used to master the meanings of words commonly used in math story problems that are somewhat different from in everyday use. For example, the word *by* is generally used to mean "close to." But in word problems, it can be used to mean two separate things: for multiplication, to mean "using as a multiplier," and for division, the meaning would be "into groups of."

Essential

The Davis Math Mastery program takes five to eight full days of one-on-one work with a trained facilitator to complete. Your child will need to do follow-up work at home, continuing to use clay to model words that represent math concepts or cause confusion in word problems. The specific techniques used are detailed in the book *The Gift of Learning* by Ron Davis.

A Davis facilitator then guides your child through a series of twelve participatory mathematical exercises to move rapidly from counting, to multiplication, to understanding fractions, to developing proficiency with pencil-and-paper math. The exercises can be done quickly because the focus is on helping your child understand the concepts underlying each mathematical function; for example, using exercises counting forward and backward in multiples to lead into the concept of multiplication.

On Cloud Nine Math

Lindamood-Bell Learning Processes offers a program called On Cloud Nine® Math, geared to developing the ability to connect imagery to language in order to express mathematical concepts. Your child is encouraged to verbalize mathematical concepts through working with manipulative stacking blocks and dialogue with the teacher. The program begins with basic concepts, such as the number line, and addition and subtraction, and progresses to more complex applications, such as place value, fractions, multiplication, and division.

The Paradox of the Math Whiz

Some children with dyslexia have very strong mathematical skills, and they are often able to understand very advanced mathematical concepts and calculations. Often the knack for math was demonstrated very early, perhaps when the child was able to understand and apply concepts of multiplication or fractions as a preschooler. Yet these budding math geniuses often encounter problems at school. Typically, they have difficulty learning their multiplication tables and problems with paper-and-pencil math, such as with the concept of "borrowing" in multidigit subtraction or with doing long division. They often are able to correctly give the answer to a complex problem but are at a loss to explain how they arrived at it.

If your child follows this pattern, he may experience difficulties in school, particularly during the elementary and middle school years, because of his inability to satisfy the teacher's expectations for written math. Your child may write the correct answer to problems on a math worksheet or exam, but be denied credit because he failed to write out the steps for solving the problem, or because he wrote the steps incorrectly. You may observe him following a process of writing the answer to a problem first, then working backward to write the steps. He may be able to understand advanced concepts in algebra or trigonometry, but be prone to frequent errors in calculation. Don't worry, he's in good company—Albert Einstein had similar problems.

 Fact

You may be surprised to find that your child with strong math skills is not interested in working with math manipulatives. This is because, unlike the math-challenged child, your son already understands the concepts and has strong internal visual imagery. He does not need help with concepts, but rather with learning to associate his intuitive answer with the words used to describe the concepts.

The reason for this disparity in skill level is that there are two separate modes of thought used for math problems. Researchers have found that when students memorize their multiplication tables or do precise mathematical calculations, they rely in part on the language processes of their brains. In one study, bilingual students who were taught math procedures in one language had difficulty doing the same procedures when the problem was presented in the other language. However, another part of the brain governs understanding of mathematical and spatial relationships—for example, recognizing that the number 56 is larger than 12. In the language experiment, the bilingual students could perform equally well on those math generalization tasks in either language. They were relying on their inherent sense of concepts of quantity or size, or their ability to visualize the problem, rather than on language.

The problem for your math whiz child, then, is actually the same as the problem experienced by a child with dyslexia who struggles with basic arithmetic. Both have difficulty using and applying words and symbols to mathematical concepts. Thus, you can help your math-capable child in the same way you would help the math-challenged child, except that, in most cases, you don't need to teach the underlying concepts.

Another reason that your child may struggle with paper-and-pencil arithmetic is that he instinctively uses different strategies for solving most math problems. Students with strong spatial reasoning skills understand that numbers can be manipulated in multiple ways, and they will tend to adopt different approaches to more efficiently resolve different problems. They are often very good with mental math, sometimes amazing others with how quickly they can answer a difficult problem, such as multiplying 19×21—the math whiz understands immediately that this problem is the same as $(20 \times 20) - 1$.

The language-based math processes that cause so much difficulty are generally functions of basic arithmetic; in more advanced mathematics, understanding of basic numerical and spatial relationships takes precedence. If your child is not discouraged by early experiences with grade-school math, he is likely to do very well in high school and college.

CHAPTER 17

Home and Family Issues

Your child's dyslexia is more than just a school problem. It affects the way your child feels about himself, and it impacts your home and family life. You may find that you spend a good deal of time worrying about trying to help your child and that you are uncertain as to how to treat him. If he seems overwhelmed at school and emotionally fragile, you may be reluctant to criticize him or enforce household rules. However, even though he has a different way of thinking and learning, he is still a growing child with normal wants and needs.

Effective Communication

One of the most frustrating aspects of living with a person with dyslexia is difficulty with communication. It may often seem as if your child is deliberately ignoring you, or purposefully mocking or disobeying you, because she does exactly the opposite of what you say or ask. But those problems arise directly from your child's language processing difficulties. She really does miss half of what you say, as her mind cannot keep pace with the flow of verbal information. She compensates by filling in the gaps with what she thinks you probably meant to say.

You can effectively address or eliminate most of these problems at home by changing your own communication style. You cannot change your child, but you can change the way that you talk to her. Here are some suggestions:

- **Make sure you have your child's attention.** Say her name and make physical contact, such as gently putting your hand on her shoulder. Try to establish eye contact; at least make sure your child is able to see your face. Announce that you have something to say, using a neutral tone of voice, so your child doesn't think you are angry. If you have a series of instructions or directions to give, say at the outset how many items you will be talking about: "There are three things I want you to do. The first is . . ." This will prepare your child mentally to listen for all three points.
- **Eliminate distractions.** Make sure your child is looking at you and not at the TV or computer screen. Wait for a break in the action if your child is watching TV, and ask to mute, pause, or turn off the TV or video game if possible. Do not allow your other children to interrupt; if they do, take a deep breath and start over from the beginning.
- **Speak clearly.** Speak slowly and use words that clearly and concisely describe what you want. Try to use "picture words"—words that will help your child visualize what you are talking about. Give accurate and specific directions, and call items by their names—that is, say, "Please go out to the car, open the trunk, and bring in the bag of groceries," not, "Go bring in the stuff from the store." If you need to give a complex set of directions, begin by stating the purpose of the instructions. Say, "I want you to start cooking our dinner while I am gone, so here's what you have to do . . ." That will give your child a context for understanding why you are talking about a chicken, a baking pan, and preheating an oven.
- **Verify that your child has gotten the message.** If you have given a set of instructions, ask your child if she understands. If "no," ask what she is confused about and answer her

questions. If "yes," ask your child to tell you what it is that you want her to do. Do not be patronizing in tone. At first, you can simply explain that you are trying to improve the way you explain things, and that you want her help in letting you know if you are being clear. Later, verbal confirmation will simply become a habit. Use the same pattern of communication when your child wants something from you. Instead of simply saying, "H'm" or "Okay," verify that you understand the message: "You need me to give your friends a ride home from soccer practice at 6 P.M. today. I'll be there."

- **If you want something done immediately, say so.** Don't assume that your child understands something that you haven't explicitly said.

 Essential

Treat your child with courtesy and respect. Say "please" when you want your child to do something, and "thank you" when he completes the job. If he makes a mistake or forgets a step, show appreciation for his efforts and gently remind him of the part that he missed. Your courtesy will set a good example and will help prevent him from habitually tuning you out.

Be careful that you don't set up situations that are bound to fail. If you know from experience that your daughter will lose track of time and forget to do a task, set an alarm or find some other way to remind her. If your child is a daydreamer and a dawdler, don't expect her habits to change—instead, plan on giving her frequent reminders or supervising the task.

Chores and Family Responsibilities

Your child's dyslexia does not affect his abilities to participate in household activities, including taking on age-appropriate responsibilities like regular chores. A child with dyslexia can care for a pet as well as anyone else. He can wash dishes, use a mop, handle a vacuum cleaner, take out the trash, or wash the family car. If your child is particularly disorganized or clumsy, there may be some tasks that you may find that you prefer he not do—but there are plenty of areas that can be his own responsibility.

Many parents are tempted to want to protect a child who has a disability, but your child will be better off if he has regular responsibilities. The more he is struggling in school, the more important it is to show him that he is a valued member of the household. Of course you do not want to overwhelm him with chores—but responsibilities like feeding a pet or setting the table for dinner are not time-consuming. If you notice that there is a task that your son does particularly well or seems to enjoy, praise and encourage him. For example, if your child likes to cook, encourage him to help with preparation of family meals; as he grows older, he can take pride in his culinary talents.

Behavior and Discipline

Just as you should not excuse your child from regular chores, you should have reasonable behavioral expectations. If your child misbehaves deliberately, then the consequences should be the same as for any of his siblings. However, you should be aware that not all misbehavior is deliberate. For example, if your child has problems with focusing or sustaining attention, then it is natural for him to lose track of time or forget to do his chores. Help him devise better ways of remembering, such as using a chart to keep track of tasks, rather than repeatedly chastising him for forgetting.

Be careful not to punish your child for his disability. Don't withhold privileges or punish him for academic problems, such as poor grades or forgetting to complete his homework, or for predictable areas of difficulty, such as a messy room or a tendency to lose track of possessions. Over time, you can help your child build skills and become more responsible, but you need to offer guidance and support. You will do better to break down tasks into manageable segments, offer praise when your child does well, and use small incentives to encourage him to succeed in areas that are within his grasp. Keep in mind that children with dyslexia tend to be very inconsistent in performance. Your goal is to help motivate your child to improve. Fear of punishment in a situation where he cannot be sure of his own abilities is demoralizing and can lead to a tendency to give up without trying.

 Alert

Keep your emotions under control. It is natural to feel frustrated at times with your child, but it is risky to lose your temper, as it is too easy to say something hurtful that you will regret. If you need to, take a timeout for yourself before trying to correct or discipline your child.

Keep in mind that your child's communication and attention-focusing difficulties may lead to confusion on his part. Children with dyslexia tend to be highly imaginative, and they have an inconsistent sense of time; they may confabulate to make up for gaps in understanding. This can lead to disputes over what someone said or did that seem like your child is lying—when in fact your child actually believes that he is reporting events accurately. Keep calm and gently question and guide your child to help him sort out remembered from imagined facts. Use questions like, "Is it possible that the teacher did say that, but you just didn't hear?"

Do be aware that frustration at school can lead to serious misbehavior. Having empathy for your child does not mean that you should tolerate acts of violence, destruction, or hostility. It is understandable why a child who is hurting inside may vent his rage by smashing a vase, but it is not excusable. But harsh punishment will also be ineffective if the reason your child's misbehavior arises is because he feels demeaned and humiliated every day at school, or is angry because other children make fun of his difficulties. The punishment will only increase the level of your child's anger. You will need to help him develop better coping strategies. Be consistent with imposing reasonable consequences that your child can directly relate to his behavior. For example, if he breaks something, working to pay the cost of replacement may be a more effective lesson than being grounded or losing privileges. You may need outside help, such as family counseling, to help understand and address the problems.

Sibling Rivalry

Conflicts among siblings usually stem from feelings of jealousy or resentment. Your child with dyslexia will feel frustrated if siblings close in age or younger than her are allowed extra privileges that are denied to her because of her learning problems. This may occur because of the need for your child to spend time outside of school receiving special tutoring, while siblings have more free time to participate in sports or social activities.

Conversely, your child's siblings may feel that she has monopolized all of the family attention and resources. For example, a sibling may resent being denied the opportunity to go to summer camp because you don't have the money after paying for intensive tutoring at a summer program for dyslexia. Or a sibling may feel frustrated that her good grades and accomplishments are not honored by the family, when you are simply bending over backward trying to make sure that the child with dyslexia doesn't feel humiliated or inadequate in a house full of honor roll students.

Maintain Balance

It is important to try to maintain balance. Your children do not have equal abilities, but each child deserves recognition and encouragement for her abilities, and support and understanding for areas of weakness. At the same time, you need to guide your children toward having respect for each other's differences. Start by making sure that your child's siblings understand what dyslexia is. At the same time, they need to know that their sibling is not fragile or inept.

 Essential

A healthy sense of humor will help everyone get along. No one likes being the butt of a joke, but everyone gains from learning to laugh at his own mistakes. You can help set the tone in your family by maintaining a lighthearted attitude.

It is important as well to avoid being overprotective of your child with dyslexia. You may wince when you hear a sibling crack a joke about his sister's spelling errors, but you can cause more strife if you overreact by yelling or punishing the offending sibling. A gentle reminder that the comment was hurtful is more appropriate. Keep in mind that healthy sibling relationships do tend to involve teasing and criticizing one another. Observe your child's reactions before lashing out in anger. You may discover that your child with dyslexia is quite capable of standing up for herself—you may even discover that the one with dyslexia is the instigator of many sibling battles.

Try to keep the family focus on more than only academics. This means that you will give your child with dyslexia recognition for accomplishments outside of school. Do not allow efforts at addressing one child's school problems prevent you from acknowledging the importance of your other children's extracurricular activities. Encourage family hobbies that everyone can participate in and enjoy.

Foster Strong Sibling Relationships

Look for ways to spend time individually with each sibling, and allow each child free rein to vent their feelings of frustration or anxiety. You may be surprised to learn that an older child is as worried about your child's dyslexia as you are. Help your older child understand ways that he can help. If he learns more about his younger sibling's learning style, he may be better equipped to offer help with homework.

Younger siblings rarely perceive the child with dyslexia as being disabled. They are more likely to simply accept their older sibling at face value, and to be fully aware of her many strengths. After all, a child's older sibling has always been bigger and stronger and quite capable in many ways. However, the younger child is also less apt to understand why so much attention is being focused on the sibling with dyslexia.

At some point, a younger sibling is likely to develop better reading and writing skills than the child with dyslexia. This can be a source of confusion and resentment. The older child may feel embarrassed, and the younger child may not understand why his older sister needs extra help with skills he has easily mastered. At this time, it is important that you answer the younger child's questions about dyslexia. Be sure to explain that it is a learning difference and not an illness. Many children mistakenly believe that their sibling has some sort of contagious or debilitating disease.

Siblings can also be a great source of support for one another. Rather than feeling resentful, a child with dyslexia may feel a sense of pride when her younger brother starts reading. While understanding her own limitations, she may feel relieved that her sibling doesn't face the same barriers, and the younger child may be eager to help the older one.

Sports and Other Activities

You should encourage any interest your child has in sports or athletic activities. If your child is good at team sports, such as basketball or soccer, his abilities will help build his self-esteem and allow him to earn the respect of his peers. Exercise and physical fitness will also improve your child's energy levels at school, and make him better able to cope with academic demands and stresses.

Try to steer your child toward activities where he can feel successful. Unless he seems to have a very strong talent or dedication to a particular sport, look for team sports where the emphasis is on having fun and developing good sportsmanship, rather than being highly competitive. Attend practices at first, and observe the coach. Look for an individual who gives his players praise and encouragement. Unlike at school, your child does not *have to* participate in any sport, so there is no point in exposing him to the additional stress of a verbally abusive coach, or the scorn of other players bent on winning every game.

If your child has problems with coordination that make it difficult for him to keep up on the playing field, look for noncompetitive activities where he can begin by taking lessons, such as gymnastics, martial arts, dance, or swimming. You should be able to find a class that takes children of varied ages; if your child sees that he is not the oldest "beginner" he will not feel embarrassed. These types of activities can help your child develop improved balance and coordination skills, which may help address some aspects of his dyslexia, as well as build confidence and improve self-esteem.

 Alert

> Athletics and fitness are an important part of your child's life; your child should not miss out on these activities because of afterschool tutoring or the need to spend extra time on homework. Your child's academic needs may mean that you have to limit the hours and days spent on sports, but make sure to reserve time for both.

You should also encourage your child's interest or aptitude in other areas, such as learning to play a musical instrument. Again, these activities are an important part of your child's emotional life and development, and they may have positive effects on his schoolwork as well. Practicing an instrument or singing in a choir, for example, may help boost your child's listening skills. Of course you shouldn't expect karate classes or violin lessons to substitute for specialized therapy for dyslexia. Just keep in mind that while these activities are primarily for your child's enrichment, they may have added side-benefits when it comes to school.

Keep in mind that your child's aptitudes or outside interests may also be the key to his future career. Of course you want your child to learn to read, to do well in school, to go on to college—but the world is full of actors, dancers, singers, musicians, and athletes whose talent is far more important to their success than was their education. For a child who struggles in school, exploration of arts and athletics is particularly important, and it may help build motivation to succeed in academics as well.

Rest and Relaxation

It is vitally important that your child also have time in his life for rest and relaxation. The tension, effort, and stress that he experiences at school make it especially important for him to have time to simply let go, and not have to worry about academics and schoolwork. If he is outgoing and sociable, he will want to have time to hang out with his friends. Introverted children have a strong need for time alone, sometimes seemingly doing nothing; for them, this is an important time to recharge. Most children need a little bit of both—time with friends and time alone.

 Essential

You can help your child sustain energy to focus on schoolwork by feeding him nutritious, high-protein snacks. Sliced cheese, peanut butter on whole grain bread, or a smoothie made with yogurt and fresh fruit are all good ideas for wholesome snacks that will help boost and maintain energy levels.

Individuals with dyslexia generally do not perform well under stress. In fact, many children will have periods in which they seem to do quite well, alternating with periods when their reading and writing regresses. When their skill level seems to inexplicably deteriorate, it is often related to stress or fatigue.

The irony is that your child needs to work harder than his peers to complete the same tasks, yet he is particularly prone to mistakes and confusion when his energy levels are low. So staying up late to study is often the worst thing that your child can do. As a parent, you need to make sure that your child has time to rest and relax. Each child has a different pattern; you need to observe your child to get a sense of his energy cycles. For some kids, it is important to do homework right away after they get home from school, as they tend to be too tired to do it later on. Other kids really need to take a break to recoup their energy after a trying day at school. Some children will fade early in the evening, and need an early bedtime. Other children are night owls who seem to get a burst of energy as the evening wears on, and may do better with a short nap in the afternoon after school, postponing homework until after dinner.

Your child may also benefit from learning some techniques for stress relief. Yoga, stretching, tossing a light Koosh ball or Nerf ball, or deep breathing are all good ways to help let go of tension and anxiety. Help your child learn what works best for him, and develop habits of self-awareness and self-monitoring. Learn these techniques for yourself, too—you will be a better and more nurturing parent if you also make sure to take time for rest and relaxation for yourself.

CHAPTER 18

The Teenage Years

As your child reaches adolescence, you will face new challenges. Your child with dyslexia will experience the same emotional and physical changes as any other teenager. However, the teenage years are also a time when children begin to think about their future. Your child's school struggles can translate into a negative self-image, which in turn may lead your teenager to become depressed or engage in risky activity. As a parent, you will need to recognize and acknowledge your teenager's needs, and at the same time help her become more self-reliant and independent.

Fostering Independence

During the elementary school years, you may find that you need to constantly monitor your child at home and intervene at school to help your child along. At home you may be in the habit of doing many things for your child, such as reading aloud to him or writing things down for him. You know that your child needs extra help, and you are happy to give it. There is a tendency for parents of children with learning disabilities to become overprotective. Partly it simply becomes habit for you to anticipate your child's needs and try to help him, and partly you have become conditioned over time to expect problems unless you take action to prevent them.

As your child moves into adolescence, it is critical that you begin to let go and start to transfer responsibility to your child. Over time, you will need to guide and encourage your child to take responsibility for keeping track of his own books and supplies, remembering to do his own homework, advocating for himself with teachers, and making his own academic choices.

 Alert

Beware of assuming too much responsibility for your child with dyslexia. This can lead to a cycle of dependence that lasts into adulthood. Your child must be given the opportunity to take risks and learn from mistakes or he will not develop the self-determination that is critical to independent adulthood.

Your child may or may not become a good reader, and he may or may not achieve academic success; but he certainly will grow to adulthood and some day need to be able to take care of himself and hold down a job. Your child with dyslexia has the potential to develop all of the skills he needs for these life responsibilities, and like all children he needs your support and guidance to make this transition to adulthood. The more difficulty your child has with academics, the more important it is that you equip him with the social and emotional skills he will need to become a productive member of society. For many young people, college is a four-year cushion between high school and the responsibilities of adult life. If your teen does not enjoy or do well in school, then he will not have that extra time—he may need to be prepared to enter the work world in his late teens. His educational limitations do not need to stand in the way of gainful employment. There are dozens of vocational skills that a young person can learn that will lead to employment in environments where high-level reading and writing skills are not necessary, and many young people do well in positions in retail business and sales. What your child does need is emotional resiliency and values like a strong work ethic, persistence, and reliability.

Taking on New Challenges

One of the most difficult—and necessary—parts of parenting a teenager is that you must be prepared to allow your child to risk making mistakes and failure. Of course you will still provide support and assistance, and you will try to exercise good judgment as to how much responsibility to take on; but you have to avoid the tendency to continue to do work for your child or intervene constantly on her behalf. At age eight, it is unfair to a child with dyslexia to expect her to "tough it out" and simply "work harder"— but at age fourteen it is important that your child begin to develop some of the work habits she will need to succeed in life.

Adolescence is a time of extraordinary mental and intellectual growth for your child. With dyslexia, there is often a pattern of "late blooming." It is very typical for a child who has struggled tremendously in the early years to suddenly develop new competencies during the teenage years. A child whose parents were told that she would never be "college material" may end up excelling in high school and later go on to earn a PhD.

 Essential

Do not push your child to take on challenges that he does not want. The key to your teen's success in meeting new challenges is his own internal motivation. A student with dyslexia with a passionate interest will overcome many odds in pursuit of that passion; but parental prodding cannot substitute for that inner drive. Just as you should support your child if he feels ready to work to a higher standard than he has in the past, you must also respect your child if he prefers to choose an easier path.

As a parent, you love your child and want the best for her, but there is a natural tendency to see your child in the light of your previous experiences with her. If she has always needed extra help to keep up in school, it is hard for you to believe that she is going to suddenly change and become an honors student. Your daughter may want to enroll in an honors or college preparatory class at school that you feel, in your heart, is too difficult for her. You don't want to see her hurt, so it is natural for you to try to steer her to something more suited to her abilities. But that is a mistake; you may find to your surprise that the more challenging the course, the better your child does. You can't know that this will be the case, of course—but you can never find out unless you allow your child to try. The fact that your child wants to meet a challenge is usually a good indication that she will be successful. Individuals with dyslexia seem to be blessed with an extra dose of persistence and perseverance, perhaps because their early struggles have conditioned them to expect to work hard to succeed.

Accept Your Child

If you have been working on getting help for your child for many years, by the time your child is a teenager you may have become something of an expert on knowing what your child needs and what programs he should have to get it. You are accustomed to advocating and planning for your child, and you have come to see his dyslexia as your responsibility.

When your child is in his early teens, it is time to reassess and allow the dyslexia to become his responsibility. That doesn't mean that you stop caring, but it does mean that you allow your child a much greater role in planning for himself. That includes giving him the right to choose what sort of special educational intervention he wishes to have, or to discontinue specialized therapy or tutoring. You don't want to give up on your child, but acceptance of limitations is not always the same as giving up. It is very rare that a teenager with dyslexia has no ability whatsoever to read; more commonly, the teen reads at an elementary school level with difficulty. Most teens in that position would like to read better, but teens also want to explore other interests. Your teen may simply decide he would rather devote his energies to something he is good at, instead of continuing to try to improve reading skills that he now feels are adequate for his needs. He may have talents in other areas, such as art, music, or athletics, where he would rather focus his energies, and he may be comfortable with the compensation strategies he has developed for areas of weakness.

It is important for your teen's self-esteem, and for family harmony, that you show him that you respect and accept him the way he is. A young child will simply accept the idea that his parents know what is best, and go along happily. Around the time of puberty, your teen may begin to see parental urging in a different light. Though your love and concern have not changed, your teen may see your well-intentioned advice as an indication that you do not have faith in him, or that you do not think he is good enough to meet your standards. During early adolescence, your teenager is essentially reshaping his own self-image and is very vulnerable to perceived negative messages. Thus it is crucial to his self-esteem that your role shift from manager to adviser, and that you allow him to exercise an increasing amount of control over his own life. Of course you are still a parent and should intervene when clearly necessary, but you need to also accept that your teen may make some decisions that do not fit with your hopes and aspirations for his future. If you secretly dream that your child will become a doctor, and instead your teen announces that he has decided medical school is too difficult and he has decided to train to be a paramedic, you need to be ready to accept that your teen's plans may be far more practical.

Extracurricular Activities

You should encourage your teen to participate in any sports or extra-curricular activities that she is interested in, including church youth groups, recreational clubs, hobbies, volunteer work, working for a political campaign or cause, theater, musical performance, or scouting. If your teen doesn't seem interested in much of anything, try to nudge her toward any activity that you think might pique her interest.

 Essential

> It is important for your teen's self-esteem for him to have social opportunities with other young people; if school is a struggle for him, nonacademic pursuits provide an opportunity for him to demonstrate competence or even to excel.

When your teenager is struggling to keep up in school, you may feel that she needs more time to study. If you see that her outside activities are taking up a large amount of her time and energy, you may wish to see her drop some activities or cut back on her participation. It is important for you to help your teen to find balance in her life, but it is vital that your teen is able to participate in activities where she has a sense of fulfillment and self-worth. If your teen is struggling to keep up in school, she is getting a message from her grade reports that she must not be very smart. Over time she is likely to get increasingly discouraged. Teens who are under stress or have a poor self-image are at risk for depression, which can lead to alcohol and drug abuse, risk-taking behavior, sexual promiscuity, eating disorders, and suicidal thoughts or attempts. Thus, it is important for your teen to have the opportunity to participate in activities that keep her active and engaged.

Your teen's activities can also be a powerful motivating force that will lead to her putting more effort into her schoolwork. If participation in a school sport or club requires that your teen maintain a minimum grade point average, she will have a motivation to work harder even if she has decided that she doesn't plan on attending college. If the sport or activity is something that she could continue in college, the participation may supply an incentive to aspire to a college education. Activities outside of school may bring your teen in contact with peers or adults who become her mentors or role models.

If your teen discovers an endeavor that she feels passionately about, or if she seems particularly talented in a sport or in visual or performing arts, do everything you can to support and encourage this activity. You will still want to help your teen maintain balance in her life. If the outside endeavor becomes all consuming or stressful, it may be time to place some limits. However, your teen's passion will be the fuel that will inspire her to succeed in life, and it may also plant the seeds of a future career.

Getting a Job

Your teen may want to get an afterschool or summer job. Although you may rightfully be worried about whether the job will cut into time needed for study during the school year, employment offers many benefits for a teen with dyslexia. Talk to your teen about how many hours of work are reasonable. You may find that your child actually becomes more disciplined about studying once he is working. The money he earns and his commitment to his employer will help motivate him to better manage his time.

 Alert

If your teen is required to fill out a written application for a job, suggest that he bring it home to fill out. Have him fill it out in pencil first, or make a photocopy for him to work with. Misspelled words, illegible handwriting, and questions left unanswered give a bad impression. You can help by proofreading and reviewing the application for your teen.

If your child struggles in school, the job can offer a welcome respite and an environment in which he feels more confident of his abilities. Your son will learn new skills through on-the-job training, where he will usually learn through observing others do a task, and then doing it on his own while being supervised. This learning-by-doing is ideal for his learning style. In the workplace, your teen may turn out to be a quick learner who earns praise from his employers. His social skills play a greater part in success here as well; a winning smile or an eager attitude is a great asset.

Of course, dyslexia can also create problems in the workplace, especially if your child takes on a job for which he is not well suited. His career in a fast-food restaurant may be cut short by a habit of repeatedly mixing up orders or incorrectly counting out change. It is important for you to help direct your child to seek jobs in areas where he has stronger interests or abilities.

Community service or volunteer work is another great way for a teen with dyslexia to build a sense of confidence and self-esteem. Helping others simply feels good, and your child will quickly see that his efforts are needed and appreciated. Volunteer work also often involves hands-on activities that your teen is well able to handle, whether it is preparing meals at a homeless shelter or wielding a hammer for Habitat for Humanity. Volunteering can also help your child meet people or gain skills that will later lead to a paying job.

Keep in mind that your teen's experience in school has been that he is expected to succeed in a wide range of academic subjects, whether he is interested in them or not. He has generally been graded and measured by comparison to same-age peers. His sense of his place in the world may be profoundly influenced by the grades he has received in school. He may have gotten the message that he is a C student and therefore cannot expect much out of life.

Through work, he will discover a different reality. Individuals of varied ages and abilities work together, and few employers expect anyone to be a jack-of-all-trades. Rather, in the workplace individuals have the opportunity to specialize based on their interests and inclinations, and nonacademic skills are often very highly valued. Through work, your teen may discover what he is "good with," and he will also likely receive positive feedback from his employer, coworkers, and customers for a job well done.

Getting a Driver's License

Learning to drive can present extra challenges to some, but not all, teens with dyslexia. Usually, by the time your child has reached high school, her reading skills will be adequate for the purposes of taking driver's education and passing a typical written test to get a permit. If not, that is a problem that may be resolved through extra study and tutoring.

Many teenagers with dyslexia have problems learning to control a vehicle or passing the behind-the-wheel test. One problem your child may face is simply the process of motor and perceptual coordination. Driving involves a heightened level of awareness and the need to perform several visual and motor tasks at once. For most people, this quickly becomes second nature with practice. For some individuals with dyslexia, it is difficult to reach this point of automatic response for the same reason that other skills involving motor coordination and balance may be difficult to master. If your child had a hard time learning to tie her shoes or ride a bicycle, she may experience the same sort of difficulties with driving. Your teenager can eventually learn to drive comfortably, but it may take longer than average to get to that point. If your child has difficulties learning to drive, you may find it worthwhile to pay for extra lessons from a professional driving school.

Alert

Some teens don't want to drive. They may be reluctant to take driving lessons, or avoid driving even after they have their licenses. They may be frightened when behind the wheel and have difficulty coping with the demands that driving makes on their ability to focus attention and respond quickly. Unless it is absolutely necessary for your teen to drive for family reasons, do not put pressure on him. Many teens simply are not ready to handle the responsibility.

Another common problem is communication between parent and teen—you tell your daughter to watch out for oncoming traffic on the left, and she looks over to the right. If your teen has difficulty with remembering left from right, you need to simply avoid using those words in giving instructions—say "driver's side" and "passenger's side" instead. Your teen may also have a slow response time to verbal commands, again a function of her language processing issues. Be sure that you give directions while she is driving well in advance. Your teen may also find it very difficult to use the rearview mirror, which can intensify the directional confusion that is part of dyslexia. These issues can also cause problems when your teen takes the behind-the-wheel test.

Fact

Some people with dyslexia are excellent drivers. Championship race-car driver Jackie Stewart and Indy 500 racer Stan Wattles both have dyslexia. After retiring from racing, Stewart became president of the Scottish Dyslexia Trust and vice president of the British Dyslexia Association; Wattles donated part of his earnings from each race to a foundation he created to help children with learning disabilities.

If your child is a very slow reader, this could also create problems while driving. Your teen will recognize most traffic signs by their shape and color, and will have no difficulty understanding signs with pictures and symbols, like arrows. But she may not read quickly enough to recognize the name of a street or freeway exit before she passes the sign; if giving directions, you should try to give other visual clues besides the name of the street.

Finally, some—but not all—individuals with dyslexia have a poor sense of direction and easily get lost or disoriented while driving. Over time, your teen will develop coping strategies, but there may be some interesting adventures along the way. A GPS device may help, but will not solve all problems; your teen may not realize if the GPS has given mistaken directions until she has driven many miles out of her way.

You should not assume in advance that your teen will have problems learning to drive. Although the problems mentioned earlier affect some individuals, many teens with dyslexia have no problem at all learning to drive and may become extremely skilled drivers. For some, the strong spatial-reasoning skills that accompany dyslexia give rise to a greater sense of awareness of the vehicle's position in relation to other cars, as well as stronger peripheral vision. Getting a license is also a great ego-booster for a teenager. If your teen is one of the first of her peers to get a license, which might happen if your teen was ever held back a year in school, the license is an important status symbol. Because driving is important in the lives of many teenagers, getting a license can feel like a great accomplishment. Additionally, the license allows your teen more independence, and may give her the means or the motivation to take on an afterschool job or volunteer activities, which can also lead to greater self-confidence.

CHAPTER 19

Making Choices in High School and Beyond

High school is a time for tremendous physical, intellectual, and emotional growth and exploration. Your teenager's life now includes an expanded array of social, athletic, and extracurricular activities. He experiences a changing relationship with teachers; some will challenge and motivate him, but he may come into conflict with others. With greater maturity and ability to shape his education, your teen's academic life may become easier. On the other hand, a teen that previously managed to cope well despite his dyslexia may be overwhelmed by increased academic demands and deadlines.

Choosing a High School

If you live in a larger community or urban area, your teen may be able to choose from several different high school programs. The choice of high school can be an important turning point in your teen's life, because he may be able to choose a school that more closely meets his individual needs or learning style, or focuses on a program geared to his interests.

Specialty Schools

Many communities have magnet schools or specialized schools, such as schools with a focus on the visual or performing arts, an emphasis on science and technology, or a strong college preparatory curriculum. If your child has a strong interest and aptitude, the magnet school may provide a more stimulating environment. Because of the high association between dyslexia and creativity, schools with a focus on arts often have a large population of kids with learning styles similar to your teen, even if they are not formally diagnosed with dyslexia. Attending a school where the students share a common interest may help keep your teen motivated and foster stronger friendships with his peers. Many magnet schools have special auditions or testing requirements to gain entry; inquire about these procedures at least a year before your child is scheduled to start high school.

If your teen continues to struggle with academics or seems to lack motivation to complete a college preparatory curriculum, he may want to choose a high school with a strong vocational or CTE (Career and Technical Education) program. These high schools will provide training geared to giving your child marketable skills, as well as including a basic academic curriculum. Many students who complete CTE programs do go on to college; some innovative high school programs partner directly with community colleges so that your child will be working toward an associate's degree in a career-related field. Often the classes given in the student's chosen area of concentration are hands-on and very practically oriented. Many students with dyslexia begin to feel comfortable with school for the first time when they are able to begin to learn and apply skills in areas of interest.

There are a wide array of skills and programs taught in CTE programs. Some examples are electronics, computer programming, graphic design, television production, carpentry, cosmetology, culinary arts, horticulture, information technology, automotive, childcare, architectural drafting, data processing, telecommunications, and marketing. Attending a vocational high school can be a rewarding experience for a student who is uncertain about his academic interests and abilities. The teen can experience increased self-confidence through gaining technical job skills, and the career-oriented training provides a valuable boost for a student whose difficulties with reading or writing might otherwise make it difficult to gain employment.

 Fact

According to the Association for Career and Technical Education, CTE graduates are 10–15 percent more likely to be in the labor force, and earn 8–9 percent more than graduates of academic programs. CTE high school students are more likely to graduate, and are less likely to fail a course or be absent from school.

Most school districts also have alternative or continuation high schools. These are schools that usually serve students who have become disenchanted with the regular high school environment. The schools provide a focus on building student self-esteem and helping disaffected high school students get back on track. Generally faculty-student ratio is quite low and the schools are very small compared to regular high schools. Many of the students have had disciplinary problems at other high schools, but students may choose to attend an alternative high school for a variety of reasons. The goal of these schools is to provide students who are not able to function well in the traditional high school environment with the counseling and teaching needed to earn a high school diploma. If your teenager is in danger of failing or considering dropping out of high school, the alternative high school environment may be the place where he is able to regroup and salvage his education.

School Size and Scheduling

Even if your district does not offer special academic or educational programs, your teen may be faced with some choices related to the way courses are scheduled or the size of the school. Traditionally, high school students will take six or seven classes daily, moving from one period of approximately forty-five minutes to another with very short breaks in between. Many high schools have shifted to block scheduling, which allows the student to take the same number of courses overall, but class periods are longer and there are fewer classes each day; usually there are also longer break periods between each class.

One advantage of the block schedule is that the student has fewer classes to worry about each day, usually only three or four. Longer class periods allow teachers to explore subjects in greater depth and give more attention to their students. Many students with dyslexia have a very difficult time handling transitions between classes, and with organizing and keeping track of assignments for their classes. For these students, the traditional high school day may simply be overwhelming, and the more sustained pace of the block schedule may prove helpful.

A drawback with block scheduling is that more material must be covered in each class. In a difficult subject, such as mathematics or chemistry, a student may find that the teacher is simply covering too much ground in a single class session. A student with difficulty focusing attention for sustained periods may simply not have the stamina for a class that lasts ninety minutes or more.

Many school districts also offer "small schools" or "learning communities," often housing several small high schools with a few hundred students each, each within a single campus once occupied by a larger, traditional high school. The small schools movement gained popularity in the 1990s, and was meant to provide a more supportive environment for students. The faculty has a better opportunity to know the students, and students have a greater sense of responsibility because they get to know one another and their teachers quite well. Discipline problems tend to be reduced, because the small school setting allows teachers to keep a closer watch on their students. Districts that embrace the concept may also offer a greater number of educational options, as different small schools can develop very specialized areas of focus. However, smaller schools have more limited resources, and within each school there will be fewer choices for classes and electives than is typical at a larger high school. There may also be limited options for special education services—a potentially important consideration if your child still relies on extra tutoring and classroom support.

The High School Guidance Counselor

High school also introduces a new person in your teenager's life, the high school guidance counselor. Your child's counselor will be working with her to help shape educational choices, including choice of classes and planning for the future. If your child has an IEP, the counselor will now also regularly be included in the IEP planning process, and IEP meetings will include transitional planning for life after high school.

Although the counselor is important in your child's life, the counselor may not understand the unique issues that are part of dyslexia. The counselor may try to guide your child toward choices that may limit future options. You will need to keep informed of your child's options. Talk to your child regularly about her plans and aspirations and about the classes she is taking at school. Find out what types of courses colleges typically require of high school students, including colleges offering specialized majors or courses of study that your teenager may be interested in pursuing. The counselor may advise course selections that seem appropriate based on your child's past performance and history of academic difficulties, but may not meet minimum requisites for admission to your state university or to colleges offering the majors likely to appeal to your child. While you should not push your child toward unrealistic goals, you also need to keep in mind that her early struggles with reading and writing may mask her true intellectual capacity.

 **Essential**

The academic performance of students with dyslexia often follows a paradoxical pattern. Students who have difficulty earning strong grades for easy courses may do very well in more challenging courses. Let your child's interest and motivation guide his path through high school. Support and encourage your teenager in his choice of courses, even if some classes are more difficult or less challenging than you would prefer.

Your teen's unique combination of strengths and weaknesses may also indicate that she should forge a specially tailored path through high school. For example, while the counselor may be used to directing college-bound students toward a uniform schedule of challenging courses, your daughter may need to strike a balance between English and history classes geared to the ordinary student, with a focus on advanced math and science courses.

Foreign Language Learning

Many high schools require students to study at least two years of a foreign language, and colleges may prefer students who have three or four years of language study. Students with dyslexia often encounter difficulties when studying a foreign language. For this reason, many students seek an exemption from foreign language requirements.

 Alert

Many colleges require their applicants to have taken at least two years of foreign language study in high school. Although it is possible that the entrance requirement might be waived for students with dyslexia, colleges are not legally required to grant exemptions from foreign language. If your child plans on attending college, it makes sense to at least attempt studying a language.

It is a mistake to assume that because your child has dyslexia, she will not be able to do well in a foreign language class. There are many ways in which your child can benefit from study of a foreign language, and your child may do well in an immersion-style classroom, where the emphasis is on developing oral communication skills. Many students find that their reading and spelling in English improves after studying a foreign language such as French or Spanish, as they become more aware of the roots and structure of English words and grammar. Students with dyslexia also sometimes find it easier to read material in a foreign language that is phonetically consistent, such as Spanish. Some students with dyslexia enjoy foreign language study and even go on to major in a foreign language in college.

Choosing a Language

In theory, it is best if your child chooses to study the language that seems easiest, but there are also other factors to consider. If your child has a choice of languages, try to learn about the individual teachers at her high school and the methods they use. Your child may do better in a class where the emphasis is on learning oral conversational skills, and where students are taught in an interactive setting, with games and songs used to keep kids motivated. If the teacher expects the students to memorize a lot of material and learn primarily through reading, or places great emphasis on writing and learning correct grammar, your child may encounter significant barriers.

If possible, encourage your child to arrange to sit in as a visitor to a class with each teacher in advance; this will help your child get a sense of where she might do best. Some students are overwhelmed simply because the teacher talks too fast for them to catch what is being said; your child will probably prefer a teacher who has a relaxed style and is careful to speak slowly and to clearly enunciate words, with many opportunities for repetition and practice.

Some factors to consider with each language include the following:

- Your child's level of motivation to learn the particular language
- Whether your child already has some familiarity with or exposure to the language
- Whether the language uses the Roman alphabet or a different alphabet
- Whether the language is written in a phonetically consistent manner
- The relative ease or difficulty of pronunciation of words in each language
- The relative complexity of the grammatical system
- Your child's preferred mode of learning and her individual pattern of strengths and weaknesses

Some students who anticipate difficulty with learning to speak a language prefer Latin. Latin generally is extremely helpful to a student in learning English morphology, which in turn may increase reading comprehension and fluency in general. American Sign Language is another very popular alternative for students with dyslexia, who generally find it easy and fun to learn a language made up of gestures rather than words.

If your teenager's high school does not offer a particular language, she may be able to satisfy the language requirement by taking a course elsewhere, such as at a local community college or a correspondence course via the Internet.

Barriers to High School Graduation

Many states now require students to pass an exit exam in order to obtain their high school diploma. While motivated by genuine concern about the educational system, these tests often discriminate unfairly against students with dyslexia. Your child may have very limited areas of difficulty, such as a disability with math, which makes it impossible for her to pass the test, even though she has studied hard and earned good grades in high school. In some cases, your child's problem may simply be with test-taking—you may observe that she is functioning quite well working at home or in the classroom, but for some reason she consistently performs poorly on tests.

Unfortunately, many states have also failed to provide adequate accommodations to students with learning disabilities when taking the exit exam. Thus you may find that your child is able to obtain high scores on SAT math exams, where students are urged to bring calculators, but cannot pass the state exit exam, where calculators are not allowed. Lawsuits have been brought in many states to compel authorities to provide appropriate accommodations on these tests, or to provide for alternate forms of assessment to enable students to obtain high school diplomas. Some states offer more than one form of diploma, certificate, or exit credential, some of which do not require the exit exam; but parents are rightly concerned that their child may be left with a second-class diploma that may be viewed negatively by prospective employers or by colleges.

If your child's dyslexia makes it hard for her to pass the exit exam, or if she cannot meet high school graduation requirements for other reasons, she can work toward obtaining a GED (General Education Diploma), which is widely accepted by community colleges and employers as the "equivalent" of a high school diploma. Many four-year colleges also will accept students with GEDs, as well as welcoming transfer students who have completed two-year degrees at community colleges.

College Entrance Exams

If your child is considering a four-year college, she will generally need to take college entrance exams. Most colleges will accept either the ACT assessment or the College Board's SAT. Some colleges also require that students take several subject-specific SAT II exams. If your teenager is unsure whether to attend a four-year college, her test scores may provide guidance and help both with choosing among different college options. If poor scores seem to indicate significant weaknesses, your child may consider attending a community college instead. If your child feels that the test scores do not reflect her true abilities, she may opt instead to apply to four-year colleges that do not require submission of test scores for admissions.

Test Descriptions

The SAT includes three separate sections on writing, critical reading, and math. The writing section includes multiple-choice questions on grammar and usage, and a student-written essay. The test is scored by awarding one point for each correct answer, and subtracting one-fourth of a point for any wrong answer. No points are deducted for answers left blank.

The College Board also administers the PSAT, an exam that students may take in the fall of their sophomore and junior years, and optional Advanced Placement (AP) tests, which may qualify your child to receive college credit for coursework completed in high school.

The ACT Assessment covers topics in English, math, reading, and science reasoning; there is also an optional written essay that is required by many colleges. The ACT is scored by counting all right answers in the multiple-choice section, without deducting points for wrong answers; thus there is no penalty for guessing. The ACT was originally created as an alternative to the SAT that would be more tied to the high school curriculum. Sometimes students who do poorly on the SAT will perform better on the ACT, but overall there is a high correlation of scores on both exams.

PSAT, SAT, and AP Testing Accommodations

In order to receive accommodations on the PSAT, SAT and SAT II, or AP exams, your child will need approval in advance from the

College Board's Services for Students with Disabilities (SSD). Your teenager can get help in making the application from an SSD coordinator at her high school. The College Board recommends beginning the process during your child's freshman year. If approved, your child will be able to receive accommodations on all tests, and will not need to reapply. Possible accommodations include extended time for testing, extra breaks between sections, or large print text booklets.

 Essential

You or your child should check with his school's SSD coordinator well in advance of any testing date to discuss current standards and requirements for obtaining test accommodations. You can also learn information from the testing agencies' websites. Policies and practices do change over the years, so it is important to seek out the most current information.

In many cases, the College Board will accept verification from your child's school. Your child will be eligible for such verification if there is documentation on file at the school supporting her need for accommodation, and she has received and used the requested accommodations for school-based tests for at least four months.

If your child does not have an IEP or there are other reasons that the school cannot submit the request, you will need to submit documentation directly, including a full diagnostic report. If your child is requesting extended time for an exam, you will also need to submit documentation relevant to performance in a timed setting.

ACT Testing Accommodations

If your child would like accommodations, such as extra time, to complete the ACT, a written request must be submitted by or before the registration deadline for the exam. The most common type of accommodation is extended time to complete the exam, but in some cases students can qualify for support of a reader or other services.

You will need to provide documentation showing that your child has been formally diagnosed with dyslexia or another learning disability, along with a recommendation for specific accommodations made by a qualified professional within three years of the testing date. Your child will also need to provide a copy of her current IEP or 504 plan detailing the accommodations she receives in high school. If your child has not already been receiving similar accommodations in school, she will need to submit a detailed "exceptions statement" from the diagnostician or school officials to support her request. A form and instruction for submitting the request is available from the ACT website.

Choosing a College

If your child pursues a college education, his choice of college will be influenced by many factors. Even the most prestigious and highly selective colleges will provide accommodations for students with learning disabilities, so his dyslexia should not be a barrier. However, in choosing a college, it is important for your teenager to consider his own learning style and preferences. He may find that he prefers a college with flexible graduation requirements, or he may want a college where class sizes are small enough to allow close interaction between students and instructors. Encourage your child to carefully review information on college websites about course offerings, degree requirements, and school policies. By comparing course sequences and general education requirements from different schools, your teen will see that requirements for the same major can differ considerably from one school to another. That can be important if there are specific types of courses that might present a barrier to graduation.

Keep in mind that there are literally hundreds of excellent colleges your child can choose from. Attending a smaller, less well-known college can be a distinct advantage for a student who sometimes struggles with learning, as the school environment may be less competitive and the instructors more willing to provide support and guidance.

College Support for Students with Dyslexia

Because of provisions of the Americans with Disabilities Act and Section 504, almost every college will make some provisions for students with learning disabilities. You will be able to learn more from each college's Office of Disability Services. The only colleges exempt from the federal legal requirements are some small religious colleges that do not accept any federal funding or benefits for their students. However, the law requires only that colleges make "reasonable accommodations" for students; it neither dictates what is "reasonable" nor mandates extra support services. Thus, the level and type of support can be very different from one institution to the next.

In addition to the usual questions your child may have about college, such as admissions requirements, academic programs, and dorm life, your teenager should make additional inquiries about support services. Find out what special programs and support services are in place at each college your child is considering, and how long the support program has existed. You and your child should specifically ask about types of assistance he is most likely to need, such as arrangements for students who need help taking notes or writing papers, or availability of recorded textbooks.

 Fact

Jonathan Mooney, coauthor of *Learning Outside the Lines*, has severe dyslexia and didn't learn to read until age twelve. He graduated from an Ivy League college, Brown University, with a degree in English literature after gaining admittance as a transfer student. He attributes his success in part to choosing a college with an "academic culture" that "values self-directed learning, independent study, and diversity."

Ask what the procedures are for negotiating accommodations and modifications with instructors. Are students on their own, or will the college help with advocacy? What is the procedure for resolving disputes over grades or assignments with professors?

Find out whether support services like tutoring or a writing lab are included in the tuition, or whether your child will be assessed additional fees. Ask whether tutoring and academic counseling are handled through the learning disabilities support center or through academic departments and general counseling offices. It is often important that advisers and tutors have experience with students who have learning disabilities. Ask whether there are courses available in basic writing and study skills, and whether such courses earn academic credit.

Ask how many students receive support each year, and what percentage of students receiving extra services graduate. Low numbers may indicate a weak level of support. Ask what sort of documentation is needed to obtain support services. Some colleges may accept the high school IEP, but others may require a more recent evaluation by a qualified professional.

College Classes and Graduation Requirements

Your child's success in college may depend on many factors unrelated to services specifically afforded to students with dyslexia. In choosing a college, encourage your child to ask these questions:

What is the average class size in his areas of academic interest? Do classes consist mostly of lectures, discussion, or laboratory sessions? Do professors usually give multiple-choice tests, or essay-based exams; or do they rely largely on student papers or projects for grading? Ask about the college grading system, and whether it is possible to take some courses on a Pass/Fail basis.

Does the college, or your child's likely major, have a mathematics or foreign language requirement? If those subjects are likely to present a problem, may other courses, such as computer courses, an international studies course, or American Sign Language, be substituted to satisfy such requirements? If not, does the college ever waive these requirements for students with documented disabilities?

Ask about the minimum number of credits required each semester or quarter in order to be considered a full-time student, and how many credits are typically earned for a single class. Find out if the college has core requirements that must be fulfilled in the first year, and what those are. Your child may do better if he is able to limit course load. You should also find out whether there are a maximum number of courses allowed, and whether there are extra fees for taking courses beyond a certain amount of credit hours; it is possible that your child may at some point have to repeat a course to make up for a failing or incomplete grade. Find out the college polices for students who take more than four years to complete their degrees, especially with regard to financial aid.

Find out what sorts of work-learn programs and internships are available. If your teenager learns best from hands-on experience, consider choosing a college that encourages and offers academic credit for work experience in his field of interest.

Career Planning

A young person with dyslexia can be successful with just about any career he chooses. In many cases, compensation strategies used to cope with continuing reading difficulties turn out to be an asset. David Boies, an American trial lawyer known for his exceptional courtroom skills, attributes his prodigious memory in part to reading difficulties—he learned to rely on his memory so as to avoid the need to read or re-read written material. Many actors with dyslexia report similar experiences with memorizing their lines: They simply don't want to have to read the script a second time, so they get it right on the first try.

Surveys show that a high number of successful entrepreneurs have dyslexia. In one survey, 35 percent of business owners surveyed identified themselves as dyslexic. Another survey of 300 self-made millionaires found that 40 percent had been diagnosed with dyslexia. A larger survey of 5,000 millionaires found that more than half reported early struggles in school.

Generally, young people with dyslexia tend to do better with jobs that allow them to express creativity through their work, such as working as a graphic artist. This can include writing, as professional writers have editors available to proofread their work, if they haven't yet mastered the nuances of spelling and punctuation. Many young adults do well with jobs involving sales and marketing, relying on their interpersonal skills.

The key to success is to mesh interests with natural abilities. For example, many teens are quite proficient with computers and will do well in computer-related fields. If your teen plans to defer college, it may be helpful for him to work with a vocational or career counselor for ideas about where to start looking for work or training when he finishes high school. Many youngsters will find their own way, led by their own interests, with long-term employment evolving from a high school job or volunteer position.

Keep in mind that making the transition from childhood to adult employment is difficult for many young adults, and your child may explore many options before he finds his niche. Recognize that success in many endeavors depends far more on social skills and personal qualities, such as persistence and resilience, than on the academic skills so important to school success. Your now-grown child will do best in areas that excite his passions. Encourage your child to follow his dreams—in the end, you may find yourself pleasantly surprised by how much your once-struggling child is able to accomplish in his adult life.

Internet Resources for Dyslexia and Learning

Advocacy Organizations and Resource Sites

CHILDREN OF THE CODE
A Social Education Project: The Challenge of Learning to Read
www.childrenofthecode.org

FAIRTEST
The National Center for Fair and Open Testing
www.fairtest.org

THE INTERNATIONAL DYSLEXIA ASSOCIATION
Promoting literacy through research, education, and advocacy
www.interdys.org

INTERNATIONAL READING ASSOCIATION
Promoting literacy by improving the quality of instruction
www.reading.org

INTERNET SPECIAL EDUCATION RESOURCES
Referral information for assessment, treatment, and advocacy
www.iser.com

LD ONLINE
Learning disabilities information for parents, teachers, and professionals
www.ldonline.org

LEARNING DISABILITIES ASSOCIATION OF AMERICA
Information, resources, and support
www.ldanatl.org

NATIONAL CENTER FOR LEARNING DISABILITIES
Online resource for parents and educators
www.ncld.org

P.A.V.E.—PARENTS ACTIVE FOR VISION EDUCATION
Resources supporting the critical link between vision and learning
www.pavevision.org

READING ROCKETS
Teaching kids to read and helping those who struggle
www.readingrockets.org

YALE CENTER FOR DYSLEXIA AND CREATIVITY
Slow Reader. Out-of-the-Box Thinker
http://dyslexia.yale.edu

Blogs

DYSLEXIA THE GIFT BLOG
http://blog.dyslexia.com

DYSLEXIA UNTIED
http://dyslexiauntied.blogspot.com

DYSLEXIC ADVANTAGE
http://blog.dyslexicadvantage.com

DYSLEXIC IN AMERICA
www.dyslexicinamerica.info

LD RESOURCES
www.ldresources.org

Educational Support Materials

ACT SERVICES FOR STUDENTS WITH DISABILITIES
Forms and information for requesting accommodations for testing
www.actstudent.org/regist/disab

BOOK SHARE
Accessible online library for people with print disabilities
www.bookshare.org

**COLLEGE BOARD SERVICES FOR
STUDENTS WITH DISABILITIES**
How to apply for accommodations on PSAT, SAT, and AP exams
http://student.collegeboard.org/services-for-students-with-disabilities

DYSLEXIC.COM
Assistive technology for dyslexia
www.dyslexic.com

KHAN ACADEMY
Learn almost anything for free (video lessons)
www.khanacademy.org

LEARNING ALLY
Recorded Books to make reading accessible to all
www.learningally.org

MY AUDIO SCHOOL
Large library of audio content for school subjects; low annual subscription cost
www.myaudioschool.com

ONION MOUNTAIN TECHNOLOGY
Low-tech tools for learning assistance
www.onionmountaintech.com

RISE SCHOLARSHIP FOUNDATION
Recognition for students who have overcome learning challenges
www.risescholarshipfoundation.org

SPARKNOTES
Free online print and video study guides
www.sparknotes.com

TEXTHELP
Reading and Writing Support Technology
www.texthelp.com

Government and Legal Resources

DYSLEGIA LEGISLATIVE TRACKING SITE
Tracks progress of U.S. state and federal legislation related to dyslexia
www.dyslegia.com

IDEA: INDIVIDUALS WITH DISABILITIES EDUCATION ACT
U.S. Department of Education Website
http://idea.ed.gov

NATIONAL CENTER ON RESPONSE TO INTERVENTION
U.S. Department of Education sponsored resource database
www.rti4success.org

NATIONAL DISABILITY RIGHTS NETWORK
Protection & Advocacy for Individuals with Disabilities—Find help
in your state
www.ndrn.org

NATIONAL READING PANEL
Read full reports online
www.nationalreadingpanel.org

PARENT TECHNICAL ASSISTANCE CENTER NETWORK
Find the nearest Parent Training and Information Center
www.parentcenternetwork.org

WHAT WORKS CLEARINGHOUSE
U.S. Department of Education Research Database
http://ies.ed.gov/ncee/wwc

Instructional Materials for Reading, Spelling, and Math

AVKO SEQUENTIAL SPELLING
Spelling system for learners with dyslexia
www.avko.org

BARTON READING AND SPELLING SYSTEM
Tutor training and materials
www.bartonreading.com

FAILURE FREE READING—HOME EDITION
Home edition of nonphonic software training program for struggling readers
www.failurefreeonline.com

K12 READER
Reading instruction resources for parents and teachers
www.k12reader.com

MATH-U-SEE
Comprehensive math curriculum using manipulatives to illustrate and teach math concepts
www.mathusee.com

PHONO-GRAPHIX READING PROGRAM
Phonetic-based tutoring system; online training, kits, and workbooks
www.phono-graphix.com

READ NATURALLY
One Minute Reader—Home software for building fluency and comprehension
www.readnaturally.com

RIGHT START MATHEMATICS
Hands-on math program using visualization, the AL Abacus, and math card games
www.rightstartmath.com

Therapies and Treatment Programs

AUDIBLOX
Cognitive exercises to build foundational skills
www.audiblox2000.com

CELLFIELD
Computer-based dyslexia training system
www.cellfield.com

DAVIS DYSLEXIA CORRECTION
Directory of licensed facilitators, training workshops, and materials for home use
www.dyslexia.com

DORE USA
Guided program of balance training exercises
www.doreusa.com

DYSLEXIA INSTITUTES OF AMERICA
Franchised learning centers offering testing and individualized therapy
www.dyslexiainstitutes.com

FAST FORWORD LANGUAGE AND LEARNING
Computer software to build language-based reading skills
www.scilearn.com

INTERACTIVE METRONOME
Sensory Integration Training: Combining Sight, Sound, and Movement
www.interactivemetronome.com

IRLEN LENSES
Colored overlays and lenses for improved vision processing
www.irlen.com

LEARNING BREAKTHROUGH
Products for balance and sensory integration
www.learningbreakthrough.com

LINDAMOOD-BELL LEARNING SYSTEMS
Tutoring to build language-processing skills; professional training workshops
www.lindamoodbell.com

VISION THERAPY RESOURCES
College of Optometrists in Vision Development
www.covd.org

For more resources, links, and updates go to *www.everything dyslexia.com.*

Index